Technology Transfer for Entrepreneurs

TECHNOLOGY TRANSFER FOR ENTREPRENEURS

A Guide to Commercializing Federal Laboratory Innovations

Clifford M. Gross and Joseph P. Allen

Westport, Connecticut
London

Library of Congress Cataloging-in-Publication Data

Gross, Clifford M.
    Technology transfer for entrepreneurs : a guide to commercializing federal laboratory
innovations / Clifford M. Gross and Joseph P. Allen.
        p. cm.
    Includes bibliographical references and index.
    ISBN 0–275–98083–9 (alk. paper)
    1. Technology transfer—Economic aspects—United States. 2. Technology and state—
Economic aspects—United States. 3. Technology innovations—Economic aspects—
United States. 4. Commercial products—United States. 5. Laboratories—United States.
6. Entrepreneurship—United States. I. Allen, Joseph P. II. Title.
HC110.T4G76   2003
338.973'06—dc21   2003053020

British Library Cataloguing in Publication Data is available.

Library of Congress Catalog Card Number: 2003053020
ISBN: 0–275–98083–9

First published in 2003

Praeger Publishers, 88 Post Road West, Westport, CT 06881
An imprint of Greenwood Publishing Group, Inc.
www.praeger.com

Printed in the United States of America

The paper used in this book complies with the
Permanent Paper Standard issued by the National
Information Standards Organization (Z39.48–1984).

10   9   8   7   6   5   4

This book is dedicated to Norman J. Latker, you had the vision and you brought it to life, and to the memory of Joel Tanenhaus for his love, inspiration, and entrepreneurial spirit.

CONTENTS

ILLUSTRATIONS

FIGURES

EXHIBITS

TABLES

ACKNOWLEDGMENTS

We would like to thank some of our colleagues and friends at UTEK Corporation including—John Allies, Tania Bernier, Jeffrey Bleil, Stuart Brooks, Arthur Chapnik, Joel Edelson, John Emanuel, Kwabena Gyimah-Brempong, John Micek, David Mooring, Diane Mueller, Carl Nisser, Bill Porter, Sam Reiber, Brenda Uhlenhopp, Keith Whitter, and Carole Wright.

In addition, we acknowledge our colleagues at the National Technology Transfer Center who worked so hard to pull this book together: Bonnie Funkhouser, who keeps everything on track; Paula Pollock, tireless reader of this book; Gerry Griffith, wordsmith par excellence; Samantha Welsh, who can find anything; Judi Kirker, Eileen Vitale, Michelle Ritz, and Linda Papini, creators of lab contact lists who never quit; Bob Reid and Liz Cousins, relentless hunters of successes; Chuck Julian, master of information; and John Yanchak, creator of reference lists.

A special thanks to Paul Abercrombie for his editorial suggestions.

To all of these individuals we express our sincere gratitude.

INTRODUCTION

The soil for innovation is cultural diversity infused with an entrepreneurial spirit. As a result of this flora in the United States, we have forged and nurtured an amalgam of federal research laboratories and university research centers that form the underpinnings of our technological renaissance.

Much of our technological innovation is taking place at more than 600 federal laboratories—government-funded *idea factories* that form a solution-set for solving many of the world's toughest problems. These federal laboratories develop and apply scientific innovation to solve problems and head off real and perceived threats. We believe these laboratories, taken together, form one of the most significant research machines ever assembled, giving flight to numerous scientific breakthroughs in almost every field of science and technology.

These great ideas need landing gear as well as wings, and five laws passed during the 1980s provided it, making it possible to introduce university and federal laboratory technologies to the marketplace.

This intellectual capital—a national treasure that is perhaps our greatest natural resource—was made available to the marketplace through the Bayh-Dole University and Small Business Patent Procedures Act (1980), the Stevenson-Wydler Technology Innovation Act (1980), the National Cooperative Research Act (1984), the Federal Technology Transfer Act (1986), and the National Competitiveness Technology Transfer Act (1989).

Although the current marketplace is not efficient, it does offer the ability to leverage federally funded research infrastructures to accelerate the growth of companies in every field of scientific inquiry.

Much has been said about the New Economy—perhaps too much. The New Economy is not so much about the Internet or the explosive growth of communications as it is about growing all types of technology companies through the use of "big idea" intellectual capital. The New Economy is really about converting brainpower into new and useful products and services.

The growth of companies and the resulting creation of wealth have led to the economic development of society, and this can often be traced to the introduction of disruptive scientific breakthroughs. Paradigm-shifting developments like the laser, the microprocessor, recombinant DNA, nanotechnology, and other seminal leaps have the ability to enhance human productivity and improve the quality of life.

This simple primer is presented to encourage the building of bridges between federally funded research centers and the companies that need an external research pipeline in order to prosper.

Chapter 1

GROWTH AND INSPIRATION OF THE FEDERAL LABORATORIES

New Frontiers of the mind are before us, and if they are pioneered with the same vision, boldness, and drive with which we have waged this war, we can create a fuller and more fruitful employment and a fuller and more fruitful life.
—President Franklin D. Roosevelt, Nov. 17, 1944

The *Exxon Valdez* oil spill was the catalyst. Kevin Costner and his brother Dan, co-owners of Costner Industries Nevada Corporation (CINC), took it from there.

Thanks to a technology transfer agreement with the Department of Energy's Idaho National Engineering and Environmental Laboratory (INEEL), the Carson City, Nevada, company successfully manufactures and markets centrifugals that separate oil from water. The company has placed 450 units in 30 countries in a variety of industries, including pharmaceutical, mining, and food processing.

"Every technology transfer case is different, but generally, it is a very efficient way to bring things to market," Dan Costner said, noting that CINC added additional patents to the original one. "For us, obviously, it was a very good move. We worked hard and continue to make improvements on the technology."

After Exxon Valdez, CINC developed an interest in cost-effective water/oil separation technologies that could be implemented for future spills. Specifically, the company was interested in collecting as much of the spilled product as possible.

A thorough search for someone with the necessary expertise led them to the Department of Energy (DOE) where they found Dave Meikrantz employed at INEEL. Meikrantz was working with centrifuges on various solvent extraction/washing applications, and he recognized the technology could be scaled up, commercialized, and used for such liquid/liquid applications as oil spills.

So what about CINC's future?

"I look to probably double production in each of the next five years," Dan Costner said, "which means we will continue to add jobs. And these are high-paying, good opportunities." CINC now has 30 employees including Dave Meikrantz.

Partnering with a government lab as part of your commercial strategy can be tough, but it is being done successfully by those who know how and where to look. This book is all about accelerating the growth of business with government laboratory inventions.

LOOKING FOR THE MOTHER LODE

The Internet, biotechnology, micro devices, hepatitis B vaccine, laptop computers, artificial lungs, record U.S. food production, smoke detectors, and cordless tools-all are just some of the everyday benefits derived from U.S. government-sponsored research. But none of those discoveries would have made it to the marketplace if some private sector entrepreneur had not turned scientific research into a commercial product.

That entrepreneurship link remains critically important. For example, the impact of the human genome project promises to revolutionize health care, and many new products are sure to develop from it. In the American economic model, government conducts research that is beyond the scope of the private sector. However, these discoveries can only benefit the taxpayers who fund them if they are turned into products or services. This is the role of the private sector.

Since World War II, the United States has created the greatest system in the history of mankind for advancing science—a system deeply rooted in universities and federal laboratories. This system is so unique that it is almost inconceivable that any country could replicate it.

However, as unique and powerful as this great research and development (R&D) system may be, there is no guarantee that its fruits will ever turn into tangible economic benefits. Efforts to derive economic wealth from this investment in R&D have begun only recently and are still in their infancy. While there may be gold in them thar hills, finding it, extracting it, protecting the claim, and getting it back to town present a tremendous series of challenges.

This book will help you map a successful strategy for extracting valuable technologies from our national laboratories—a vein of relatively unmined "gold." Success is never guaranteed, but the payoffs can be significant. The miners who put in the effort are more likely to find the gold.

HUNDREDS OF LABS, BILLIONS OF DOLLARS

Every year, hundresd of billions of dollars are invested in R&D in the United States. Of this total, the federal government funds approximately $63 billion, with about $21.6 billion going to federal laboratories and $14 billion going to universities. The remainder of the government's funding goes to private sector contractors.

So how many federal labs are there, anyway? Like most things concerning the government, the answer is complex. Estimates of the number of

Figure 1.1
U.S. R&D Funding by Source, 1953–2000, expenditures in billions of constant 2000 dollars

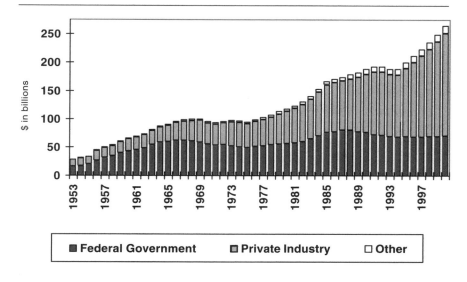

Source: American Association for the Advancement of Science (AAAS), based on the National Science Foundation's *National Patterns of R&D Resources 2000.* (Data for 2000 are preliminary.) March 2001 © 2001 AAAS

federal laboratories run as high as 700. However, the General Accounting Office (GAO) identified 515 federal R&D laboratories in a 1996 report. These laboratories are operated by 17 federal agencies. The majority of the federal labs are staffed and operated by government employees. However, most DOE labs are operated by private industry or university contractors.

Why are the labs so hard to count? Here's what the GAO had to say (GAO 1996):

> Each laboratory has a specific mission, or R&D program, designed to support the parent agency's overall mission. In fiscal year 1995, the operating budgets of 361 laboratories were less than $10 million; 101 laboratories were at least $10 million but less than $100 million; and 53 laboratories were at least $100 million. In addition, 65 federal R&D laboratories have 221 satellite facilities.
>
> Overall, the Department of Agriculture's 185 R&D laboratories were the most reported by any agency. However, these laboratories were among the smallest, with an average operating budget of $2.1 million in fiscal year 1995. Laboratories in the Departments of Defense, Energy, and Health and Human Services, and the National Aeronautics and Space Administration accounted for $23.4 billion, or 88 percent, of the funding for all federal R&D laboratories.

The most prominent laboratories are listed in chapter 6, along with their main research focus and how to contact them.

Whichever methodology we use to count laboratories, there are a number of labs with significant budgets. These labs are performing cutting-edge research and employ some of the smartest scientists and engineers in the world. Their research helps meet the missions of their agencies or further the frontiers of human knowledge.

But neither of these purposes includes commercialization of the research results. This is where the private sector must come in.

The development of the Internet in the 1970s as a communications system for Department of Defense scientists is a good example. The seed the government planted for one purpose has evolved into a worldwide communications system of unprecedented power. At the time of its creation, no one foresaw its ultimate application. Its evolution combined two powerful American institutions—government-funded R&D and small business entrepreneurship. It was the entrepreneurs who saw how this tool could be applied in a new direction. The government funds about 57 percent of the nation's basic research. This is an area where industry has been cutting back because of its long-range nature. However, it is also the area where "disruptive" technologies can completely change both existing and emerging markets.

Figure 1.2
U.S. R&D Funding by Performer, 1953–2000, expenditures in billions of constant 2000 dollars

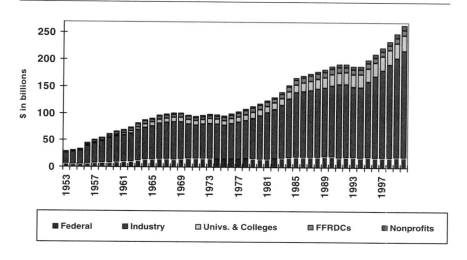

Source: American Association for the Advancement of Science (AAAS), based on the National Science Foundation's *National Patterns of R&D Resources 2000.* (Data for 2000 are preliminary.) March 2001 © 2001 AAAS

Biotechnology is another example. At the time that the Boyer-Cohen process patent was licensed by Stanford University and the University of California in 1981, the large pharmaceutical companies took little interest in it.

Small companies sprang up around the universities. Some, like Genentech, evolved into giants; others died. But biotechnology companies still tend to cluster around our research universities. No other country has successfully created a system like ours, where new companies spring from publicly funded research and create new industries.

The *Wall Street Journal* ran a story September 9, 1999, titled "Yes, America Has a New Economy: Technology." The story had this to say about a fundamental change in the law allowing companies to partner with our universities and federal laboratories:

The Bayh-Dole Act of 1980 allows recipients of government grants to retain title to their inventions. Says a study of basic research by the Committee for Economic Development: "The law has stimulated intense growth in university patenting and a subsequent technology transfer from basic research institutions to industry." As a result, industry is increasingly involved in collaboration with, and sponsorship of, university-based researchers.

For example, the Committee for Economic Development report notes that there are approximately 1,000 companies in Massachusetts with relationships with MIT. Their worldwide sales are $53 billion. Similar developments have taken place in California's Silicon Valley and Research Triangle in North Carolina.

But many places elsewhere in the world are lacking one or more of the magic ingredients that have made the U.S. the great dynamo of the technological revolution. No country, for example, can currently match America's vast network of colleges and universities, teaching hospitals and private research institutions, not to mention the labs of its multinational corporations. These centers of research attract aspiring scientists and engineers from all over the world and many find the intellectual climate so much to their liking that they settle permanently in the U.S.

U.S. national laboratories, though suffering from the usual inefficiencies of tax-supported institutions, nonetheless direct grants to thousands of individuals who are pursuing promising lines of research, and the ease with which individuals can start businesses in the U.S., in sharp contrast to Europe and Asia, means that good ideas spawn new firms, which often grow large and provide the financial infrastructure and stimulation for new generations bent on making their marks in research and development.

Sounds great. But why is the government such a major player in R&D, and why does it spend so much time and effort running the laboratory system?

THE ORIGINS OF THE MODERN FEDERAL LABORATORY SYSTEM

One of the Republic's earliest debates was over the role of the government in the economy. From the beginning, the government played a role in conducting research, particularly in the area of national defense. During the Civil War two significant activities affected the federal role in performing research and development—the creation of the Department of Agriculture and the enactment of the Morrill Act, which donated lands for colleges of agriculture and mechanical arts. Both took place in 1862, and both resulted in federal support for research at state-supported colleges and universities.

It says a lot about the American spirit that at the lowest ebb of Union fortunes in the war, the Lincoln administration and Congress had such confidence and focus on the future. It also underscores the importance President

Lincoln placed on education and research as key foundations of the Republic.

Even so, the federal government provided relatively little direct funding for research. But this changed dramatically with World War II, a war that was fought and won in the laboratories and factories as much as on the battlefield.

An example was the government's development and utilization of penicillin, discovered in the 1930s by Dr. Alexander Fleming, but not patented or developed for general use until the federal government stepped in.

This and other improvements in health care dramatically reduced the GI death toll from disease from 14.1 per thousand in World War I to 0.6 per thousand just 20 years later in World War II. These military benefits soon translated to dramatic improvements in civilian health. A visitor to an old graveyard will routinely see headstones for young children who died from diseases that the drugs of the 1940s began to contain.

Government research wasn't limited to the Allies' during World War II. The Germans developed and deployed jet fighters capable of flying at twice the speed of the Allies' prop-driven planes. German V1 and V2 missiles rained down on England until the last launch sites were captured in 1945.

The race to develop the atomic bomb was also close, but with the assistance of émigré German scientists fleeing the Nazis, the United States was able to bring the war to an end in the skies over Japan.

As the war wound down, the Roosevelt administration began wondering what to do with the prodigious research machine America had created. The United States emerged from the Great Depression only as the war economy became white hot. Factories hummed around the clock to supply the needs of millions of men in arms. Some feared that without careful planning, the United States might experience the boom and bust cycles of the post-World War I era that destroyed the world economy after the First World War, paving the way for the totalitarian economies of Germany and Russia.

VANNEVAR BUSH—SEER OF PUBLIC RESEARCH

Six months after D-Day, President Roosevelt charged a remarkable man with the task of recommending what should be done with the new American research behemoth. Not long after France had fallen to Hitler and more than a year before America would enter the war, Vannevar Bush was named director of the Office of Scientific Research and Development, an agency charged with creating a national pool of leading U.S. scientists. Ultimately, 30,000 scientists under Bush's leadership became an integral part of the war effort. Bush became involved in the development of radar, the proximity fuse, fire control mechanisms, and amphibious vehicles.

After witnessing the power and success of the U.S. R&D system, in 1944 President Roosevelt charged Bush with answering several fundamental questions to frame the postwar era:

- What could be done to let the world know, as soon as national security permits, of the possible scientific contributions that resulted from war research?
- What could be done to organize "the war of science on disease"?
- What could the government do to aid research activities of both public and private sector organizations?

Bush addressed these concerns in *Science, the Endless Frontier,* a report transmitted to President Truman on July 25, 1945, a few months after President Roosevelt's death. Bush saw basic research as seed corn for the future, and an appropriate role for government to perform. He wrote,

> To create more jobs we must make new and better and cheaper products. We want plenty of new, vigorous enterprises. But new products and processes are not born full-grown. They are founded on new principles and new conceptions, which, in turn, result from basic scientific research...Moreover, we cannot any longer depend on Europe as a major source of this scientific capital. Clearly, more and better scientific research is one essential to the achievement of our goal of full employment.

With remarkable clarity, Bush laid out a role for government in the research process that today remains the centerpiece of much of our federal R&D system.

In a section he titled "Science Is a Proper Concern of Government," he wrote,

> It has been basic United States policy that government should foster the opening of new frontiers. It opened the seas to clipper ships and furnished land for pioneers. Although these frontiers have more or less disappeared, the frontier of science remains. It is in keeping with the American tradition— one which has made the United States great—that all American citizens shall make frontiers accessible for development.

Bush was also concerned that small businesses have a seat at the table when he added,

The benefits of basic research do not reach all industries equally or with the same speed. Some small enterprises never receive any of the benefits. It has been suggested that the benefits might be better utilized if "research clinics" for such enterprises were to be established. Businessmen would thus be able to make (more) use of the research than they now do. This proposal is certainly worthy of further study.

He worried that the patent system was not functioning to promote entrepreneurship. Abraham Lincoln (himself a patent holder) once remarked that the patent system's purpose was "adding the fuel of interest to the fires of genius." Believing, as did Lincoln, in the value of a strong patent system, Bush told the President,

> Research is also affected by the patent laws. They stimulate new invention and they make it possible for new industries to be built around new devices or new processes. These industries generate new jobs and new products, all of which contribute to the welfare and the strength of the country. Yet, uncertainties in the operation of the patent laws have impaired the ability of small industries to translate new ideas into processes and products of value to the nation. These uncertainties are, in part, attributable to the existence of certain abuses, which have appeared in the use of patents. The abuses should be corrected. They have led to extravagantly critical attacks, which tend to discredit a basically sound system.

Although Bush's work, *Science, the Endless Frontier,* led to the creation of the National Science Foundation, it really set the philosophical tone for the entire *civilian* federal laboratory system. The report emphasized the need for publication of scientific research, while stressing that the government should limit its patent rights to research it helps create in the form of a royalty-free license for governmental purposes.

Even now, the publishing ethic remains very strong in agencies like the National Institutes of Health. However, government also funds billions of dollars in research in departments such as Defense and Energy (home to nuclear weapons research), and the new Department of Homeland Security that are marching to a much different drummer.

NATIONAL SECURITY AND A CONTRADICTORY TRADITION

At the close of World War II in 1945, a new threat emerged that would shape the next 50 years for our defense-oriented federal laboratories.

As Russian troops occupied much of Eastern Europe, Winston Churchill said that an iron curtain had descended on the continent. Thus, even before the dust of World War II settled, the cold war began. For virtually the remainder of the twentieth century it was feared the cold war might heat up into a nuclear exchange. Several times this fear almost became fact.

The Western Allies and the Soviet Union both eagerly acquired German scientists in the chaos surrounding the collapse of the Third Reich. The Soviet spy system quickly secured access to vital information on the American atomic bomb.

In spite of the science system envisioned by Vannevar Bush, information security became the watchword in national defense laboratories. Thus, from its earliest days, the national laboratory system developed two contradictory cultures—an emphasis on openness of information for the civilian agencies, and a corresponding need to restrict access and information on the defense side.

In the 1950s and 1960s, the United States created the most productive economy in history. With much of the industrial world still recovering from World War II, there was little concern for economic competition. Attention was focused on meeting the military and political threats represented by communist Russia and China. From the 1950s through much of the 1980s, national defense dominated federal R&D spending. Government was the customer, and secrecy surrounding research was of paramount importance.

As the Vietnam War raged, government R&D spending soared. The Johnson administration tried to fund both "guns and butter," and the result was an increase in domestic spending, including a rise in federal R&D that exceeded what all other developed countries spent on civilian, industrial, and defense R&D combined.

However, a wedge had developed between the U.S. public sector research institutions and the U.S. private sector that was to have serious economic consequences. Although economic benefits did occur from defense- and civilian-funded R&D in industries like aerospace, electronics, and computing, government policies placed inventions created by the federal government in the public domain, making them freely available to all. This policy destroyed the incentives normally provided by the patent system to encourage private-sector investment and development. Because of the nature of federal funding, significant industry development dollars are usually required, because government R&D rarely develops off-the-shelf commercial products for a competitive marketplace.

A fundamental principle of capitalism is that risk takers must feel that their research and development investments can be legally protected by the intellectual property system. Without this important leg up on competitors, innovation ceases because the costs and risks are no longer justifiable. Unfortunately, federal patent policies created precisely such a system with regard to the commercialization of government-funded inventions—with dire consequences that would soon surface from a most unexpected quarter.

It was a rude awakening when America learned that its former World War II military foes were back on the world stage as formidable economic competitors, determined to seize commercial markets from U.S. firms.

Being strapped for research dollars themselves, countries such as Japan developed highly effective systems of scouting other countries—particularly the American universities and federal laboratories—for research leads. The Japanese government funded "study teams" to systematically find and report back on developments and recommend commercial applications. This system proved highly effective and profitable for Japan.

Meanwhile the rift between the U.S. public and private sectors continued to widen. Even American companies working as government contractors segregated their own commercial and government-funded research operations. They feared the feds would take inventions they created with federal funding and give them away to competitors. Thus, even technologies the government funded in companies would have difficulty reaching the marketplace.

JAPAN DOES WHATEVER IT TAKES

While the relationship between U.S. government-sponsored R&D and the American private sector was growing further apart, a quite different model was being built in Japan and Germany. Prevented by their postwar constitutions from engaging in military activities, these nations depended on the United States for their defense and were able to focus their considerable energies on economic development. There was no soul-searching about the niceties of the relationship between their public and private sectors-economic prosperity was the goal, and government and industry worked diligently to achieve it. In Japan, especially, the government worked with large commercial concerns to target industries considered vital to the effort. Favored companies got active government assistance. Government, industry, and financial institutions worked closely together.

The first step was helping companies secure internal markets. Foreign firms were effectively denied entry through subtle and not-so-subtle means. The Japanese patent process required applicants to make their inventions known while the patent was pending, rather than being held secret as required by U.S. law. The Japanese system made copying easier. Ironically, the Japanese system effectively negated any role for innovative small companies, a characteristic that would cause major problems for Japan later on.

Japan developed highly efficient manufacturing processes; intense attention to quality; a knowledgeable, quality-oriented workforce; and a new, just-in-time system for the delivery of parts and supplies to keep inventories low. Seemingly oblivious to this shift, American companies complacently assumed they would always enjoy a dominant role in their traditional markets.

The erosion of the U.S. steel industry began in the 1960s. This caused ripples through the traditional heavy-manufacturing sectors. However, the bottom appeared to be falling out of the whole economy in the 1970s, when the United States suddenly confronted an energy crisis caused by the Arab oil-producing countries cutting supplies in retaliation for America's support of Israel. The U.S. economic base was centered on inexpensive energy, and the reduced oil supply posed a significant economic threat to the nation.

A steady loss of market share in the automotive industry became apparent as U.S. consumers turned to fuel-efficient cars. Consumers found that while Detroit ignored their preferences for styling and creature comforts, Japanese and German models not only reflected customer desires, but were also better built. American workers were tagged for not working as hard as their Asian competitors. Jokes about the quality of U.S. products became commonplace.

The crisis seemed to come to a head in 1979, when Chrysler turned to Congress for a bailout to prevent being driven entirely from the market. A series of significant international events soon followed-the Russian invasion of Afghanistan; a U.S. boycott of exports to the U.S.S.R., which hurt American farmers; a communist-government takeover in Nicaragua; the seizing of American hostages in Iran. Double-digit inflation added to the witches' brew.

It all seemed like the American colossus was tottering, soon to be eclipsed economically by its former World War II foes and stalemated in its political war with communism. Japanese industrialists began to patronize American government and business leaders with management advice on competing in the new economic order.

The American electorate was not at all happy. It would make its feelings crystal clear in the elections of 1980. Having dominated government power for almost 30 years, the Democratic Party took the hit. President

Carter lost in a landslide to Ronald Reagan. Even more astounding to the political establishment, the Democratic Party lost control of the U.S. Senate for the first time since the Eisenhower administration.

America was not willing to settle for second place. It was time to regroup. It was also time for a fundamental reexamination of the role of government and industry in building effective economic partnerships.

It was time to act quickly. The stakes were sky high.

Chapter 2

PROPERTY RIGHTS AND THEIR IMPERATIVE

There are times when doing your best is not good enough; you have to do what is necessary.

—Winston Churchill

AMERICA AWAKENS

Americans began to debate the best course for competing effectively on the world stage. Some felt the United States should adopt an industrial policy such as Japan's, where government and large companies planned the future. This position was underlined by a feeling that the "cowboy competitors" and independent inventors who successfully built small companies in the past could not survive in the new world economy as defined by Japan and Germany.

Others felt that it might be too late for such a radical approach so different from the typical American model. Perhaps, these people felt, the United States should resign itself to inevitable decline. Rather than emphasizing high-tech products, the United States would have to be content as a provider of services and food production.

The Reagan administration argued that getting government off the back of industry by removing unnecessary regulatory burdens would revive the entrepreneurial spirit still smoldering beneath a federal bureaucracy that kept expanding its powers.

The debate included heated discussions regarding what, if any, role the public sector should play in supporting the private sector. This debate continues to this day.

A focal point in examining the role of government was asking what economic benefits the U.S. taxpayers received from the billions of dollars invested each year in universities and federal laboratories. The answer soon became apparent—not very much.

Quietly in the fall of 1978, a little-noted meeting took place at the Russell Senate Office Building that was to have a profound impact on the outcome of the debate. The meeting involved staff representing Senator Birch Bayh (D-Ind.) and visiting representatives of Purdue University, the University of Wisconsin, and the patent counsel from the Department of Health, Education, and Welfare. Bayh was a prominent senior senator who had recently run for president in the Democratic primaries in 1976. He was well respected as a thoughtful liberal surviving in a state increasingly dominated by conservative Republicans.

The visitors complained that the government policy of taking patent rights away from their creators was keeping important discoveries from development. They contended that allowing universities to retain rights to the inventions they created could pay important economic benefits to the nation if those inventions were developed. Examples were provided of Purdue making discoveries with DOE funding that were lying dormant because the inventors could not secure the patent rights to their own inventions.

Because of the importance of Purdue University to the State of Indiana, Bayh's staff looked into the problem. They determined that the problem was legitimate and widespread. Senator Bayh decided to act.

Another prominent senator was also discovering the same issue. Senator Robert Dole (R-Kans.) was the Senate minority leader and a well-established conservative. His staff had also met with university representatives and reached the same conclusions as Bayh's—it was time to cut the bureaucratic red tape strangling government-funded inventions.

Thus, a potent political team was born that was uniquely able to communicate to both sides of an increasingly heated national debate. In 1979, Bayh and Dole introduced legislation allowing universities and small businesses to own the inventions they discovered under federal grants and contracts. Provisions also allowed for the exclusive licensing of inventions arising from the federal laboratories. This marked a significant change in the relationship between federally funded R&D and the private sector.

The 96th Congress (1979–80) would prove a turning point in the "competitiveness debate." With what would be a seminal election looming in

November 1980, Congress and the administration had to provide answers to the American public addressing the economic morass engulfing the country.

Hearings on the Bayh-Dole proposed law began in 1979. They revealed that of the 28,000 patents the government owned, fewer than 4 percent had been licensed. The comptroller general of the United States added that the policy of making these discoveries freely available to anyone had effectively destroyed the incentives the patent system was designed to provide for subsequent development and deployment.

Several examples were provided by universities and small companies where potentially important discoveries made with government funding were languishing in the bureaucracy.

A series of policy pronouncements from Presidents Kennedy, Johnson, and Nixon seeking to relieve the situation had instead led to the creation of 24 different patent policies in the federal agencies. This meant that often there was more than one policy in place for the same agency. The resulting uncertainty ground the process to a halt.

Agency policies typically allowed inventing organizations to petition to claim patent ownership for inventions they created under federal funding. However, the resulting process frequently took two years for the bureaucracy to complete, and even then the answer could easily be "no."

Not surprisingly, these policies had a chilling effect on small businesses. A number of small business representatives testified that they simply could not accept government funding knowing that the resulting discoveries—usually heavily underwritten by them—would end up being taken by the government. These companies had to choose between being full-time government suppliers or full-time commercial entities—the government's patent policies did not allow them to be both.

Some of the most innovative small companies declined to even consider accepting government funding. This meant that the agencies were not able to tap into some of the best talent in the country to meet their needs.

The solution Senators Bayh and Dole proposed was to cut through the federal procedures strangling innovation with a Jeffersonian approach. The best way to commercialize new discoveries was to leave them with their creators and get the bureaucracy out of the way. The bill that resulted from the hearings allowed small companies and universities to own inventions they made under government grants and contracts.

Rather than seeking to copy the then-in-vogue Japanese/German big government style, Bayh and Dole chose a traditional American entrepreneurial response.

Other important provisions of the bill were

- Universities would be required to provide the government with a royalty-free license, as had been suggested by Vannevar Bush.
- University inventors would share in whatever royalties were generated.
- Domestic companies would receive a preference in licensing university inventions.
- Universities would be required to give a preference in licensing to small companies because they had proven to be the most reliable creators of new technologies and jobs over the years.

Not everyone was happy with the bill. Bayh-Dole was attacked from several directions. Admiral Hyman Rickover, the father of the nuclear navy, testified strongly against the bill, claiming it was a perversion of taxpayer-supported research and that the policy of open dissemination of government-funded inventions had served the nation well.

From the other direction, the proponents of a more Washington-centered approach floated competing legislation. The Carter administration backed a bill written by Senators Stevenson (D-Ill.) and Schmitt (R-N.Mex.), embodying a big-business approach to the problem.

A more subtle attack was launched within a few federal bureaucracies that saw the Bayh-Dole bill as transferring power from Washington to the universities and small businesses performing research. Their desire to recentralize these authorities within the Washington Beltway remains a constant theme even now, 20 years later.

Many senators felt that past policies, while creating impressive scientific knowledge and significant progress in federal mission-related R&D, had not generated significant economic benefits for all of the billions of dollars spent each year. Bayh-Dole garnered impressive cosponsors from all across the political spectrum.

Although the debate centered on whether to allow the decentralized management of research by universities and small businesses, another section of Bayh-Dole began to open the federal laboratories. The bill set clear guidelines for licensing inventions arising from the federal labs. Again, domestic small businesses were to be given preferential treatment. There was little discussion of these sections tucked in the back of the bill at the time. Even so, these sections were the first attempts to open up the federal laboratories. This effort would continue over the rest of the decade.

Exhibit 2.1
Embrex: A Small Business Reaping the Benefits of Technology Transfer

How has technology transfer benefited Embrex, Inc.? Just ask Randy Marcuson, the company's president and chief operating officer.

"The technology we licensed from the USDA (United States Department of Agriculture) is the foundation of the company. We would not be here without it."

Here is the story. Embrex is an international agricultural biotechnology company focused on developing patented biological and mechanical products that improve bird health, reduce bird and production costs, and provide other economic benefits to the poultry industry. Based on a technology it licensed from the USDA in the late 1980s, Embrex has pioneered the development and use of Inovoject®, an approach to poultry disease prevention that improves consistency and reliability by inoculating chicks while they are still in the egg. It was commercialized in 1993.

Just check out the numbers:

- Inovoject® systems are capable of injecting up to 50,000 eggs per hour.
- Nearly all U.S. poultry producers, including Tyson Foods, Perdue Farms, and ConAgra, use *in ovo* technology in their hatcheries.
- More than 80 percent of the eight billion broilers produced annually in North America are inoculated *in ovo* by the Inovoject® system.
- Embrex has systems installed in 30 countries in Europe, Latin America, Australia, North America, and Asia.

"Our revenue last year was just under $39 million," Marcuson said, noting that the company has grown from a half dozen employees in 1995 to in excess of 200 today, with offices in England, Brazil, Argentina, Korea, and Thailand, to name just a few countries. Its corporate headquarters is located near Research Triangle Park, North Carolina.

"This transfer is the foundation of the company," Marcuson said. "It is my understanding that this is the most successful out-licensing project the UDSA has ever undertaken. It is a wonderful example of where a technology transfer worked. We created a company that has successful sales and generated jobs for the local community."

Embrex offers its customers its proprietary platform delivery system called the Inovoject® automated egg injection system on a fee-per-egg-injected lease basis. This automated system punches a tiny hole into the egg's shell and then lowers a needle through the hole, delivering the therapeutic product to the embryo. This usually occurs on day 18 of the bird's 21-day incubation period.

"This technology is really the sparkplug for all we do today," Marcuson added.

THE NEXT STEP—REVERSING TRADITION

At the time Bayh-Dole was debated in 1979–80, the government had amassed some 28,000 patents, many of which had been created in the federal government's own labs.

Even before Bayh-Dole, it was recognized that because of the early stage of development of most federal inventions, significant private investment was needed to bring them to market. A 1968 General Accounting Office study of the Department of Health, Education, and Welfare (now the Department of Health and Human Services, the home of the National Institutes of Health) revealed a key weakness in the system.

"We found that hundreds of new compounds developed at university laboratories had not been tested and screened by the pharmaceutical industry because manufacturers were unwilling to undertake the expense without some possibility of obtaining exclusive rights to further development of a promising product," the study reported.

The study showed that companies would not invest their own funds in technologies if intellectual property protections were not available. The reason was simple: competitors had a great advantage by simply waiting until the "bugs" were worked out by the prior company. They then would ask for a similar nonexclusive license from the funding agency. Thus, the first company entering the system assumed the development risks, while copycats waited in the wings. Companies were no more willing to develop federal laboratory technologies than those of universities under such a system.

A report of the Senate Judiciary Committee (U.S. Senate 1979)on the Bayh-Dole bill summarized the efforts to license government-owned inventions under these circumstances: "The central problem seems to be that the agencies seek to issue nonexclusive licenses for these patents that are generally available to all interested persons. Nonexclusive licenses are generally viewed in the business community as no patent protection at all, and the response to such licenses has been lackluster."

The marketplace was quite clear—a "socialistic" technology licensing system was not going to work in a competitive economy. In essence, the U.S. policy was very similar to an approach expected of the Soviet

Union—no incentives were offered for risk taking, and subsequently, few government inventions were being commercialized.

As the election of 1980 approached, the Bayh-Dole bill passed the Senate. The House of Representatives, meanwhile, had backed an approach favored by the Carter administration emphasizing patent rights for large company contractors.

On the first Tuesday in November 1980, the frustration of the American public swept President Carter from office in a landslide victory for Republican nominee Ronald Reagan. The electoral tidal wave also pulled down many Democrats such as Birch Bayh. So many Democratic Senators lost that a Republican-controlled Senate was created, sending political shockwaves throughout Washington.

Because Congress had not wrapped up its business, a special lame-duck session was necessary, in which officeholders like Bayh and Carter were still actively engaged in the business of government until the next Congress convened in 1981.

Passing any legislation in this environment was very difficult. Only those bills with unanimous support were being processed. Most members of Congress simply wanted to go home. A game of legislative "chicken" ensued, with Bayh's staff eyeballing their House counterparts to see who would blink first. At the last possible moment, the House Judiciary Committee staff called and offered a deal—Bayh-Dole would be accepted in return for Senate support of a larger package dealing with reforms of the Patent and Trademark Office. With a staff phone call, the bargain was struck.

Bayh-Dole was added to a House bill that was sent to the Senate for unanimous approval.

Senator Russell Long (D-La.) had been a vocal opponent of Bayh-Dole and previously had forced consideration of the legislation off the Senate floor. However, the Senate is a close community in many respects. As a tribute to his departing colleague, Birch Bayh, Senator Long agreed to look the other way as the bill was brought up for unanimous approval. It passed and was on its way to President Carter's desk for signature.

Congress then went out of session.

With Congress finally gone, President Carter could pocket veto any legislation he didn't like by simply not signing it. Opposition to Bayh-Dole was particularly strong at DOE, which had a significant cadre of lawyers to oversee the department's tangled patent policies. There was a legitimate fear that enactment of Bayh-Dole would remove much of their reason for existence.

An active behind-the-scenes campaign began with small companies and universities encouraging acceptance of the bill by the outgoing administration. In the murky atmosphere typical of defeated administrations, it was very difficult to get a read on how President Carter would act.

Finally, prompted by the university and small business communities, President Carter signed the bill on the last day before it would die. After a three-year struggle, Bayh-Dole became the law of the land.

The fight was not over, however. The bureaucracy had another shot at Bayh-Dole, which required implementing regulations laying out exactly how the agencies would use its authorities. Many laws are undone behind the scenes when hostile agencies get a chance to interpret legislation. It remained to be seen whether or not Bayh-Dole would survive this new challenge.

STEVENSON-WYDLER—ANOTHER ARROW IN THE QUIVER

As Bayh-Dole inched through final approval, another key piece of legislation was also fighting its way along the legislative process. The Stevenson-Wydler Act was a more centralized approach, creating centers around the country to manage publicly funded R&D projects rather than leaving them with the universities and federal laboratories that created them. The bill emerged from the Senate Commerce Committee at almost the same time Bayh-Dole was being born in the Senate Judiciary Committee. Thus, these two pieces of legislation moved on parallel tracks, taking policy in different directions. During the confusion typical of lame-duck sessions of Congress, they were enacted at almost the same time.

Stevenson-Wydler did contain several sections that complimented Bayh-Dole. (A copy of the Bayh-Dole Act is in appendix II. A copy of the Stevenson-Wydler Act is in appendix III.) For example, the Stevenson-Wydler Act gave a charter to the Federal Laboratory Consortium (FLC), which originated as an informal group of Defense Department technology transfer officials meeting periodically to exchange notes. Stevenson-Wydler also taxed the R&D agencies to fund the FLC. This created a unique forum for interagency cooperation and education and what would become an increasingly important focus for professional development.

The Stevenson-Wydler Act also mandated that R&D-intensive agencies create Offices of Research and Technology Applications (ORTAs) to serve as focal points for disseminating information to industry about potentially commercially relevant R&D. However, the legal authorities needed for labs to actually make deals for commercialization were not significantly changed.

Another change enacted by the Stevenson-Wydler legislation was the establishment of the Center for the Utilization of Federal Technology (CUFT) at the Department of Commerce. CUFT was to be the clearinghouse and manager for licensing federally owned inventions.

The incoming Reagan administration would have to sort out what to do with these new laws as it began formulating its R&D policies. It quickly and categorically rejected calls for a centralized industrial policy to combat Japan. Less government and less control of the private sector became watchwords for the Republican revolution.

The decentralization-from-Washington thrust for technology management embodied in Bayh-Dole struck a chord with the incoming Reagan administration. Over the first years of the Reagan administration, attempts were made by DOE in particular to defang the new law through the implementing regulations. Through a series of complex maneuvers, these actions were beaten back.

The new administration also refused to fund, and thereby killed, the innovation centers envisioned in Stevenson-Wydler, but the FLC was established across the agencies. The stage was being set for a new approach to commercializing federally owned technologies across the board.

BAYH-DOLE KICKS IN FOR UNIVERSITIES

Soon after passage of the Bayh-Dole Act, universities began to license processes and products that evolved into the biotechnology industry. Because the law was in place, Washington could not take these inventions away from the universities. The result was an increase in patents, licenses, and industry funding, and the creation of new small businesses based on university R&D, a trend that continues.

President Reagan wondered why there were not similar developments around federal laboratories and in 1983 called on businessman David Packard to investigate the laboratory system.

The resulting Federal Laboratory Review Panel reported,

The United States can no longer afford the luxury of isolating its government laboratories from university and industry laboratories. Already endowed with the best research institutions in the world, this country is increasingly challenged in its military and economic competitiveness. The national interest demands that the federal laboratories collaborate with universities and industry to ensure continued advances in scientific knowledge and its translation into useful technology. The federal laboratories must be more responsive to national needs.

The ultimate purpose of federal support for R&D is to develop the science and technology base needed for a strong national defense, for the health and well-being of U.S. citizens, and for a healthy U.S. economy. Federal laboratories should recognize that they are an important part of the partnership with universities and industry in meeting this goal. A strong cooperative relationship must exist between federal laboratories, universities, industry, and other users of the laboratories' research results.

Federal laboratories have traditionally felt that they are part of the government, committed to its highest service, and totally dependent on it for support. They perceive industry as an awkward partner with a different value system. Although the degree of interaction with universities and industry varied among the laboratories visited, the Panel feels that this interaction could be increased at all federal laboratories.

While the Packard report was being prepared, Senator Dole (now the new Senate majority leader) became increasingly frustrated with continued bureaucratic resistance to Bayh-Dole, especially in DOE. Dole argued that not only was Bayh-Dole good for the universities, it would reinvigorate the department's own laboratories. Most of the DOE labs are operated by contractors, many of which are universities.

Dole introduced legislation to allow all federal laboratories to operate with similar technology transfer authorities as those in Bayh-Dole. The legislation was particularly aimed at DOE, which was the most resistant agency to decentralization. Most witnesses supported the concept. DOE opposed it. Finally running out of patience at this resistance, Dole ran the amendment through the Senate.

The House did not have similar legislation and wanted to look more carefully at what to do to overhaul the federal laboratory system. There was not sufficient time remaining in that legislative session to begin this investigation. However, the House finally agreed to accept a scaled-down version of Dole's bill. The legislation that was enacted allowed university-operated federal laboratories to operate under the Bayh-Dole authorities.

Even in its modified version, the Dole amendment was an important step forward. Congress was making its interest in overhauling the federal laboratories' commercialization efforts apparent. The Dole concept of giving all the federal labs more autonomy for linking their R&D with U.S. industry was not forgotten. This idea would be reintroduced in the next Congress. It became the landmark Federal Technology Transfer Act of 1986.

Because it is essential to understand how the Federal Technology Transfer Act works to successfully interact with the labs, we will explore its key provisions in the next chapter.

Exhibit 2.2
Additional Lab Partnership Opportunities

Technical Assistance

Federal laboratories often provide industry with technical assistance regarding unique government expertise. Small businesses in particular benefit from technical assistance and suggestions from laboratory staff. Depending on the circumstances, there may be no charge for this assistance. Experience has shown that technical assistance often opens the door to future technology transfer activities.

Personnel Exchanges

The exchange of personnel between federal and nonfederal laboratories is a key means of technology transfer. Personnel exchanges provide an opportunity for federal lab engineers and scientists to receive an insider's look at external laboratories where new ideas, process improvements, enhancements, and shortcuts can take place. Federal laboratory personnel can also learn from the contributions of external engineers and scientists who are temporarily assigned to their laboratories.

Through personnel exchanges, each party gains insight into the problems of the other partner. This helps to facilitate the transfer of technology between federal and commercial applications. The benefits of personnel exchanges are extensive.

Use of Laboratory Facilities

Universities, industry, the technical community, and other government facilities may utilize equipment and expertise at a federal laboratory, which was designed by the government for use by these groups. Features of this sharing arrangement, which involves designated user facilities and other resources, include the following:

- Research may be conducted on a proprietary or nonproprietary basis.
- Full cost recovery is required to offset any federal lab expenses for proprietary R&D.
- Class patent waiver, in which title goes to the user, may be granted, and the user's proprietary data can be protected.
- For nonproprietary R&D, title to inventions goes to the user, but data generated are freely available.
- If funded under another government contractor or international agreement, users are subject to those intellectual property clauses.
- Availability of federal laboratory facilities for use by nonfederal entities will vary by agency and by laboratory.

PEORIA HELPS CHANGE FEDERAL
LABORATORIES' MISSION

The economic doldrums cast over traditional U.S. industries in the 1970s and early 1980s was particularly apparent in the industrial heartland. This region, once the keystone in the industrial race that helped win World War II, was now derisively termed the "Rust Belt." And no town better epitomized the Rust Belt syndrome than Peoria, Illinois.

Like many moderately sized American cities of the time, Peoria's economy was directly linked to the dominant company in town, Caterpillar Tractor. Caterpillar was a leading provider of heavy industrial and farm machinery, but during the 1970s and early 1980s its market share eroded because of pressure from Japanese companies. The resulting downsizing threw the local economy into a tailspin.

City leaders realized they must take action or the situation would only worsen. Looking for diversification opportunities, they noted that their local university and a Department of Agriculture laboratory had complimentary competencies in biotechnology.

A delegation from Peoria visited Washington to meet with the U.S. Department of Commerce, the lead agency on technology transfer. They wanted guidance on how to form a research consortium around their publicly funded institutions.

They were informed that as a result of the Bayh-Dole Act, the university could be utilized. But they also learned that the local federal laboratory could not fully participate because it lacked the legal authority to conduct proprietary joint research.

Refusing to give up, the Peoria delegation learned of the Dole proposal to open up the federal labs to industry. Unfortunately, as amended the final Dole bill would not cover labs like the one in Peoria that are operated by federal employees.

Still persisting, the Peoria delegation interested their congressman, House Minority Leader Bob Michel (R-Ill.) in the idea. Rep. Michel agreed to introduce new legislation in the next session of Congress. A sympathetic Senate sponsor was found in Senator Slade Gorton (R-Wash.), who served on the Senate Commerce Committee.

Because this committee did not have jurisdiction over the Bayh–Dole Act (which arose from the Senate Judiciary Committee), the legislation was reintroduced as an amendment to the Stevenson-Wydler Act.

This law made it clear that Congress and the administration expected the federal labs to ally with industry and to include small business in a significant way. Transferring technologies to the private sector was becoming an important part of the lab mission.

By the time the Federal Technology Transfer Act was debated in Congress in 1986, a number of factors led to an atmosphere that was conducive to limited cooperation between the public and private sectors. Universities using the Bayh-Dole Act were meeting with successes; the American people were frustrated with economic stagnation; and there was an alarming loss of jobs across America.

Under the Reagan administration, U.S. policy was clear. Government should not try to direct commercial innovation, but it should instead continue to fund its mission and basic research while encouraging U.S. companies to create partnerships that could take federally funded research into the marketplace.

The intent of the Senate sponsors of the Federal Technology Transfer Act was clearly laid out in the committee report that sent the legislation to the full Senate for approval.

The report stated (U.S. Senate 1986),

> Despite the Bayh-Dole Act as amended in 1984 and the Stevenson-Wydler Act, the federal laboratories still face problems and disincentives in trying to transfer technology. This is especially true for those laboratories operated by the federal government, as opposed to those operated by contractors. Many of them have no clear legal authority to enter into cooperative research projects.

The secretary of commerce, in his February 1984 report to the president and Congress on operations under the Stevenson-Wydler Act, stated,

> It appears to be no accident that technology complexes such as Silicon Valley, Route 128, Research Triangle, and Princeton's Forestall Center have evolved around major universities. Direct access to the university and the university's right to transfer the results of its research on an exclusive basis is an important incentive for business to invest in the further development and commercialization of new technologies. In contrast, federal laboratories generally have not served as nuclei for similar arrangements. They often perceive themselves as unable to enter into cooperative development arrangements because of organizational and legal restraints. This is one reason why national reviews of federal laboratories have concluded that too little of the results of laboratory research is used in the private sector. To improve technology transfer, the federal laboratories need clear authority to do cooperative research, and they need to be able to exercise that authority at the laboratory level. Agencies need to delegate to their laboratory

directors that authority to manage and promote the results of their research. A requirement to go to agency headquarters for approval of industry collaborative arrangements and patent licensing agreements can effectively prevent them. Lengthy headquarters approval delays can cause businesses to lose interest in developing new technologies.

Working closely with their counterparts in the House Science Committee, legislation was crafted that allowed the federal laboratories to enter into cooperative R&D agreements (CRADAs) with private industry. (Appendix V contains a sample CRADA form.) Preferences in these partnerships, as in Bayh-Dole, were given to small companies and to those manufacturing the resulting products substantially in the United States. Companies could contribute funds, expertise, or equipment to the CRADA. Agencies would link these resources with ongoing research and could grant the company partner appropriate intellectual property protection so that resulting discoveries were moved to the marketplace.

The law also mandated that agencies must share royalties arising from CRADAs with their inventors. The labs were allowed to reward other employees involved with the project and to use remaining funds for performing R&D at the lab. In the next chapter, we will explore in more detail how this important bill works. It is essential for partnering with the federal laboratory system and understanding its in's and out's.

Coming up six years after the enactment of the Bayh-Dole Act of 1980, the Federal Technology Transfer Act was not subject to the same philosophical debate about the appropriateness of promoting R&D partnerships between the public and private sectors. Rather a new issue emerged. A small intellectual property trade association attacked the bill during consideration in the House Science Committee because one section provided that royalties must be shared with federal laboratory inventors. Fearing that this might become a precedent for government mandating how private companies must reward their inventors (as in Germany), the association successfully had the section stricken. Again the House and Senate staff worked a horse trade—the royalty-sharing section was restored in exchange for expanding the charter of the FLC. This historic bill then moved through the Congress and was promptly signed by President Reagan.

Enactment of the Federal Technology Transfer Act of 1986 heralded a new era for the federal laboratory system. The 40-year policy debate was effectively over. It was now clear that the federal laboratories were to partner with American companies. Now the hard work began. Laboratories and industry would have to learn to walk this new path together. This was not a simple task.

EXECUTIVE ORDER 12591—ANOTHER MESSAGE TO FEDERAL LABORATORIES

The enactment of the Federal Technology Transfer Act in 1986 and its endorsement by President Reagan in Executive Order 12591 the next year began a new phase in which the labs received a new national mission—to link with U.S. industry in economic development as well as continuing their traditional role of conducting mission-related research and basic research.

A pattern also emerged after the passage of Bayh-Dole in 1980. Almost like clockwork, every two years Congress pushed the agencies to become more aggressive in using the significant new authorities given them. The general feeling was that the labs were too timid and didn't move quickly enough to finalize deals with industry. There were also fears that agency headquarters did not really allow the labs to use the authorities Congress gave them by continuing to second-guess the labs' decisions on licenses and CRADAs.

Much of this tension was caused by the original emphasis placed on the labs for public disclosure of all research unrelated to national security, dating back to the 1945 Bush report; some came from the reluctance of the headquarters' bureaucracies to allow their labs to manage their R&D without significant review and "guidance."

There were other reasons: the lack of familiarity with time-to-market and other imperatives that drive the private sector; lack of skills in deal making; and a lack of high-level support for technology transfer. We will address these factors in chapter 4.

Still, without minimizing the learning curve the labs have gone through, significant progress has been made.

PEORIA'S REPORT CARD

Soon after enactment of the Federal Technology Transfer Act of 1986, Peoria successfully crafted a biotechnology consortium built around a federal lab and a university. Six companies signed up. Despite the lack of precedent, the Peoria consortium took root and grew.

The Department of Commerce is required to report to the president and Congress on utilization of the Federal Technology Transfer Act by the federal agencies. Here is what the May 2000 report had to say about Peoria's Biotechnology Research and Development Corporation (U.S. Department of Commerce 2000):

> Another interesting example of collaboration aimed at achieving economic development and involving a federal agency, state and local government, universities, and industry is the Biotechnology Research and Development Corporation (BRDC). BRDC resulted from the collaborative efforts of the Department of Agriculture's Northern Regional Research Center, local government authorities in Peoria, Illinois, and a number of private sector companies interested in agricultural technologies.
>
> BRDC currently has 10 publicly traded companies as stockholders. It helps to fund collaborative research at the Agricultural Research Service's (ARS) laboratories and 26 universities, looking for embryonic technologies that it can push to proof of concept. Early-stage commercial development is generally handled by finding a suitable private sector partner to work with the inventors (generally a BRDC shareholder but sometimes a BRDC licensee). During 1989, BRDC filed 11 new patent applications, had 24 patents issued or applications allowed, and executed eight license and option agreements.
>
> Many interesting and important technical achievements have come out of BRDC-backed research. ARS scientists, working with Dow Chemical Company scientists, have developed a family of composite materials derived from starches and flours that exhibit remarkable mechanical and strength properties and can be fabricated into injection and compression molded and extruded articles. BRDC also funded research at Purdue University producing a plant gene promoter useful in genetically engineered crops and has granted licenses or options to license to nearly every major agriculture biotechnology company in the world, as well as making it available to researchers. This technology has generated more than 50 percent of BRDC's licensing income. BRDC, in collaboration with the University of Illinois, has also filed for the first patent on stem cell technology involving an animal other than the mouse. This technology may provide the means of reproducing superior genetic versions of production animals. Licensing of this technology is now underway.

The Peoria delegation served as pioneers of the federal laboratory system. They realized the significant potential that combining the resources of their local federal laboratory and research university held for the region. They learned from the mistake of relying on one company or industry for their economic well-being in a changing world. Even more importantly, they paved the way for others by providing the impetus for legislation opening up the federal labs. Like true pioneers, they blazed a trail for others to follow.

We will now examine in more detail how the technology transfer laws work. For those who know how to use them, these statutes allow companies to leverage their own R&D and bring new products to market by tapping into some of the brightest minds in the world—the scientists and engineers in the federal laboratory system.

Chapter 3

HOW TO USE FEDERAL LABORATORIES

Let us develop the resources of our land, call forth its powers, build up its institutions, promote all its greatest interests, and see whether we may also, in our day and generation, perform something worthy to be remembered.

—Daniel Webster

LICENSING

There are two kinds of federal laboratories: those operated by contractors and those operated by government employees. The enabling statutes vary, but the major provisions for patent licensing are the same with the exception of the public notification clause. Here is what you need to know.

Notification—Except for laboratories operated by contractors (e.g., most of the DOE labs and the National Aeronautics and Space Administration's [NASA's] Jet Propulsion Laboratory), the law determines how federal agencies must notify the public about government-owned inventions that are available for licensing. Contractor-operated labs are given discretion on how they will advertise that their inventions are available for licensing.

Before exclusively licensing any invention, the government employee operated labs must provide a public notice in the *Federal Register* that the patent is available for development. Most labs also routinely list patents available for licensing on their Web sites. (See the Web site listings in chapter 6.)

Nonexclusive licenses may be granted without this notification, although most federal agencies post notices of any patent available for licensing anyway.

The regulations normally require agencies to provide notices for three months. If a company indicates an interest in an exclusive license, a further 60-day notice is published in the *Federal Register,* allowing affected persons to object or comment. This second notice identifies the patent for which the exclusive license is being sought and names the interested company. In highly competitive fields, rival companies closely follow notices of exclusive licenses being sought.

Before granting an exclusive license, the government must consider any comments and must also believe that granting the exclusive license will not substantially reduce competition, is in the national interest, and enhances U.S. competitiveness.

The agency then determines how to proceed.

Companies are advised to seek only the license protections they really need. For example, it would be much easier to secure an exclusive field-of-use license linked with a specific commercial application being pursued than to seek an across-the-board exclusive license that may include markets the company has no ability to enter.

Because industry worried that the *Federal Register* requirements could discourage timely development of federal inventions, Congress enacted legislation in 2000 written by former Rep. Connie Morella (R-Md.) allowing agencies to collapse both notices into a 15-day notification. Agencies are wrestling with how to utilize this new provision, but Congress is clearly pressing them to move quickly on these issues.

The new law also allows companies to license inventions and further develop them under a cooperative R&D agreement (CRADA) with the creating agency. How to secure a CRADA is described in the next section. This is an important benefit because most federal technologies require significant development and testing. Keeping the lab inventors involved in this process is extremely valuable.

PREFERENCE FOR U.S. INDUSTRY

In establishing technology transfer laws, Congress hoped taxpayers would receive maximum benefits for the development of any technology they helped fund in our federal labs and universities. Consequently, the laws require the labs and universities to consider where the development of a licensed technology will occur. The laws provide a preference for those seeking exclusive rights in the U.S. market when *the subject invention will be manufactured substantially in the United States.* Because what is *substantial* varies with each technology, the laws leave it up to the agency to determine when a potential licensee meets this test. Also, this provision can

Figure 3.1
Income from Licenses for Federal Laboratory Intellectual Property

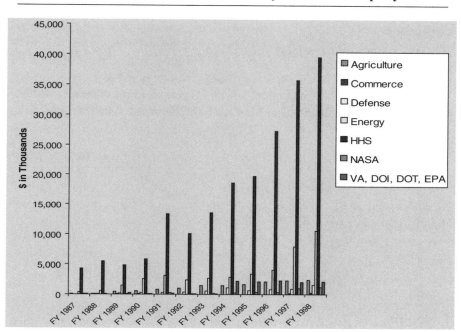

HHS–Health & Human Services; VA–Veterans Administration; DOI–Department of
Interior; DOT–Department of Transportation; EPA–Environmental Protection Agency

be waived when legitimate efforts to secure domestic development prove
unsuccessful.

This provision has caused major discomfort with multinational firms that
would like to manufacture products in the most cost-effective location—
often overseas. Congress has shown no inclination to change it, however.

PREFERENCE FOR SMALL BUSINESSES

The law states,

First preference in the exclusive or partially exclusive licensing of federally
owned inventions shall go to small business firms submitting plans that are
determined by the agency to be within the capabilities of the firms and
equally likely, if executed, to bring the invention to practical application as
any plans submitted by applicants that are not small business firms.

Whether a company is a small business depends in part on the industry. The determination is made by regulations formulated by the U.S. Small Business Administration.

NEED FOR A DEVELOPMENT PLAN

No agency may license its patents to an applicant until it has received a *plan for development and/or marketing of the invention.* Plans submitted to the agencies are confidential and exempt from the Freedom of Information Act.

Exhibit 3.1
Rogers Corporation: A NASA License Leads to Ownership of Niche Market

Hundreds of millions of computers in the United States, made by scores of different manufacturers, have one element in common: they each contain a laminate now offered by Rogers Corporation through Polyimide-Laminate Systems, LLC (PLS), its 50/50 joint venture with Mitsui Chemicals, Inc. The laminate is converted into part of the suspension assembly inside the hard disk drive.

"We are the only supplier of this laminate to fabricators of computer manufacturers," said Dr. Richard Traskos, director of product development at Rogers. "We have developed the material, and our joint venture is the sole company serving this niche market."

Rogers worked with NASA Langley Research Center to license the patent for a NASA-developed laminating adhesive. In the mid-1980s, Traskos and the company's patent attorney worked with NASA's attorneys to write the laminate patent, which was tailored to Rogers's development plans for the adhesive.

"Rogers evaluated the adhesive, but our goal was to develop a laminate made by using the Langley-type adhesive," said Traskos. "The laminate ends up as part of the suspension assembly used to hold the read/write head inside the hard disk drive. It can best be described as a "sandwich" of stainless steel, adhesive, and copper that has both electrical conductivity and mechanical properties."

In 1999, Rogers's sales included more than $30 million of the specialty laminate.

Rogers Corporation, headquartered in Rogers, Connecticut, develops and manufactures specialty materials focusing on the growing wireless communications and computer markets. Rogers operates manufacturing facilities in the United States and Belgium and has sales offices in Japan, China, Hong Kong, Taiwan, Korea, and Singapore. Rogers has joint ventures in Japan with

Inoac Corporation, in Taiwan with Chang Chun Plastics, and in the United States with Mitsui Chemicals and 3M Corporation. The company manufactures printed circuit materials, high-performance foams, electroluminescent lamps, and moldable composites, among other specialty materials.

"When we started this project, NASA was new to the technology transfer concept. We helped each other through this process," Traskos said. "Rogers Corporation is looking at another NASA technology, which could potentially develop into a further relationship with them."

The implementing regulations governing how agencies apply the provision requiring a development and/or marketing plan list the following factors that the potential licensee should address:

- Identification of the invention being licensed, including the patent number, title, and date, if known.
- Identification of the type of license sought (exclusive for all fields, exclusive for a specific field of use, nonexclusive, etc.).
- Name and address of the person/organization applying for the license.
- Nature/type of business, including products and services the applicant has already commercialized.
- Approximate number of applicant's employees.
- Where the applicant learned about the availability of the patent for licensing.
- Whether the applicant is a small business. (Remember: small businesses get preferential treatment.)
- A detailed description of applicant's plan for development and/or marketing of the invention.
- A commitment to update the agency on development of the patent if the application is approved.

The regulations then list what the plan should include:

- How much time, investment, and other resources the applicant expects to need *to bring the invention to practical application.*
- How capable the company is of fulfilling its plan, including information regarding manufacturing, marketing, finance, and technical resources.
- What markets (fields of use) the company plans to pursue.
- The geographic regions in which the company intends to use or sell the invention.

- Whether the company ever licensed a federal technology before.
- Whether the potential licensee knows if the invention is currently in use by industry or the government itself.
- Any other information the applicant believes will support a determination to grant the license.

The development plan is obviously the heart of things. Look over the comments in our confidential survey of agency licensing officials in the next chapter. They will help you hit the bull's-eye with your plan!

The government has the right to modify or terminate a license it has granted if the licensee does not meet its obligations. The licensee must first be notified in writing. Agencies are reluctant to take this sort of action unless it becomes clear that a company can't or won't develop the patent.

Applicants denied a license may appeal. The agency licensing official can tell you who receives such petitions.

OTHER PROVISIONS

Agencies may include additional provisions in the licensing agreement as long as they do not conflict with the law. The license may allow a company to sublicense, but licenses cannot be completely assigned to another company without agency approval.

Licenses may or may not include royalties, and they may include other compensation.

Agencies may terminate a license if such an action is deemed necessary to meet the public need, as specified by regulations issued after the license is approved and which the licensee cannot reasonably satisfy. Also, a license can be terminated if the applicant provided false or misleading information.

The government has the right to use the invention for research, procurement, or other purposes, and any company sublicense must include that provision. In practice, however, the government's rights provision has rarely, if ever, damaged the commercial rights of the licensee. Even if the government should want to buy the product for its own purposes, it is much more likely to work with the licensee than to try and take the technology back.

COOPERATIVE R&D AGREEMENTS

The ability to perform CRADAs with federal agencies falls under the provisions of the Federal Technology Transfer Act except in the case of NASA, which uses the Space Act. The provisions of both laws are similar.

Here are the main provisions you need to know:

Agencies may accept funds, personnel, services, and property and may provide personnel, services, and property to the collaborating party. However, agencies may not provide funding. The purpose of the CRADA is to leverage research the lab is conducting so that commercial as well as agency mission research is developed. The CRADA is not intended to substitute for government contracting, where labs are paying for services. Congress does not want the labs diverting from their missions in order to attract industry sponsors. Rather, the concept allows the lab and its industry partner to leverage their capabilities to their mutual benefit.

The lab must ensure that the industry partner may receive an exclusive field-of-use license for patents created under the CRADA. This is a relatively new provision, added to the law by Rep. Morella in 1998. It is intended to send a message to the labs that Congress is serious about the industry partner enjoying the commercial benefits of the CRADA.

Exhibit 3.2
New Software Makes Humans and Environment Healthier

An environmental software technology—a product of a CRADA between Technical Database Services, Inc. (TDS), New York, New York, and the U.S. Environmental Protection Agency's National Risk Management Research Laboratory—is a commercial product with a potentially bright future.

PARIS II—the Program Assisting Replacement of Industrial Solvents, Version 2—is a powerful Windows-based tool for the selection and design of solvent systems that have a lower impact on human health and the environment. It became commercially available in early 2001. Chemical and environmental engineers, chemists, industrial hygienists—anyone involved in the evaluation or replacement of solvents—will find PARIS II easy and efficient to use, said Dr. Mildred R. Green, president of TDS.

"PARIS II can help reduce the risk of exposure to substances that are a hazard in the workplace or the environment," Green added.

The user specifies a solvent system by its chemical composition, or by its physical properties, and sets a tolerance level for the properties and the health and environmental effects deemed to be acceptable. PARIS II will then draw upon its extensive knowledge base to identify alternatives that are safer and less costly to manage and dispose of.

In addition to its advanced solvent design algorithms, PARIS II utilizes a database of physical properties and information in four main categories of environmental concern to identify pure chemicals and mixtures that can perform as well as or better than solvents that are more hazardous. The environmental impact categories in PARIS II include local human toxicity (dermal, inhalation, and ingestion), local ecological toxicity (aquatic and terrestrial), regional effects (photochemical oxidation and acidification), and global effects (ozone depletion and green house effect). A weighting scheme allows users to adapt each analysis to a specific site or application.

As for sales so far, Green said they have been "good," despite the fact that it sometimes "takes a while to establish a foothold" in software. "We will continue to look for innovative ways to make it available."

What about Green's thoughts on technology transfer and working with the federal government?

"It has been good for our business," she said. "For technology transfer to work, you have to make sure the product in question will fit into your product line at the time. Is it a product you like? Do you have a market for it?"

Because the federal government has an investment in the laboratory's research, the government may use the invention for its own purposes, as is the case with university patents under Bayh-Dole. The lab can require the CRADA partner to license others only if such licensing is necessary to meet public health or safety needs that "cannot be satisfied by the collaborating party." Such actions may also be taken if the industry partner does not substantially manufacture the developed patent in the United States, as agreed. Any actions taken by the agency under this provision are subject to administrative and judicial appeal by the company.

Any invention made solely by a company employee under a CRADA is owned by the company, with the government having the right to use the invention for its own purposes—normally research. Any confidential or privileged information the laboratory has received from its CRADA partner is protected if the government uses the invention.

The agencies must give special consideration to small business firms or consortia seeking CRADAs.

Agencies must consider whether resulting technologies are "substantially manufactured" in the United States. In the case of foreign companies, agencies must consider whether U.S. companies are provided the opportunity to engage in similar activities with national laboratories in the foreign company's country.

Provisions aimed at DOE require agency headquarters to quickly approve or disapprove CRADAs with contractor-operated labs. Laboratories may permit employees to work with the CRADA partner on commercial development of the patent.

No trade secrets, confidential business information, or commercial or financial information the lab receives from a CRADA partner may be disclosed.

The laboratories also have the ability to protect for up to five years after development any information created under the CRADA that in the private sector would be considered a trade secret or privileged or confidential commercial or financial information.

As mentioned earlier, legislation now permits companies to license a government-owned invention and then work with the laboratory under a CRADA for its further development. Such agreements have been routine between companies collaborating with universities or university-operated labs. Now, any federal lab can license a patent and agree to perform additional R&D under a cooperative agreement with the partner company. Given the embryonic nature of most federal technologies, this is potentially a major benefit to an industrial developer.

The bottom line: Agencies, like any business partner, favor those who have done their homework and have a plan to succeed, not simply a dream. By knowing how agencies and laws work and what agencies look for in a partner, you may successfully stake your claim.

Chapter 4

VIEW FROM THE BRIDGE: ADVICE FROM INSIDE

> All of the glory that goes with winning, all of the turmoil, all of
> the winning, all of the money, they don't last. But the spirit that
> it takes to try to get there—these are the things that really endure.
> —Vince Lombardi

We have discussed how labs were formed, what they do, how they do it, why they were directed to work with industry, how they must give preference in licensing or CRADAs to small companies, and how the laws work. So, all you have to do now is knock on the door and off you go, right?

Well, it's not quite that simple.

There are challenges any industry "miner" must face in working with the federal labs. We will share some very candid advice from several veteran federal technology managers on how you can succeed.

THE JOHN PRESTON TOUCH

Massachusetts Institute of Technology (MIT) has long been recognized as a real technology transfer engine. It is not only a significant catalyst for the New England economy, but an important national asset as well.

However, MIT was not particularly successful in transferring its world-class research to the commercial marketplace until it overhauled its technology transfer office in the mid-1980s. John Preston was brought in to energize the office, and he has gone on to be a key member of several small business start-ups. He now serves as chief executive officer and president of Atomic Ordered Materials in Massachusetts.

Preston has been very active in moving technologies to market. He has testified before Congress, been honored by the government of France, advised the government of Singapore, and even held a meeting with Prince Charles on how to successfully integrate public sector research facilities into the national economy.

Preston believes the most important ingredient in any business alliance is *passion*. He notes that in the world of developing partnerships, things will inevitably go wrong, take longer than expected, cost more, or go off in an unanticipated direction. If all the partners do not share a burning *passion* to succeed, they will not survive the pitfalls.

Preston has composed a concise list of "passion killers":

1. Greed
2. Greed
3. Greed
4. Destructive criticism
5. Lawyers and committees
6. Bureaucracy and red tape

PASSION KILLERS ON PARADE

People in the public sector certainly are not greedier than others, and many top researchers have passed up lucrative opportunities in private industry because they are truly passionate about their research. The simple fact is, they are either very committed to achieving such important national missions as defense or space exploration, or they enjoy performing basic research to further the frontiers of science.

This does not mean you will never encounter greed as a factor in dealing with the labs, but it is not the driving force for the labs to work with industry.

That takes care of items one through three on Preston's list. Now, let's examine the other issues.

What is your mental image of government? Do conformity, delays, aversion to risk, endless meetings, and emphasis on process pop up? That generalization would certainly be unfair to the many dedicated public servants who work very hard at their jobs. However, it is fair to say the public sector has more than its share of destructive criticism, lawyers, committees, bureaucracy, and red tape.

The single biggest criticism of federal labs that has been brought to the attention of Congress time and time again is that the labs are slow to complete commercialization deals. There certainly are two sides to this complaint, and delays can be cited on the industry side as well. However, make no mistake about it—institutional factors in government cause delays.

Unlike industry, government lawyers rarely report to the federal dealmakers, and most see their essential task as *preventing bad things from happening, not as getting deals done.* Particularly deals that break new ground or use new legal authorities make government lawyers nervous.

Such situations can result in a three-way negotiation: (1) the company with the lab, (2) the lab with headquarters, and (3) back to the company. Many times it's the middle negotiation within the agency that is the more complex. This can cause confusion with the company partner, which the lab then wonders why things that seemed okay in the first place are now being rehashed.

For this reason, most agencies use *model agreements.* If your deal can fit into an existing model, that's great. If it doesn't, things can bog down.

As Einstein observed in another context, *time is relative.* Government and industry concepts of timeliness are two very different things. Companies frequently bemoan that agencies simply do not understand how competitive markets work. Small companies are especially sensitive, because they often understand that quick time-to-market is their most significant advantage over larger competitors.

We have already seen that delays in licensing government inventions are created by the federal notification process. Although most federal technology transfer officials are keenly interested in clearing pending deals quickly, agency approval procedures can be quirky. Typically, more experienced agencies are faster because their systems have done this before. Still, with patience, companies can successfully negotiate the system.

Exhibit 4.1
Partnership with Lab Spurs Company Growth

Thanks to a technology it developed with Brookhaven National Laboratory, Novagen, Inc., of Madison, Wisconsin, has a product that has achieved a fivefold sales increase from 1997 to 2000. Under the terms of the CRADA, Novagen has the right to sublicense the invention to other companies. There is growing interest in using the technology in the development of pharmaceutically useful materials. Novagen expects a substantial increase in its sublicensing activities in the next few years.

"It is a pleasure to work with them and to see their success continue. Their success in this highly competitive field of the manufacture and sale of research reagents is attributable to their excellent exploitation of specific product arenas, their maintenance of the ability to collaborate, and their good business acumen," said Christine L. Brakel, Ph.D., a licensing associate at Brookhaven National Laboratory.

In 1990, prior to the CRADA, Novagen became Brookhaven's first licensed distributor of products known as the T7 Gene Expression System, arising from a lab patent. Novagen became the world's best-known supplier of T7 Gene Expression System reagents. Under the subsequent CRADA, a new patent resulted that was exclusively licensed by Novagen. This discovery modifies a T7 virus so that a protein-coded gene can be displayed on the surface of a virus. Brookhaven scientists will use genetic engineering techniques to create a library of millions of T7 viruses, each displaying a different protein or variant of a protein. Powerful methods of selection can be applied to the library to isolate viruses displaying proteins with desirable properties—for example, improved antibodies. Growth of the select virus provides the cloned gene for further analysis and for making large amounts of the protein.

This success led to the company being purchased in 1998 by a large research reagent manufacturer and supplier, CN Biosciences of San Diego, California. However, Novagen maintains its own corporate identity while working with CN Biosciences.

IF YOU DON'T LIKE TODAY'S POLICY, JUST WAIT FOR TOMORROW

Laboratory officials know technology transfer goes in and out of style in Washington. The GAO issued a report in July 2001 on tech transfer in DOE's nuclear weapons and production facilities, which include world-class research labs like Los Alamos, Sandia, Oak Ridge's Y-12 facility, and Lawrence Livermore (GAO 2001).

DOE provided funds as incentives for these labs to do more R&D with industry.

With the Clinton Administration taking office in 1993 and the election of a new Congress in 1994, the original intent of the program was lost and DOE's defense programs requested that funding for this activity be eliminated, which it was. Not surprisingly, the GAO report found that this abrupt policy reversal caused the number of CRADAS created in the labs to plummet. The labs then emphasized licensing, which increased dramatically.

Policy change is not always bad for technology transfer. For years, the Department of Veterans Affairs (VA) sat out the tech transfer revolution. It was on the sidelines when the Federal Technology Transfer Act passed in 1986 and again when President Reagan endorsed the principles in his 1987 executive order.

The VA is an important source of a wide range of health-related research. Unfortunately, because its links with the private sector were so weak, its commercial development of medical research was sporadic.

When Anthony Principi was named secretary of the VA by President George W. Bush, Principi convened a meeting of key VA stakeholders in Washington. The secretary succinctly summed up VA's situation: "For many years, VA did not establish the ownership rights to new technologies our researchers developed. As a result, our department has lost the revenues those rights generated and the opportunity to show America's veterans and others the results of our research."

Principi made clear to his staff that he was committed to tech transfer, "This new system will help us serve veterans better. Veterans are the reason VA exists, and if we can find a way to improve the care we provide them, that is what we will do."

The result is that VA now has several major deals working their way through the system.

Still, strong support from the top of an agency does not always exist. This shifting of agency priorities was pointed out in a study conducted in 1997 for the Federal Laboratory Consortium (Chapman and Lundquist 1997):

> Perhaps the most important (pitfall) was the lack of top support at the departmental or agency level. Quite obviously, the policy case FOR technology transfer IS NOT BEING MADE effectively at the top levels of the executive departments and agencies. Even where there were coordinating activities at Washington, D.C., headquarters, this was limited via either advocacy or resources—at the level of political leadership.
>
> Also there is a "clash of cultures" apparent at the program management levels in departmental or agency Washington, D.C., headquarters that undercuts effective technology transfer efforts at the lab/facility level; many program managers have yet to accept technology transfer as an integral part of their respective programs.

The FLC report made several recommendations for creating a more efficient tech transfer system in their labs:

- Incorporate tech transfer into lab strategic planning.
- Develop systematic valuation of tech transfer to capture economic and other impacts.
- Adopt more aggressive management of intellectual property by the labs.
- Use CRADAs more innovatively.

- Better align tech transfer activities with the core mission of the lab/facility to tap needed external skills to improve lab performance of its core mission through tech transfer activities.

This critique was bolstered in an unusually candid article by Jeffrey Mobley, former director of licensing and business development at the Idaho National Engineering and Environmental Laboratory (Mobley 1999).

Coming to the lab from industry, Mobley observed, "Most labs have focused technology transfer efforts on communications rather than commercialization and the creation of information rather than licensing income.... What is missing is a strategy that provides economic incentives for all players and a businesslike approach to implement them."

The already mentioned U.S. Department of Commerce report on the labs' performance with the Federal Technology Transfer Act (U.S. Department of Commerce 2000) made these recommendations for building a more vigorous national technology transfer system:

- Provide additional help for companies looking for the right lab partner.
- Make managing intellectual property an agency priority.
- Maximize the effective use of the flexibility CRADAs provide in forming partnerships.
- Call on industry regularly to critique the tech transfer system to identify and remove barriers.
- Develop better metrics.

VIEW FROM INSIDE

All the agencies reported that 70 to 80 percent of their licenses and CRADAs were with small companies, so these firms are successfully working their way through the system.

Still, the in's and out's of the federal system can be daunting for any company, large or small, that has not worked it before. For this book, several leading technology managers were asked to provide candid, confidential insights for how to successfully work with labs. This information provides a real insight of how those making decisions on which partnerships to accept actually apply the laws and policies already discussed.

Here are the questions and the answers:

QUESTION: What advice would you give a small company before it approaches your lab?

Almost unanimously the response was *look at our Web site.* Lab and agency Web sites will explain what research, expertise, and technologies a particular lab has and how it does business. Many Web sites also provide model license and CRADA agreements employed by that facility.

The experts emphasized that companies should maximize *face-to-face* time when deals begin to form. Don't waste time asking general questions that a few minutes of homework could have answered.

Two respondents said companies should talk with lab scientists to gauge if there is real *passion* for working together before approaching the tech transfer office. *Any company wanting to work with a lab should feel sure the scientists will actively support the agreement before going further. When they get into development and need help, will the scientists take their calls? This can make all of the difference in a successful collaboration, and both parties should know upfront how serious they are.*

The need for active involvement with the lab scientists was underscored by another comment: *Companies should understand that the average federal technology is years away from the market. It can easily take five years to develop.*

QUESTION: For exclusive licenses, what are you looking for in a business plan from a potential licensee? What key features are you looking for in the plan? How long or detailed should it be?

Agencies look for serious commitments to the commercial development process. Particular emphasis is placed on companies demonstrating they either have or can secure funding for development.

A clear understanding of the market, realistic sales projections, and milestones are essential. *"I'm looking for reasonable sales projections— not wild-eyed optimism,"* one lab representative said.

Several technology managers said they want to see serious commitment to commercial development from those seeking nonexclusive licenses as well as those seeking exclusivity.

The clear emphasis was on a realistic chance for companies to reach the market, not on maximizing initial royalty income back to the agency. This does not imply that lab officials don't care about royalties; they do. Rather, it shows the importance they place on products actually reaching the market.

"I would much rather have low or nonexistent royalties up-front and get in the market than try and maximize my initial dollars. After all, in the long run I'll get more from a low royalty rate on a successful product than a high rate on a market failure," one official observed.

Two respondents said companies should demonstrate seriousness in 10 pages or less. "This is an iterative process," one official said. " If I need more, I'll ask. And please spare me the nonsense. What I'm looking for is, is this a *must-have technology* or simply a 'nice to have' technology?"

Added another, "I want to know if the company is realistic about the development costs they face. It normally costs 10 times as much in development as in research. I want to make sure they are coming in with their eyes open."

Some officials advised that small companies should make better use of state and local economic development programs for developing business plans, locating needed resources and expertise, and seeking tips for working with the government. Many of these resources are free.

QUESTION: What are frequent mistakes you see small companies making?

Three respondents said, "Hiring a lawyer to negotiate for them."

"I've seen several cases where a company was paying a lawyer by the hour, and he was haggling with us over clauses that are required by law."

"Companies should put their resources into commercial development—not lawyers."

Other observed mistakes noted by respondents included the following:

- Failure to really understand the market
- Not having financial support but hoping to get it once they get an exclusive license
- Not having any commercial experience or understanding of competitors

"Medium-sized companies (200–500 employees) are ideal partners for us," one said. "These are the ones that know their markets, have been around the block, have resources, and can move fast. Unfortunately, these are also the companies that tend to avoid working with us unless they are bidding on a government contract."

QUESTION: What issues do you frequently see in your CRADA/license negotiations?

Some answers:

- Companies demanding across-the-board exclusivity when what they really want is a specific field-of-use application.
- Companies seeking a license when what they really need is a CRADA.
- Lack of understanding of what rights to the technology the government must retain by law and great fear that the government's license will be

used to harm them. I've never seen or heard of a case where this has happened.

- Lack of understanding that different agencies use CRADAs in different ways. Sometimes when a company has worked with another agency, they are very frustrated that we operate differently.

Bottom line: Federal labs can be valuable partners for American industry. The public and private sectors march to different drummers. Deals are not automatic, but are certainly possible if you anticipate the bottlenecks and if both parties share a common passion to succeed.

Chapter 5

EFFECTIVELY MANAGING INTELLECTUAL PROPERTY

Discovery consists in seeing what everybody has seen and thinking what nobody has thought.
—Albert Szent-Gyorgyi von Nagrapolt

By its very nature, sifting through discoveries of any large R&D institution seeking diamonds in the rough is tough work. It is hard in companies where everyone knows that the goal is bringing new products to market. It is even harder in the public sector.

As mentioned previously, government conducts R&D for one of two purposes: advancing the mission of the federal agency or advancing basic scientific knowledge. As inventions arise, federal laboratories tend to patent from these perspectives. Additionally, the Department of Defense laboratories add another factor—protecting their interests in case they need to procure a product or technology in the future. From an industrial standpoint, none of these facets include the most important consideration—what is the commercial value of the invention?

Reconciling these perspectives can be a real challenge. Research-intensive companies also wrestle with how to maximize their investment in technologies. Over the last 20 years, companies such as IBM developed very robust patent management strategies. These widely publicized successes stoked great interest in developing similar strategies in other companies.

An astute public sector technology manager can learn much from this experience. Of course, an inherent advantage in the private sector is a much greater familiarity with the commercial marketplace. Even so, the unpredictable nature of research leaves many companies seriously concerned, lest they leave an undiscovered jewel in their inventory that has an important application outside the intended field of its discovery.

With the costs of patenting increasing, government agencies are facing the fact that they simply can no longer afford to patent an invention simply because it is patentable. Since patenting costs typically are subtracted from a federal lab's budget, pressures begin to mount for developing an effective intellectual property management strategy. Such efforts are in their infancy in most federal laboratories.

How can agencies bridge this gap? Much can be learned from the approaches developed by industry.

An interesting model is The Dow Chemical Company. Dow overhauled its processes to increase efficiency and maximize its return on investment. After an effective sorting process, intellectual property is grouped into three broad bundles:

- Those applying to the core business that are not licensed and constitute the seed corn for future growth;
- Those with applications outside the core business that have value to others if they are licensed or donated; and
- Those with little or no immediate value, which are simply abandoned.

The utility of such a strategic approach to intellectual property has been proven by increased profitability for the company.

Sam Khoury was a pioneer at Dow in developing this highly effective approach. As the "intangible asset appraiser" for Dow, Khoury saw firsthand how the lack of an intellectual property management system was costing the company. He developed an effective interdisciplinary approach to the problem that is worth studying in more detail.

Khoury now leads Inavisis International, Inc., a recognized international leader in the valuation of intellectual property.

Here's Khoury's summary of how he approached the problem:

As in any large organization, there was a need to keep all the parties that can benefit or be negatively impacted by a decision informed relating to intellectual property decisions.

The process initially was to have one person trying to communicate and gather information from R&D, manufacturing, business, marketing and sales, and the patent departments. It is critical that these viewpoints be considered and shared to make an informed decision. Unfortunately, all the information was disseminated by one individual who then had to make a decision that sometimes was not the right call. Further, decision making was taking too long and usually required someone not actually familiar with the needs of the stakeholders to interpret their wants.

The solution was to create intellectual asset management teams that included all the stakeholders. All functions for that business were invited to attend. Any function that did not attend had to live with the decisions of the team. So not attending would forfeit the rights of that function to come and cancel the decision of the team. We found that this team approach was very successful because when all the functions are present, the discussion would allow in-depth analysis and explanations of the why we should proceed with a certain technology or not.

Rather than just reading someone's input as before, now we had a real exchange of views. This not only helped us reach a consensus on the potential value of an invention for the company, but just as importantly, helped educate the other stakeholders. We found that we really began to understand how the various entities making up a large company like Dow functioned, what they needed, and how they thought.

Any action items and follow-ups were documented, and when the different representatives left the meeting they knew what decisions were made and why.

This was very helpful in a big organization such as The Dow Chemical Company, which competes in dynamic markets where timely decisions are critical—especially about our products and technologies of the future.

Another important plus is to see how these evaluation teams "get smarter" the more they function. After the light bulb goes on and we agree what our goal is, the process really picks up speed. The team members are more valuable employees because when they return to their home units, they carry with them a valuable insight into the strategic needs of the parent company that is hard to get from just knowing your own piece of the puzzle.

The group that led the facilitation of the meeting was the intellectual asset managers. For business units with small IP [intellectual property] portfolios, the patent attorneys had the dual role of patenting and managing the IP of that business.

When I worked at Dow, intellectual asset management was a stand alone function. As the businesses took ownership of their intellectual properties, they had their own intellectual asset manager operating within the business unit. Thus, a small expert group evolved that acted as a central technology center to support the different businesses with their intellectual asset management.

Outside Dow

Inavisis International, Inc., now consults with companies on all aspects of intellectual asset management. The most frequently asked question we get from our clients is, "How can we make intellectual asset management more effective within our company?"

The bottom line is a realization by top management that developing technology and protecting it in patents, trademarks, and copyrights is an expensive proposition for a company. The most efficient way is to have one group responsible to upper management to bring together all the stakeholders from all the functions to be involved in the process. The successful companies understood this concept and have a team approach. Other companies that are not comfortable with dedicating the resources are seeing some benefit, but at a much slower rate.

Team management of these assets is the prudent thing to do, with one function being held accountable to do the planning, call the meeting, and follow up on the decisions of the team. I believe the reason for the success of the Dow program is all functions saw the impact of their contribution to the bottom line of the business.

If a technology becomes obsolete, it should be abandoned. If a technology becomes very relevant to the business strategy, then it should be developed into a business unit. If a technology is very important, but does not fit the business, then it should be licensed, sold, or donated.

These concepts developed when organizations started treating IP as an asset or property of the business. If a company owns a building, it would commit the resources to maintain it. If the building fits its needs, it has its people use it as offices. If the location or configuration does not fit, then the company would lease it, sell it, or donate it. The concept of treating IP as an asset is real, and companies are realizing significant revenues. Companies that are proactively managing their intellectual properties are realizing revenues in the tens and hundreds of millions of dollars.

It is estimated that by implementing proactive management of intellectual property, Dow realized approximately $40 million in savings just from abandoning patents that the reviewing team felt did not fit the company's needs or have significant market values. This savings is on top of the income generated from an aggressive licensing program for technologies that fell outside Dow's core business areas, but still had value to others. Like many other major corporations, Dow also donated intellectual property with value but requiring more development to nonprofit organizations such as universities. Thus, a comprehensive team-based approach maximizes the value Dow enjoys from its significant investment in R&D.

How can these lessons be applied by the public sector? Let's examine how federal laboratories typically manage their inventions now.

When a federal researcher reports an invention, the technology transfer office normally alerts its patent attorney. If the invention appears to have relevance to the agency mission, a patent may be filed. If there is obvious commercial application, this is factored in. However, these efforts can be cursory, particularly when the commercial potential lies outside the main research area familiar to the laboratory personnel. A danger exists that the patent claims may not cover all of the potential commercial applications because these may not be known.

Over time, the patent portfolio grows larger. As the technology transfer office mulls over where to begin its efforts, the marketplace begins to ask questions like

How unique is the discovery?

Do the patent claims cover potential applications?

How does it benchmark with rival techniques or technologies?

How strong is the patent if challenged?

How far is the discovery from application?

These are important points to know. Since this market expertise frequently does not exist in a federal laboratory, how can a teaming approach like that of Dow be replicated?

One way is by having an outside experts involved in the process as early as possible.

Having an industry-savvy viewpoint even before filing a patent may suggest unanticipated applications that neither the inventor nor the agency realized. There are many organizations, expert consultants, and retired industry executives whose input at this critical stage can be invaluable. Such insights can present an opportunity for broadening the patent claims so that its appeal to industry is stronger. If the patent issues without sufficient claims, its market potential may be minimized or lost altogether.

Getting outside advice can also trigger a discussion on whether or not the time and expense of filing a patent, or even a provisional patent, are warranted. As shown at Dow, the team begins to internalize these viewpoints so that a management strategy develops that is appropriate for that entity.

Because of the basic nature of a great deal of federally funded technology, unanticipated industrial applications are not uncommon. When these applications are realized, it is a "Eureka!" experience. These occur in industry as well. The case of 3M's Post-It Notes is a good example. In looking for a new adhesive, the discovery was considered a failure—until some very creative person realized the utility for having a note that could easily be peeled on and off. The result was one of the company's most lucrative products. A fundamental skill for those involved in assessing these discoveries is to step back and look at a reported invention "with new eyes."

Having a brainstorming session as this juncture can be very fruitful as the characteristics of the invention are considered and alternative applications are bandied about. The scientist offers an important perspective as to whether or not the invention in question can perform various functions. For example, information-scanning technologies designed for NASA space missions led to the supermarket bar code. It took a very creative mind to realize this application, which most of us now use daily. As many applications as possible should be considered before the patent is filed so that potential markets, which are vastly different, are protected.

In government all too often this step is omitted. The patent is filed and, when issued several years later, a relatively passive marketing approach is initiated, consisting of listing a patent on a government Web site as available for licensing. Obviously such an approach will have minimum returns to the agency, to the inventor, and ultimately to the American public.

The lack of perspective on the utility of a patent causes another serious problem for those trying to manage federal laboratory patent portfolios. With limited time and resources, where should efforts be focused? A good rule of thumb that top university technology managers have devised is get in, get out, and go on. In other words, don't waste too much time on run-of-the-mill inventions. One or two "crown jewels" normally carry top universities—and many companies—that are astute in analyzing their intellectual property portfolios. These entities typically are very strong in areas like medical research or specialized computer software and have a good handle on the commercial utility of resulting inventions. They also have strong industry recognition as world-class research institutions in their fields and enjoy the luxury of having companies seeking them as partners.

Institutions falling below this exalted category that haven't developed an effective patent management strategy can spend too much time on trying to license "the living dead," technologies that have limited appeal. This means that valuable staff time is tied up when it might be more effectively applied to inventions with a much greater return on investment—if they can be identified.

By better applying an industrial approach to their portfolios, agencies can be more confident about waiving rights to those technologies that are not strong commercialization candidates. Indeed, federal laws require agencies to give such inventions back to their government inventors if the inventor is interested in personally pursuing them. All too often this requirement is ignored by the agencies, as they tend to err on the side of caution in case an unexpected application for the invention arises. Such "dog in the manger" behavior can be demoralizing to inventors forced to stand by while their inventions gather dust in government files.

CLOSING THE GAP BETWEEN THE LAB AND THE TECH TRANSFER OFFICE

In building an effective teaming approach, often a critical gap exists between the government scientist and the laboratory technology transfer office. Remarkably, more than 77 years after the passage of the historic Federal Technology Transfer Act, many federal scientists and middle managers still have little idea that they can partner with industry in collaborative R&D arrangements.

Some leading scientists view the technology transfer functions at their labs as a decidedly less important activity than their own research missions and do not see a linkage between the two.

Because there is frequently little knowledge of the value of the technology transfer function, reporting inventions can be hit or miss. Frequently inventions are reported in order to build academic credentials similar to publishing research results, not for capturing their commercial potential. The "publish or perish" culture of the labs when they are conducting nonclassified research is still strong. Like their university counterparts, federal government scientists and engineers often gain prominence through revealing their research results to their international peers. Such actions without establishing intellectual property protections negate the possibility of development. Even though U.S. patent law allows for filing claims within a year of publication, in many fields like health care, where international markets are the norm, such actions may reduce commercial interest.

Conversely, many scientists are very interested in attracting industrial sponsorship of the research. They also greatly enjoy seeing their discoveries actually utilized. These interests represent a natural way to bridge the interests of the researcher and the technology transfer office.

Frequently companies are much more interested in funding research for which they can secure resulting intellectual property than they are in just licensing an existing invention. Corporate-government R&D partnerships allow the best public and private sector scientists and engineers to work together, rather than having an invention "thrown over the fence." Since most government patents will require substantial development, these research partnerships are vital to prompt commercialization efforts.

Unfortunately, communication gaps at the laboratory can mean that the technology transfer office is in the dark about the exciting research going on in the lab. To be effectively matched with a company, research projects should be marketed as close to commencement as possible. If the technology transfer office is not involved until an invention is made, many exciting possibilities are lost.

This gap is a fundamental problem in maximizing the potential of the federal laboratory system. To address it requires a strong buy-in from agency and laboratory management. A continuous educational campaign is required so that laboratory personnel understand that without commercial development of their research, the job is only half done.

Nothing makes these abstractions about the importance of working with industry more believable to government researchers than a success story involving one of their peers. The incentives in a successful deal for the individual, the research department, the lab, the agency, the partner company, and the taxpayer are vital. Federal education and training efforts must emphasize that moving technology to market is a key part of the laboratories' job.

When an effective technology transfer office is located with cutting edge research, the impact can be dramatic. Just ask Dow.

Chapter 6

OVERVIEW OF FEDERAL LABORATORIES AND CAPABILITIES

Government is a trust, and the officers of the government are trustees; and both the trust and trustees are created for the benefit of the people.

—Henry Clay

Here is a quick guide to the major federal R&D agencies and their top laboratories.

DEPARTMENT OF DEFENSE (DOD)
HTTP://WWW.DOD.MIL/

Federal R&D obligations, total and intramural by agency: FY 1998

Total R&D obligations: $34,832.6 million

Total R&D obligations as a share of federal total: 48.30 percent

Intramural R&D: $7,750.6 million

Agency R&D obligations that are intramural: 22.25 percent

DoD trains and equips the armed forces through three military departments—the Army, Navy, and Air Force. The Marine Corps, being mainly an amphibious force, is part of the Department of the Navy. The primary job of the military departments is to train and equip personnel to perform fighting, peacekeeping, and humanitarian/disaster assistance tasks.

DoD Defense Technical Information Center (DTIC)

http://www.dtic.mil/
Technology Transfer Contact: Wendy Hill
Phone: (703) 767-8225
Fax: (703) 767-9161
Fort Belvoir, VA 22060-6218

DTIC collects all scientific or technological observations, findings, recommendations, and results derived from DoD endeavors, including both in-house and contracted efforts. DTIC, a major component of the DoD Scientific and Technical Information Program, contributes to the management and conduct of defense research, development, and acquisition efforts. It provides access to and transfer of scientific and technical information for DoD personnel, DoD contractors and potential contractors, and other U.S. government agency personnel and their contractors. DTIC has eligibility and registration requirements for use of its services.

DEPARTMENT OF THE ARMY (ARMY)
HTTP://WWW.ARMY.MIL/

The Army operates in more than 50 countries, performing such duties as securing the South Korea border and keeping the peace in Kosovo, in addition to its primary mission of defending the United States and its territories, commonwealths, and possessions.

DoD Army Cold Regions Research and Engineering Laboratory (CRREL)

http://www.crrel.usace.army.mil
Technology Transfer Contact: Sharon Borland
Phone: (603) 646-4735
Fax: (603) 646-4448
Hanover, NH 03755-1290

CRREL conducts research on the nature and effects of cold-related processes and properties. This knowledge is used to develop measures to minimize the adverse effects of cold, monitor the impact of cold-stressed environments on human activity, and develop recommended mitigative measures for all seasons. Moreover, the solution to the cold aspects of certain problems, such as predicting the physical state of terrain based on weather and the associated signatures measured by sensors, has led to an expanded all-weather capability and expertise in this topic area. CRREL's

Remote Sensing/GIS Center of Expertise conducts research related to knowledge management capabilities where new, enhanced or specialty GIS database, spatial database technologies, and/or software systems are required to support the national environmental and water resources needs.

DoD Army Natick Soldier Center (Natick)

http://www.natick.army.mil
Technology Transfer Contact: Robert Rosenkrans
Phone: (508) 233-4928
Fax: (508) 233-5223
Natick, MA 01760-5015

Natick personnel have expertise and experience in the following areas: chemical and biological protection, combat field feeding systems, hardened shelters, chemical-protected tentage, advanced personnel and cargo airdrop systems, advanced field organizational equipment, sustainment (food, field feeding systems, and airdrop systems), and protective clothing and shelters. Natick maintains the following facilities and resources: nuclear magnetic resonance spectrometer for multinuclei and solids, high-resolution mass spectrometer, peptide synthesizer to produce proteins, scanning transmission electron microscope, bacteriology laboratory equipment, laser laboratory for evaluation of high-energy lasers on textiles and dyeing and finishing laboratory.

DoD Army Research Laboratory (ARL)

http://www.arl.army.mil/
Technology Transfer Contact: Norma Cammarata
Phone: (301) 394-2952
Fax: (301) 394-4795
Adelphi, MD 20783-1197

ARL is the Army's major resource for basic and applied research and technology development. ARL's primary mission is to provide a technological edge through military product-oriented scientific research and advanced technology development. The laboratory was formed by a recent Army reorganization that integrated the activities of seven laboratories of the former Army Laboratory Command, seven other technology base elements, and close to 3,600 people across the United States. ARL R&D efforts are directed toward new and improved materials, components, subsystems, techniques, and manufacturing processes, which are then transferred to Army research, development, and engineering centers.

DEPARTMENT OF THE NAVY (NAVY)
HTTP://WWW.NAVY.MIL/

The mission of the Navy is to maintain, train, and equip combat-ready naval forces capable of winning wars, deterring aggression, and maintaining freedom of the seas.

DoD/Navy National Center for Excellence in Metalworking Technology (NCEMT)

http://www.ncemt.ctc.com
Technology Transfer Contact: Ed Coyle
Phone: (215) 697-9530
Philadelphia, PA 19111-5078

NCEMT activities are focused on casting technology, forming technology, joining technology, powder metallurgy and ceramic materials, and surface treatment. The advanced tools used to support these activities include concurrent engineering; product analysis; process modeling; advanced materials testing and materials characterization; expert systems; intelligent processing of materials; systems integration; and demonstration facilities for welding, machining and cutting, forming, semisolid metalworking, wire drawing of high temperature superconductors, and powder metallurgy processes.

DoD Naval Research Laboratory (NRL)

http://www.nrl.navy.mil/
Technology Transfer Contact: Dr. Catherine Cotell
Phone: (202) 404-8411
Fax: (202) 404-7920
Washington, DC 20375

NRL, the Navy's corporate laboratory, is responsible for Navy-wide leadership in the following areas: primary in-house research for the physical and engineering sciences, a broadly-based exploratory and advanced development program in response to identified and anticipated Navy needs, and development of space systems for the Navy. Examples of R&D areas available for technology transfer include advanced materials, biomolecular engineering, chemical processing, microelectronics, photonics, sensors, and radar technologies. Examples of programs available for licensing or cooperative research and development (CRADAs) include chemical sensors for toxins, explosives and environmental pollutants, pulsed laser deposition of biocompatible ceramics, fluoropolymers, advanced optical data storage systems, controlled release systems, silicon-on-insulator technology, and the neural network vector multiplier device.

DoD Naval Surface Warfare Center (NSWCDD), Dahlgren Division

http://www.nswc.navy.mil/dahl.htm
Technology Transfer Contact: Ramsey Johnson
Phone: (540) 653-2680
Fax: (540) 653-2687
Silver Spring, MD 22448-5600

NSWCDD is one of six divisions of the Naval Surface Warfare Center. The three major sites are the Dahlgren Laboratory and the Coastal Systems Station. It is the Navy's principal research, development, and test and evaluation (RDT&E) activites for surface ship combat systems, ordnance, mines, and strategic systems support. It performs warfare analysis, research, design, development, testing and evaluation, systems integration, strategic missile systems support, and special and amphibious warfare and fleet engineering services. NSWCDD expertise includes devices, information and system sciences, pulsed power technology, sensors, electro-optics, simulation and modeling, electromagnetic interference, diver and life support, solid state technologies, chemical/bacteriological detection, advanced computation technology, and engineering of complex systems.

DoD Naval Undersea Warfare Center (NUWC)

http://www.nuwc.navy.mil/
Technology Transfer Contact: Dr. Theresa A. Baus
Phone: (401) 832-8728
Fax: (401) 832-1725
Newport, RI 02841-1708

The NUWC Division, Newport, performs research, development, engineering, testing, and evaluation, as well as field support for surface ship, submarine, and autonomous underwater vehicle sonar and weapons systems. Areas of special expertise include acoustic arrays and components; acoustic signal processing; multiple-source information management; turbulent and laminar-flow hydrodynamics; high-power density underwater propulsion; communications, especially very low and very high radio frequency; underwater testing of systems and vehicles; numerical modeling and analysis, including large-scale computations; and modeling and analysis of very complex systems.

UNITED STATES AIR FORCE (USAF)
HTTP://WWW.AF.MIL/

In its more than 50 years of existence, the USAF has become the world's premier aerospace force. Its mission is simple in words, yet awesome in meaning—defend the nation through the control and exploitation of air and space.

USAF Air Force Research Laboratory (AFRL)

http://www.afrl.af.mil/
Technology Transfer Contact: Douglas Blair
Phone: (937) 656-9176
Fax: (937) 255-3521
Wright-Patterson Air Force Base (AFB), OH 45433-7131

Located in the AFRL, Wright-Patterson AFB, Ohio, the Air Force Technology Transfer Program was created to assure all USAF science and engineering activities promote the transfer or exchange of technology with state and local governments, industry, and academia. These activities enhance the economic competitiveness of industry and promote the productivity of state and local government, while leveraging the DoD research and development investment. The end result is a strong industrial base the USAF and DoD can utilize to supply their needs. Each of the nine technology directorates has a technology transfer focal point that is responsible for establishing and executing the directorate's technology transfer program.

USAF Arnold Engineering Development Center (AEDC)

http://www.arnold.af.mil
Technology Transfer Contact: Robert Crook
Phone: (931) 454-6510
Fax: (931) 454-3559
Arnold AFB, TN 37388-9011

AEDC tests aircraft and missile and space systems and subsystems at flight conditions to be experienced during a mission. The Research and Technology Program develops advanced testing techniques and instrumentation and supports development of new test facilities. Current programs are Peacekeeper testing, including aerodynamic and rocket motor firings; strategic defense initiative testing; F-110 alternate fighter engine development and testing; advanced tactical fighter propulsion and flight dynamics testing; and inertial upper stage rocket motor firings.

USAF Materials and Manufacturing Directorate (Directorate)

http://www.ml.afrl.af.mil/
Technology Transfer Contact: Greg McGath
Phone: (937) 255-5669
Fax: (937) 256-1422
Wright-Patterson AFB, OH 45433-7746

The directorate develops materials, processes, and advanced manufacturing technologies for use in aircraft, spacecraft, missiles, rockets, and ground-based systems and their structural, electronic, and optical components. Areas of expertise include thermal protection materials, metallic and nonmetallic structural materials, nondestructive inspection, materials used in aerospace propulsion systems, electromagnetic and electronic materials, bio-derived or bio-synthesized materials, nanotechnology, nanopolymer technology, computational materials science, polymer characterization, and laser-hardened materials. The directorate is also responsible for USAF technology programs that address environmental issues.

DEPARTMENT OF HEALTH AND HUMAN SERVICES (HHS)
HTTP://WWW.OS.DHHS.GOV/

Federal R&D obligations, total and intramural by agency: FY 1998

Total R&D obligations: $13,717.8 million

Total R&D obligations as a share of federal total: 19.02 percent

Intramural R&D: $2,957.2 million

Agency R&D obligations that are intramural: 21.56 percent

HHS is the U.S. government's principal agency for protecting the health of all Americans and providing essential human services, especially for those who are least able to help themselves. The department includes more than 300 programs covering a wide spectrum of activities. Some highlights include medical and social science research; preventing outbreak of infectious disease, including immunization services; assuring food and drug safety; Medicare (health insurance for elderly and disabled Americans); and Medicaid (health insurance for low-income people).

HHS Centers for Disease Control and Prevention (CDC)

http://www.cdc.gov/
Technology Transfer Contact: Dr. Andrew Watkins
Phone: (770) 488-8610
Atlanta, GA 30341

CDC seeks to accomplish its mission by working with partners throughout the nation and world to monitor health, detect and investigate health problems, conduct research to enhance prevention, develop and advocate sound public health policies, implement prevention strategies, promote healthy behaviors, foster safe and healthful environments, and provide leadership and training. CDC has developed and sustained many vital partnerships with public and private entities that improve service to the American people.

HHS Food and Drug Administration (FDA)

http://www.fda.gov/
Technology Transfer Contact: Beatrice Droke
Phone: (301) 827-7008
Fax: (301) 827-7029
Rockville, MD 20857

The mission of the FDA is to ensure that foods are safe and wholesome. It also makes certain that human and veterinary drugs, human biological products, medical devices, and consumer products that emit radiation are safe and effective. In addition, the FDA ensures that regulated products are honestly, accurately, and informatively represented, and that these products are in compliance with FDA regulations and guidelines. Noncompliance is identified and corrected, and any unsafe or unlawful products are removed from the market.

HHS National Cancer Institute (NCI)

http://www.nci.nih.gov/
Technology Transfer Contact: Kathleen Sybert
Phone: (301) 496-0477
Fax: (301) 402-2117
Bethesda, MD 20892

NCI conducts comprehensive programs in laboratory and clinical research on cancer treatment; basic research on cancer biology, immunology, and diagnosis and their application in studies of metabolism, dermatology, and pathology of neoplastic diseases; and research on the cause and natural history of cancer and methods of prevention. The institute has extensive laboratory facilities and equipment, animal facilities, and general services for biomedical research related to cancer.

HHS National Heart, Lung, and Blood Institute (NHLBI)

http://www.nhlbi.nih.gov/index.htm
Technology Transfer Contact: Dr. Carl Roth
Phone: (301) 496-6331
Fax: (301) 402-1056
Bethesda, MD 20892

The NHLBI provides leadership for a national program in diseases of the heart, blood vessels, lung, and blood; blood resources; and sleep disorders. Since October 1997, the NHLBI has also had administrative responsibility for the National Institutes of Health's Woman's Health Initiative. The NHLBI plans and directs research in development and evaluation of interventions and devices related to prevention, treatment, and rehabilitation of patients suffering from such diseases and disorders. It also supports research on clinical use of blood and all aspects of the management of blood resources.

NATIONAL AERONAUTICS AND SPACE ADMINISTRATION (NASA)
HTTP://WWW.NCTN.HQ.NASA.GOV/

Federal R&D obligations, total and intramural by agency: FY 1998

Total R&D obligations: $9,850.7 million

Total R&D obligations as a share of federal total: 13.66 percent

Intramural R&D: $2,462.7 million

Agency R&D obligations that are intramural: 25.00 percent

Since its inception in 1958, NASA has accomplished many great scientific and technological feats in air and space. NASA technology also has been adapted for many nonaerospace uses by the private sector. NASA remains a leading force in scientific research and in stimulating public interest in aerospace exploration, as well as science and technology in general.

NASA Ames Research Center (ARC)

http://www.arc.nasa.gov
Technology Transfer Contact: Carolina Blake
Phone: (650) 604-1754
Fax: (650) 604-1592
Moffett Field, CA 94035

ARC is responsible for the performance of a tightly coupled, multidisciplinary research base directed toward NASA's missions. ARC has core scientific competencies in fundamental space biology and all disciplines of the agency's multifaceted astrobiology thrust. ARC performs fundamental research and technology development of nanoscale assembly, computational nanotechnology, nanoscale computing and sensing elements, and nanoscale architecture and systems integration. ARC is pursuing the development of protein-based nanotubes, a crossover technology, potentially capable of self-organization and replication.

NASA Dryden Flight Research Center (DFRC)

http://www.dfrc.nasa.gov
Technology Transfer Contact: Jennifer Baer-Riedhart
Phone: (661) 276-3689
Fax: (661) 276-3088
Edwards, CA 93523

DFRC has developed unique and highly specialized capability for conducting flight research programs. Its versatile and unmatched test organization of pilots, engineers, scientists, technicians, and mechanics has demonstrated capabilities with high-speed research aircraft and unusual flight vehicles, such as the lunar landing research vehicle and wingless lifting bodies. Research emphasis includes flight research, remotely piloted vehicle research, shuttle landing and recovery, and contingency landing site. Primary research tools are research aircraft, from B-52 carrier aircraft to high-performance aircraft capable of speeds to mach 3; the F-15 ACTIVE; and the ERAST alliance.

NASA George C. Marshall Space Flight Center (MSFC)

http://nasasolutions.com/
Technology Transfer Contact: Vernotto McMillan
Phone: (256) 544-2615
Fax: (256) 544-1815
Huntsville, AL 35812

MSFC's primary mission is research and development of large launch vehicles, both reusable and expendable, and the development and integration of payloads and experiments. Technical expertise spans the disciplines required for the definition, design, and development of space-related hardware, payloads, and experiments from inception to flight operations. The center has a broad science and engineering base with seven laboratories dedicated to support in areas of: information and electronic systems, materials and processes, space science, propulsion, systems analysis and integration, structures and dynamics, and mission operations.

NASA Goddard Space Flight Center (GSFC)

http://techtransfer.gsfc.nasa.gov
Technology Transfer Contact: Nona Cheeks
Phone: (301) 286-5810
Fax: (301) 286-1717
Greenbelt, MD 20771

Research at GSFC is conducted on space and earth science applications. Atmospheric science activities are directed toward the use of space technology in advancing the understanding of the atmosphere of the Earth and other planets and applying that knowledge to problems in weather, climate, and environmental quality. Expertise includes advanced optics, advanced software development, artificial intelligence, sensors, microelectronics, photonics, cryogenics, thermal systems, environmental monitoring systems, and information systems and data handling.

NASA Jet Propulsion Laboratory (JPL)

http://www.jpl.nasa.gov/
Technology Transfer Contact: Merle McKenzie
Phone: (818) 354-2577
Fax: (818) 354-1360
Pasadena, CA 91109

The JPL at the California Institute of Technology (Caltech), a federally funded research and development center, is NASA's lead center for the unmanned exploration of the solar system. The leading U.S. research center for lunar and planetary missions since the space age began, JPL also performs other research, development, and space flight activities for NASA and other agencies. The laboratory's technical expertise includes astrodynamics and space flight navigation, autonomous systems, chemical systems and processes, image processing, information systems, materials, mechanical and thermal systems, operations technology, optics and optoelectronics, propulsion, remote sensing, solid-state electronics, and telecommunications.

NASA John C. Stennis Space Center (SSC)

http://technology.ssc.nasa.gov/
Technology Transfer Contact: Kirk Sharp
Phone: (228) 688-1914
Fax: (228) 688-2408
Stennis Space Center, MS 39529

SSC in southern Mississippi is one of four NASA centers responsible for the human exploration and development of space. As NASA's lead center for rocket propulsion testing, it manages the agency's rocket propulsion test assets. This includes facilities at the Marshall Space Flight Center in Alabama, the White Sands Test Facility in New Mexico, and the Glenn Research Center's Plumbrook Station in Ohio. SSC's primary role is the testing and flight certification of the space shuttle main engine, but it also has on-site developmental testing facilities for turbomachinery and other components for future generation rocket engines.

NASA John F. Kennedy Space Center (KSC)

http://technology.ksc.nasa.gov/
Technology Transfer Contact: James Aliberti
Phone: (321) 867-6224
Fax: (321) 867-2050
KSC, FL 32899

Research is conducted on aerodynamic, inertial, and ballistic technology for devices and system operation; navigation and flight control integration; atmospheric gases as applied to ionization absorption and instrumentation anomalies; meteorology; man-machine integration and operation; bionics and artificial intelligence; design, installation, test, maintenance of space and terrestrial equipment and supporting ground-tracking radar; microwave radio refrequency and carrier bay relay systems; mechanical, electronic, printed, chemical, alphanumeric, plotting, static, and dynamic displays design operation maintenance; image enhancement techniques and analysis; radar and laser instrumentation and systems; radio frequency detection; antenna devices and systems; circuit design; and navigation, guidance, and control.

NASA John H. Glenn Research Center at Lewis Field (GRC)

http://www.grc.nasa.gov/
Technology Transfer Contact: Larry Viterna, Ph.D.
Phone: (216) 433-3484
Fax: (216) 433-8551
Cleveland, OH 44135

GRC is NASA's lead center for research, technology, and development in aircraft propulsion, space propulsion, and space power and satellite communication. GRC has been advancing propulsion technology to enable aircraft to fly faster, farther, and higher and also has focused research on fuel economy, noise abatement, reliability, and reduced pollution. GRC has responsibility for developing the largest space power system ever designed to provide the electrical power necessary to accommodate the life-support systems and research experiments aboard the Space Station. GRC will support the station in other major areas, such as auxiliary propulsion systems and communications. More than 2,500 scientists and engineers conduct nearly every kind of physical research in fluid mechanics, physics, materials, fuels, combustion, thermodynamics, lubrication, heat transfer, and electronics.

NASA Langley Research Center (LaRC)

http://www.larc.nasa.gov/
Technology Transfer Contact: Wilson Lundy, Ph.D.
Phone: (757) 864-7717
Hampton, VA 23681

LaRC conducts basic and applied research necessary to advance aeronautics and space flight and generate new and advanced concepts for related goals. It also provides research advice, technological support, and assistance to other sources. Research includes fundamental and applied research in aerothermodynamics, fluid mechanics, propulsion aerodynamics, performance, stability and control, stall/spin, airfoil development and STOL/VTOL in all flight regimes; configuration development and testing of transonic and supersonic decelerators; digital flight controls; active controls technology; aeronomy; dynamic meteorology; application of aerospace instrumentation and materials to biomedicine and bioengineering; basic and synthetic chemistry; and analysis.

NASA Lyndon B. Johnson Space Center (JSC)

http://www.jsc.nasa.gov/
Technology Transfer Contact: Charlene Gilbert
Phone: (281) 483-1175
Fax: (281) 244-8452
Houston, TX 77058

JSC has expertise and is actively involved in space power, electrical power control, medical sciences, software development, robotics, information systems, and communications for space systems. JSC was established in 1961 as NASA's primary center for design, development, and testing of spacecraft and associated systems for manned flight; selection and training of astronauts; planning and conducting manned missions; and extensive participation in the medical engineering and scientific experiments carried aboard space flights. JSC also has program management responsibility for the space shuttle program and major responsibility for development of the Space Station.

DEPARTMENT OF ENERGY (DOE)
HTTP://WWW.ENERGY.GOV/

Federal R&D obligations, total and intramural by agency: FY 1998

Total R&D obligations: $5,833.1 million

Total R&D obligations as a share of federal total: 8.09 percent

Intramural R&D: $535.1 million

Agency R&D obligations that are intramural: 9.17 percent

DOE's mission is to foster a secure and reliable energy system that is environmentally and economically sustainable, to be a responsible steward of the nation's nuclear weapons, to clean up our own facilities, and to support continued U.S. leadership in science and technology.

DOE Ames Laboratory

http://www.ameslab.gov
Technology Transfer Contact: Debra Covey
Phone: (515) 294-1048
Fax: (515) 294-4456
Ames, IA 50011

Ames Laboratory conducts basic and applied research to advance understanding of chemical, engineering, materials, mathematical, and physical sciences underlying energy technologies and other technologies essential to national interests. Areas of particular emphasis include advanced materials synthesis and processing, including preparation of ultrahigh-purity and well-characterized metals, alloys, composites, and single crystals and new nontraditional materials, such as organic polymers and organometallic materials, processable preceramics, and nonlinear optical systems.

DOE Argonne National Laboratory (ANL)

http://www.techtransfer.anl.gov/index.html
Technology Transfer Contact: Cynthia Wesolowski

Phone: (630) 252-7694
Fax: (630) 252-5230
Argonne, IL 60439

ARL is a leading center for R&D in basic and applied energy sciences and engineering, with more than 200 programs spanning many technologies. The laboratory's Office of Technology Transfer helps move ARL technologies to the industrial sector. ANL is a "multiprogram" laboratory, which, for industry, translates into broadly applicable technology relating to energy production and use, advanced materials, manufacturing processes, waste minimization, and environmental remediation.

DOE Brookhaven National Laboratory (BNL)

http://www.bnl.gov/
Technology Transfer Contact: Margaret C Bogosian
Phone: (631) 344-7338
Fax: (631) 344-3729
Upton, NY 11973

BNL conducts basic and applied research in physical, biomedical, and environmental sciences and selected energy technologies. The BNL National Synchrotron Light Source, the world's brightest dedicated source of synchrotron light, annually supports about 1,500 research projects ranging from developing an x-ray microscope to studying surfaces of various materials. The laboratory led a national effort to design a prototype production facility for manufacture of the next generation of computer chips in partnership with private industry.

DOE Ernest Orlando Lawrence Berkeley National Laboratory (LBNL)

http://www.lbl.gov/
Technology Transfer Contact: Cheryl Fragiadakis
Phone: (510) 486-6467
Fax: (510) 486-6457
Berkeley, CA 94720

LBNL is a major multiprogram national laboratory, managed by the University of California for the DOE. Transferable technologies and expertise are available from 14 principal research divisions: Genomics Division; Life Sciences Division; Physical Biosciences Division; Computing Sciences Division; Advanced Light Source; Chemical Sciences Division; Earth Sciences Division; Environmental and Energy Technologies Division; Materials Sciences Division; Accelerator and Fusion Research Division; Nuclear Science Division; Physics Division; Engineering Division; and Environment, Health, and Safety Division.

DOE Idaho National Engineering and Environmental Laboratory (INEEL)

http://www.inel.gov/
Technology Transfer Contact: Chuck Briggs
Phone: (208) 526-0441
Fax: (208) 526-0690
Idaho Falls, ID 83415-3805

INEEL is a multiprogram laboratory. Historically a leader in DOE reactor technology programs and engineering projects, INEEL conducts applied R&D to support the missions of DOE and other government agencies. Expertise includes biotechnology, chemical sciences, engineering sciences, instrumentation development, materials and materials processing, nuclear reactor research technology, information and communications technology, sensor development and measurement science, mechanical and electronic system development, robotics, computational intelligence, and environmental and waste treatment technology.

DOE Lawrence Livermore National Laboratory (LLNL)

http://www.llnl.gov/
Technology Transfer Contact: Annemarie Meike
Phone: (925) 422-3735
Fax: (925) 423-8988
Livermore, CA 94550

The LLNL physics and chemistry departments maintain a spectrum of capabilities for studying the micro- and macroscopic defect properties of materials, using unique mono-energetic positron facilities and associated instrumentation. Of particular interest to potential industrial partnerships is the demonstrated ability to measure critical quality management parameters in advanced materials systems. Other areas in which successful industrial applications have been explored include metallurgical defect studies, especially related to reliability issues, and critical components for high-technology energy and transportation systems.

DOE National Energy Technology Laboratory (NETL)

http://www.netl.doe.gov/
Technology Transfer Contact: Dee Dee Diane Newlon

Phone: (304) 285-4086
Fax: (304) 285-1301
Morgantown, WV 26507-0880

NETL's objective is to provide Americans with a stronger economy, healthier environment, and more secure future by resolving the environmental, supply, and reliability constraints of producing and using fossil resources. NETL works to support development and deployment of environmental technologies that lower the cost and reduce the risk of remediation of DOE's Weapons Complex and contribute to best business and management practices within the DOE complex.

DOE Oak Ridge National Laboratory (ORNL)

http://www.ornl.gov/
Technology Transfer Contact: Louise Dunlap
Phone: (865) 576-4221
Fax: (865) 241-4265
Oak Ridge, TN 37831

One of the largest DOE multiprogram energy laboratories, ORNL is a world leader in isotope development, especially isotopes for medical research and imaging, and reactor technology and safety. Other important programs include energy technology, including magnetic fusion, renewable energy, fossil energy, and conservation; and environmental and waste management research and development. The laboratory conducts experimental and theoretical research in physics (nuclear, atomic, and solid-state), chemistry, materials science, computing and mathematics, genetics and other biomedical research, environmental and life sciences, and genetics.

DOE Pacific Northwest National Laboratory (PNNL)

http://www.pnl.gov/
Technology Transfer Contact: Cheryl Cejka
Phone: (509) 375-3700
Fax: (509) 372-4589
Richland, WA 99352

PNNL conducts R&D activities in the physical, biological, chemical, environmental, materials, and computational sciences. Program areas include developing technologies for waste management, environmental restoration, efficient energy usage, nuclear energy utilization, and national security; transferring technology to users in the public and private sectors;

developing and operating scientific user facilities; and contributing to the enhancement of science and mathematics education.

UNITED STATES DEPARTMENT OF AGRICULTURE (USDA) HTTP://WWW.USDA.GOV/

Federal R&D obligations, total and intramural by agency: FY 1998

Total R&D obligations: $1,441.9 million

Total R&D obligations as a share of federal total: 2.00 percent

Intramural R&D: $954.9 million

Agency R&D obligations that are intramural: 66.23 percent

USDA remains committed to assisting America's farmers and ranchers. But it also does much more. USDA leads the federal antihunger effort with the Food Stamp, School Lunch, School Breakfast, and WIC Programs. USDA is the steward of our nation's 192 million acres of national forests and rangelands. USDA is the country's largest conservation agency, encouraging voluntary efforts to protect soil, water, and wildlife on the 70 percent of America's lands that are in private hands. USDA brings housing, modern telecommunications, and safe drinking water to rural America. USDA is responsible for the safety of meat, poultry, and egg products. USDA is a research leader in everything from human nutrition to new crop technologies that allow us to grow more food and fiber using less water and pesticides. USDA helps ensure open markets for U.S. agricultural products and provides food aid to needy people overseas.

USDA Agriculture Research Service (ARS)

http://www.ars.usda.gov/
Technology Transfer Contact: Rick Brenner
Phone: (301) 504-6905
Fax: (301) 504-5060
Washington, DC 20250

ARS conducts research to develop and transfer solutions to agricultural problems of high national priority and provides information access and dissemination to ensure high-quality, safe food and other agricultural products; assess the nutritional needs of Americans; sustain a competitive agricultural economy; enhance the natural resource base and the environment; and provide economic opportunities for rural citizens, communities, and society as a whole. To achieve these objectives, ARS identifies critical problems affecting American agriculture, then plans and executes the strategies needed to address these problems by mobilizing resources (both human and financial); fostering multidisciplinary research; linking research to program and policy objectives; and communicating and interacting with customers, stakeholders, partners, and beneficiaries to ensure program relevancy.

USDA Crop Science Research Laboratory

http://msa.ars.usda.gov/ms/msstate/csrl.htm
Technology Transfer Contact: Dr. Johnie Jenkins
Phone: (662) 320-7387
Fax: (662) 320-7528
Mississippi State, MS 39762-5367

The mission of the Crop Science Research Laboratory is to (1) conduct genetic, entomological, pathological, chemical, and plant resistance studies on cotton, corn, and forages for major insect and disease pests; (2) expand the knowledge of molecular processes of cotton and corn; (3) develop site-specific precision agricultural technologies and systems, applying cotton growth and development models in conjunction with remote sensing capabilities and improved entomological sampling methods; and (4) improve nutrient removal from lands heavily fertilized with waste from confined poultry and swine operations.

USDA Land Management and Water Conservation Research Unit

http://www.wsu.edu:8080/~lmwc/
Technology Transfer Contact: Donald McCool
Phone: (509) 335-1347
Fax: (509) 335-7786
Pullman, WA 99164-6421

The unit conducts multidisciplinary research on the principles and practices that enhance soil/water/air quality in economically feasible and environmentally sound agro-ecosystems. The unit conducts research on (1) water-erosion prediction and control under freeze/thaw and unfrozen conditions; (2) wind-erosion impacts on soil degradation and air quality and prediction and control of wind erosion; (3) best management practices for no-till and reduced tillage for soil quality, weed management, and sustainable crop production; (4) cropping systems, alternative crop selection, and microbial technology that improves plant growth and soil, water, and air quality; and (5) the biology and ecology of weeds in dry land crops.

Controlling soil erosion, managing weeds, and enhancing soil/water/air quality are major present and future issues.

USDA Pacific Basin Agricultural Research Center

http://pbarc.ars.usda.gov/
Technology Transfer Contact: Dr. Dennis Gonsalves
Phone: (808) 932-2100
Fax: (808) 969-6967
Hilo, HI 96720

The Pacific Basin Agricultural Research Center works to (1) increase the economy and well-being of Pacific Basin societies by strengthening their agricultural sectors, thus providing opportunities in agricultural for the next generation of island inhabitants; (2) strengthen small farm culture by focusing research on the development of crops and farming systems that will provide necessary profitability and efficiency; (3) develop farming practices consistent with the preservation of fragile island environments; (4) develop crop varieties adapted to island conditions to allow agriculture diversification for export; and (5) develop pest and postharvest technologies that satisfy quarantine requirements, thus allowing crop export from the Pacific Basin region.

USDA Plant Sciences Institute (PSI)

http://www.barc.usda.gov/psi/
Technology Transfer Contact: Harry Danforth
Phone: (301) 504-6421
Fax: (301) 504-6001
Beltsville, MD 20705-2350

The research mission of the PSI is to discover and develop biological, chemical, and physical processes and principles (including bioregulation) that will improve pest management systems, crop production efficiency, conservation of natural resources, and environmental quality. PSI supports regulatory and action agencies to contribute to advances in biotechnology and biocontrol to the benefit of agriculture and society. PSI's mission is accomplished through complex and exceptionally difficult fundamental and applied research programs in 14 laboratories.

USDA Microbial Food Safety Research Laboratory

http://www.arserrc.gov/www
Technology Transfer Contact: Dr. John Luchansky

Phone: (215) 233-6620
Fax: (215) 233-6581
Princess Anne, MD 21853

In cooperation with the University of Maryland Eastern Shore and the Food Safety and Inspection Service of USDA, this laboratory seeks to develop quantitative risk assessment and predictive models to provide the scientific basis for use of Hazard Analysis Critical Control Point (HACCP) systems in poultry production, processing, and distribution. The laboratory works to ensure a safe and wholesome food supply for consumers by preventing pathogen spread, growth, and/or survival under a variety of environmental conditions. Research includes studies of the natural incidence of bacterial pathogens, such as Salmonella and Campylobacter, in poultry.

USDA Soil and Water Management Research Unit

http://www.soils.agri.umn.edu/research/ars/Index.html
Technology Transfer Contact: Phillip O'Berry
Phone: (515) 294-7762
Fax: (515) 294-8125
St Paul, MN 55108

The mission is to understand the fundamental soil properties and processes affected by conservation tillage and residue management and to develop process-oriented models of these properties and processes applicable to a broad spectrum of agricultural management problems, including the quality of our ground water (potential drinking supplies). These understandings and models are to prevent ground water contamination and manipulate and control the environment of plants and other biota. A unique focus of the research unit's mission is the integration of multidisciplinary experimental research and predictive model development.

DEPARTMENT OF COMMERCE (DOC)
HTTP://WWW.DOC.GOV/

Federal R&D obligations, total and intramural by agency: FY 1998

Total R&D obligations: $978.7 million

Total R&D obligations as a share of federal total: 1.36 percent

Intramural R&D: $695.1 million

Agency R&D obligations that are intramural: 71.02 percent

The DOC promotes job creation, economic growth, sustainable development, and improved living standards for all Americans by working in partnership with business, universities, communities, and workers to (1) build for the future and promote U.S. competitiveness in the global marketplace by strengthening and safeguarding the nation's economic infrastructure, (2) keep America competitive with cutting-edge science and technology and an unrivaled information base, and (3) provide effective management and stewardship of the nation's resources and assets to ensure sustainable economic opportunities.

DOC National Institute of Standards and Technology (NIST)

http://www.nist.gov/
Technology Transfer Contact: Public Inquiries Office
Phone: (301) 975-6478
Fax: (301) 926-1630
Gaithersburg, MD 20899

NIST laboratories, located in both Gaithersburg, Maryland, and Boulder, Colorado, conduct research in a wide variety of physical and engineering sciences. The labs respond to industry needs for measurement methods, tools, data, and technology. NIST researchers collaborate with colleagues in industry, academic institutions, and other government agencies.

ENVIRONMENTAL PROTECTION AGENCY (EPA)
HTTP://WWW.EPA.GOV/

Federal R&D obligations, total and intramural by agency: FY 1998

Total R&D obligations: $606.0 million

Total R&D obligations as a share of federal total: 0.84 percent

Intramural R&D: $289.3 million

Agency R&D obligations that are intramural: 47.74 percent

EPA will be a major contributor to both solving America's energy crisis and accelerating the protection of our environment through the use of technology, market-based incentives, and the building of partnerships across traditional boundaries.

EPA National Exposure Research Laboratory (NERL)

http://www.epa.gov/nerl/
Technology Transfer Contact: Larry Fradkin

U.S. EPA Office of Science Policy
Phone: (513) 569-7960
Fax: (513) 569-7132
Cincinnati, OH 45268

NERL performs research to reduce causes of human and ecosystem exposures to harmful components in air, water, food, soil, sediment, and waste. The laboratory's goal is to provide exposure methods that represent state-of-the-art science. NERL scientists and engineers develop methods to predict human and ecosystem exposures to microbes, chemicals, and effects of physical disturbances. Included are models to predict and evaluate causes of exposures; methods to characterize stressors to sensitive ecoregions and atmospheric contaminant sources, transport, and flux; procedures to assess regional vulnerabilities resulting in human and ecosystem exposures; and high-performance computing technology and algorithms to enhance visualization and modeling.

EPA National Health and Environmental Effects Research Laboratory (NHEERL)

http://www.epa.gov/nheerl/
Technology Transfer Contact: Larry Fradkin
U.S. EPA Office of Science Policy
Phone: (513) 569-7960
Fax: (513) 569-7132
Cincinnati, OH 45268

NHEERL, located in Research Triangle Park, North Carolina, works to formulate and implement a comprehensive research program to investigate the effects of environmental pollutants and other anthropogenic stresses on human health and the ecosystems in which we live. NHEERL is the focal point for toxicological, clinical, epidemiological, ecological, and bio-geographic research within the agency. To improve the scientific underpinnings of EPA's risk assessments and regulatory policy decisions, NHEERL scientists create and apply biological assays and toxicological assessment methods, predictive pharmacokinetic/pharmacodynamic models, ecosystem function theory, and advanced extrapolation methods.

EPA National Risk Management Research Laboratory (NRMRL)

http://www.epa.gov/ORD/NRMRL/
Technology Transfer Contact: Larry Fradkin

U.S. EPA Office of Science Policy
Phone: (513) 569-7960
Fax: (513) 569-7132
Cincinnati, OH 45268

NRMRL is the agency's center for investigation of technological and management approaches for reducing risks from threats to human health and the environment. The focus of the NRMRL's research program is on methods for the prevention and control of pollution to air, land, water, and subsurface resources; protection of water quality in public water systems; remediation of contaminated sites and ground water; and prevention and control of indoor air pollution. The goal of this research effort is to catalyze development and implementation of innovative, cost-effective environmental technologies; develop scientific and engineering information needed by EPA to support regulatory and policy decisions; and provide technical support and information transfer to ensure effective implementation of environmental regulations and strategies.

DEPARTMENT OF VETERANS AFFAIRS (VA)
HTTP://WWW.VA.GOV/

Federal R&D obligations, total and intramural by agency: FY 1998

Total R&D obligations: $299.3 million

Total R&D obligations as a share of federal total: 0.42 percent

Intramural R&D: $299.3 million

Agency R&D obligations that are intramural: 100.00 percent

The VA Web site is a worldwide resource that provides information on VA programs, veterans' benefits, VA facilities worldwide, and VA medical automation software. Made available in September 1994, the site serves several major constituencies, including the veteran and his or her dependents, veterans service organizations, the military, the general public, and VA employees around the world.

VA Rehabilitation Research and Development Center

http://guide.stanford.edu
Technology Transfer Contact: David L. Jaffe
Phone: (650) 493-5000 x64480
Fax: (650) 493-4919
Palo Alto, CA 94304

The VA Center of Excellence on Mobility in Palo Alto, California, is dedicated to developing innovative clinical treatments and assistive devices for veterans with physical disabilities in order to increase their independence and improve their quality of life. The clinical emphasis of the center is to improve mobility, either ambulation or manipulation, in individuals with neurologic or orthopedic impairments. The center specifically targets four conditions that cause significant loss of mobility to veterans and non-veterans alike: stroke, spinal cord injury, arthritis, and osteoporosis. The approach is based on the belief that rehabilitation strategies of high impact will arise from scientific understanding of the underlying impairment. Rehabilitation science research includes, therefore, experimental and theoretical investigations of tissue properties and muscular coordination.

VA Rehabilitation R&D Center for Function through Electrical Stimulation (FES)

http://feswww.fes.cwru.edu
Technology Transfer Contact: P. Hunter Peckham
Phone: (216) 231-3257
Fax: (216) 231-3258
Cleveland, OH 44106

The Cleveland FES Center mission is developing technology that improves the quality of life of individuals with disabilities through the use of functional electrical stimulation and enabling the transfer of the technology into clinical deployment. FES is a leader in developing advanced techniques to restore function for persons with paralysis. The focus is on functional electrical stimulation systems that improve health, productivity, and quality of life. FES engages in a full range of research and development activities, including conceptual design, prototype development, *in vivo* testing, clinical evaluation, and technology transfer to industry.

VA Rehabilitation R&D Center for Wheelchair and Related Technology

http://www.herlpitt.org/
Technology Transfer Contact: Rory Cooper
Phone: (412) 365-4850
Fax: (412) 365-4858
Pittsburgh, PA 15206

This R&D center is a worldwide leader of research and development that is continuously improving the mobility and function of people with disabilities through advancing engineering and clinical research in medical rehabilitation.

Chapter 7

A NEW MODEL FOR TRANSFERRING GOVERNMENT LABORATORY DEVELOPED TECHNOLOGIES TO THE PRIVATE SECTOR

Discovery consists not in finding new lands, but in seeing with new eyes.

—Marcel Proust

Technology companies need new discoveries to invigorate their product pipelines. Yet the cost of a basic research program is formidable and its value is difficult to assess. In addition, technology development cycles are long and often fraught with setbacks and disappointments. For public companies this is not just a tough patch in the corporate landscape but an ever-present conundrum because a company's value is largely based on the strength of its technology franchise. For management, this weakness— the lack of control over ongoing innovation—must be neutralized to meet customer needs and to achieve an optimal marketplace valuation.

From another perspective, it has been well documented that the majority of innovations developed at universities and federal laboratories never reach the marketplace. This is a profound waste of the intellectual capital produced by some of the most creative scientific minds in the world. To address this twofold problem a new model for technology transfer has been developed called U2B. In essence, the model states that to facilitate technology transfer, a financial instrument is needed that can monetize the present value of intellectual capital in the form of common stock or another equity instrument. U2B technology transfer bridges the gap between basic research and marketplace commercialization. To allow for the systematic closure of technology transfers, it is helpful for both the buyer and seller to value technologies with a common currency. This enhances the potential for creating an efficient market between producers and purchasers of intellectual capital in much the same way that a mortgage helps to create an efficient market between buyers and sellers of real estate.

THE U2B MODEL

An initial premise of this U2B intellectual-capital-to-equity exchange is that technology transfer must be market driven to enhance efficiency. Therefore, an entrepreneur should start with a well-defined technology acquisition need. Once a profile is constructed describing the type and state of development of the technology needed, an experienced technology transfer company can supply this profile with some of the many technologies available for license from federal laboratories and research universities.

A second premise is that companies need to minimize invention risk to maximize shareholder return on equity. Invention risk is defined as the total cost of the invention process, including capital, manpower and equipment. Most basic research programs do not result in the development of breakthrough technologies. Therefore, it is difficult to determine *a priori* the financial outcome of a basic research program. In contrast, outsourcing often produces a higher or better-understood rate of return on investment, when compared with deploying capital in-house in a non-core area.

Market-driven technology transfer begins when the technology need is directly fulfilled by the technology available for license (figure 7.1). To facilitate acquisition of the license, the technology transfer company may help in setting up a special-purpose portfolio company to negotiate the license from the laboratory and facilitate the transfer. Once the portfolio company and the laboratory agree to the terms of the license, a stock sale agreement must be negotiated between the portfolio company and the public technology company, the final acquirer of the license. The portfolio company is then sold to the end acquirer for stock. This is a stock-for-stock exchange, whereupon all of the shares of the portfolio company are exchanged for a mutually agreed upon number of shares of the technology company. To obviate the buildup of inventory of depreciating assets (such as technology licenses), it is best to envision the U2B exchange as a "just-in-time" exchange of intellectual capital for acquirer company shares. The portfolio company contains the license to the intellectual property of interest, and therefore the ownership of this license is in effect transferred to the public technology company at the close of the transaction. In addition to the license agreement, the portfolio company may contain other intellectual-capital assets that the parties desire to transfer,

Figure 7.1
U2B® Model for Technology Transfer

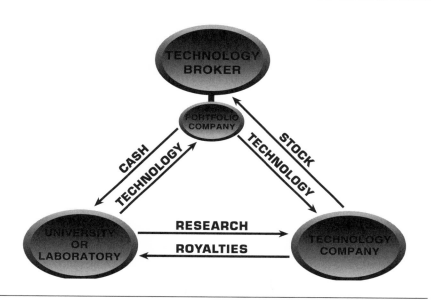

Association of University Technology Managers Licensing Survey: FY 2001 Survey Summary, AUTM, Inc., Northbrook, IL (2001). U2B® is a Registered Trademark of UTEK Corporation.

such as a sponsored research agreement, a consulting agreement, a material transfer agreement, real property or cash. At the close of the transaction, 100% of the license royalties are paid to the research institution by the public technology company.

VARIATIONS ON THE THEME

In practice, consideration paid to a university or federal laboratory for the acquisition of a technology license may also, in whole or part, be made in the form of equity depending upon the risk tolerance or applicable laws guiding the university or laboratory.

In our experience, technology transfer is facilitated by the use of the U2B model. We have applied this model successfully to close technology transfers from both universities and federal laboratories to a wide variety of technology companies. In using this model, some common features emerge:

- Intellectual capital may be acquired using common stock as a currency.
- Intellectual capital may be acquired in a profitable manner, with the assistance of a technology-transfer company, without imposing a sharing of royalties on the inventing institution. Rather, the U2B equity model uses corporate equity to finance the transfer of intellectual capital.
- The technology transfer process appears to be accelerated by the U2B model as a result of the sharing of risk among the inventing institution, the corporate purchaser and the technology transfer company.

FINANCIAL CONSIDERATIONS

In the U2B model, technology transfer is structured as a "mergers and acquisitions" transaction, which more fairly accounts for the present value of the technology on a company's balance sheet. Also, according to generally accepted accounting principles (GAAP), research and development costs are required to be expensed as incurred, the near-term effect of which is the reduction of operating income. In contrast, the outsourcing of research with the U2B model structures the technology transfer transaction as a stock-for-stock acquisition; therefore the value of the acquisition may be capitalized based on the consideration provided (stock). The net effect is that a technology license acquired through the U2B model strengthens the balance sheet by the value of what is acquired. Therefore, outsourcing basic research may enhance both corporate intellectual capital and the asset value of an organization immediately after it acquires a license.

In summary, U2B is the first just-in-time technology-transfer tool that empowers companies to grow their intellectual capital in exchange for common stock without diminishing the inventing institution's royalties. This tool has the potential to increase the value of a wide range of companies by allowing them to outsource basic research to taxpayer-funded research institutions and finance this outsourcing with the one currency that most growing companies are long in: their common stock.

Chapter 8

BUILDING SUCCESSFUL ALLIANCES WITH FEDERAL LABORATORIES: COOPERATIVE RESEARCH AND DEVELOPMENT AGREEMENTS (CRADAs)

Success is a ladder that cannot be climbed with your hands in your pockets.

—American Proverb

The U.S. government provides the nation's largest individual source of funding for research. This funding empowers the researchers at more than 600 national laboratories to move science forward in almost every area of technology. Most of this research is focused on the development or refinement of specific deliverables to aid in the national defense against geopolitical threats; environmental, safety, and health concerns; industrial competitiveness; the detection, evaluation, treatment, and prevention of diseases; and the assurance of the availability of safe and cost-effective energy sources.

THE GAME IS AFOOT

Since the 1980 passage by Congress of both the Bayh-Dole Act and the Stevenson-Wydler Technology Innovation Act, government labs have been repositioned as tools to help accelerate the development of technologies and products for the commercial sector, in addition to their primary mission of solving science problems that affect the national interest.

As a next step, the Federal Technology Transfer Act amended Stevenson-Wydler in 1986 and created cooperative research and development agreements (CRADAs). The CRADA empowered federal labs to enter into technology transfer agreements; it is basically a time- and project-limited joint venture aimed at producing a mutually beneficial research and development outcome. Both parties may contribute personnel, services, and intellectual capital, but the private partner contributes the money to effectively sponsor the research. In practice, a CRADA is the government laboratory equivalent of a university-sponsored research agreement. Normally, the corporation that funds the CRADA receives an option or an outright license to any intellectual capital that results from the project. For a corporation, the effect is similar to a work-for-hire or outside consulting arrangement—the difference is the amount of leverage that can be obtained through the use of extensive government laboratory facilities coupled with world-class subject matter experts.

As part of a CRADA, a company may agree up-front to pay a royalty on sales of any product that is derived from the CRADA in exchange for an exclusive license to the technology. To further reward government researchers, the 1986 act empowered government labs to reward inventors with royalty sharing similar to what is done at research universities throughout the United States.

With the establishment of the CRADA, Congress created one of the most entrepreneurial statutes for facilitating technology transfers between federal labs and private concerns. Federal labs are defined as any federally funded laboratory or federally funded research and development center

Figure 8.1
Active CRADA Projects at Federal Laboratories

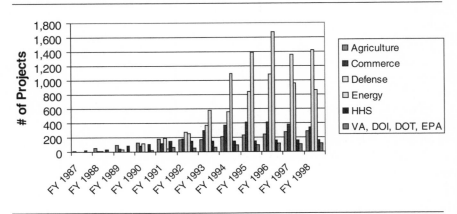

Source: U.S. Department of Commerce 2000
Note: The numbers presented here do not include "Material CRADAs." HHS–Health & Human Services; VA–Veterans Administration; DOI–Department of Interior; DOT–Department of Transportation; EPA–Environmental Protection Agency

that is owned, leased, or used by a federal agency. This applies whether it is operated by the government or by a contractor.

Single-handedly, CRADAs facilitated a rapid increase in technology transfer agreements between government and the private sector. From 1987 to 1998 the number of CRADAs increased from 34 to 3,201, testimony to the success and need for the program (figure 8.1).

As the number of CRADAs rapidly expanded, an appreciation of the importance of intellectual property in the transference and securing of ownership rights encouraged federally funded laboratories to be proactive in securing intellectual property protection. Both the number of patent applications applied for over a 12-year period (figure 8.2) and, more recently, the number of patents issued (figure 8.3) underscore the strategy.

Figure 8.2
Number of Patent Applications on Federal Laboratory Inventions

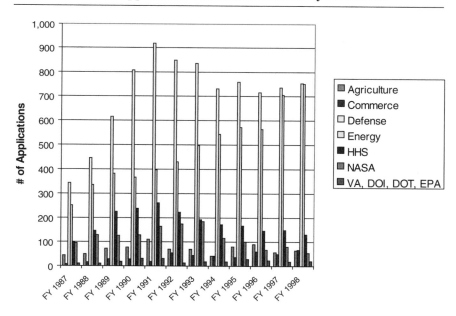

Source: U.S. Department of Commerce 2000
HHS–Health & Human Services; VA–Veterans Administration; DOI–Department of Interior; DOT–Department of Transportation; EPA–Environmental Protection Agency

Figure 8.3
Number of Patents Issued on Federal Laboratory Inventions

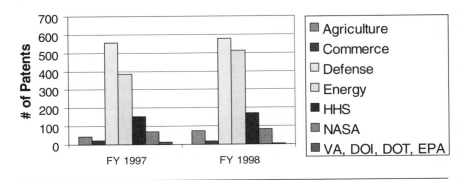

Source: U.S. Department of Commerce 2000
HHS–Health & Human Services; VA–Veterans Administration; DOI–Department of
Interior; DOT–Department of Transportation; EPA–Environmental Protection Agency

STEPS TO PROGRESS

The National Competitiveness Transfer Act of 1989 and the 1991 American Technology Preeminence Act defined and expanded the types of government entities that could enter into CRADAs. The former helped make CRADAs more practical by protecting confidential corporate information from release under the Freedom of Information Act. Confidential information developed under CRADAs is outside the domain of the Freedom of Information Act for a period of five years. This is not the case for information developed under traditional work-for-hire arrangements with the government, such as grants and contracts. This protection for confidential information reinforces the fact that a CRADA is not a procurement contract, and therefore federal laboratory directors are not required to comply with competitive bidding and many other requirements governing federal procurements.

In 1995, Congress passed the Technology Transfer Improvements Act. This gave exclusively licensed CRADA collaborators the right to any invention from a government researcher under a CRADA. Also, should the CRADA parties agree, it was now possible to transfer the patent itself to the corporate partner.

The 1995 act clarified that inventions made by the corporate partner during the performance of the CRADA belonged to the corporation. The government does, however, retain a paid-up, nontransferable, nonexclusive license to use the invention. It also has the right under emergency conditions to require the licensee to transfer its license to a third party if the licensee is unable to deliver the technology. In other words, the *march-in* rights of Bayh-Dole were extended to the intellectual capital licenses that the CRADA empowers. Under the Stevenson-Wydler Act, lab directors are authorized to negotiate license agreements for intellectual property and other intellectual capital with industry.

Under CRADAs, federal labs may accept, retain, and use money, personnel, services, and property received from collaborating parties and provide personnel, services, and property, but not money, to collaborating parties. In other words, under a CRADA, federal labs can leverage their intellectual capital to enhance the likelihood of success of an industry-partnered research and development program. In consideration for entering the CRADA, federal labs may agree to grant options, licenses, or assignments to the collaborating party for any invention made in whole or in part by the laboratory employee. Inventions made by the collaborating party under the CRADA are owned by the collaborator. In all cases, the government retains a nonexclusive, nontransferable, paid-up license to practice the invention, or have the invention practiced, throughout the world. This should not serve as a financial disincentive to industry, because having the right to intellectual property and being skilled in making and delivering high quality goods and services are quite separate matters.

Figure 8.4
Number of Licenses Granted for Federal Laboratory Inventions

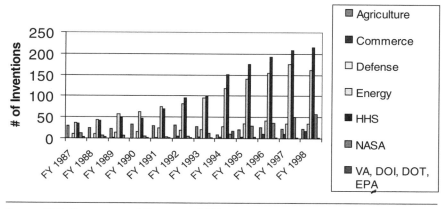

Source: U.S. Department of Commerce 2000
HHS–Health & Human Services; VA–Veterans Administration; DOI–Department of Interior; DOT–Department of Transportation; EPA–Environmental Protection Agency

The concept behind a CRADA is to create a *mutually beneficial* situation in which federal lab intellectual capital can be deployed to accelerate the development of new or improved products and services for industry. The win-win nature of the CRADA is highly evident in the growth of the number of licenses granted for federal laboratory inventions (figure 8.4). It is important to note that licenses for federal laboratory inventions translate into enhanced product and service sales for the companies that have licensed the technology.

Specifically, CRADAs offer smaller companies the availability and leverage of intellectual capital to help provide outsourced technology to their product development programs. With CRADAs, federal labs can provide an ongoing vehicle for innovation and product development for companies of all sizes. For emerging growth companies, CRADAs may be viewed as a vital new competitive tool in a rapidly evolving technology landscape—a straightforward way for businesses to create marketplace value by leveraging federally funded innovation.

Chapter 9

INTRODUCTION TO INTELLECTUAL CAPITAL

The whole of science is nothing more than the refinement of thinking.

—Albert Einstein, 1936

INTELLECTUAL PROPERTY

If you are a scientist at a federal lab or a business executive, chances are you will want to patent important new technologies before you make them public (Gross, Reischl, and Abercrombie 2000). But is patenting the idea really the right thing to do?

Let's look at what comprises "intellectual property," the creation of human intellect that is protected by law, and how companies can safeguard it.

Intellectual property includes patents, copyrights, trademarks, and trade secrets. Copyrights protect literary and artistic works; trademarks, or brands, are words, designs, or other symbols that identify and distinguish products and services. Both copyrights and trademarks are registered with the U.S. Patent and Trademark Office.

WHAT A PATENT IS AND ISN'T

Originally conceived as a way to spur invention and investment, U.S. patent and copyright laws were created in 1790. The Constitution authorizes them to "promote the progress of science and useful arts."

Parts of this chapter are adapted from chapters 5 and 6 of *The New Idea Factory* (Gross, Reischl, and Abercrombie 2000).

The word "patent" has meant different things over the centuries, but today it is most commonly known as a document that conveys specific rights to a person or group. These rights give incentives to inventors and their employers to create new technology and invest in commercializing technology. Many agree that our strong patent laws have contributed greatly to positioning the United States as the world's technological leader.

A patent provides the right to exclude others from making, using, or selling your invention. The owner of a patent may or may not be the inventor. The inventor's employer, or someone who has acquired the rights from the inventor or the employer, can be the patentee. Indeed, universities and federal labs often license their technologies to companies, which use them to make products and services, in return for payment and/or royalties.

To be eligible for a patent, an invention must be "new" and must be sufficiently different so that it is " nonobvious" to a person skilled in the field. This doesn't mean an invention has to be an improvement, only that it be distinguishable. Every kind of applied technology can be patented, but scientific principles and naturally occurring materials are not patentable.

Curiously, a patent does not necessarily guarantee the right of the patentee to make, use, or sell the invention. Indeed, in some instances, a patentee cannot make, use, or sell the invention without a license from yet another patentee. Sometimes, the practice of a patented invention actually violates the prior patent rights of a patent owned by another. This is what's known as "infringement."

Picture this scenario:

You hold the dominating patent on a motor-powered vehicle, a preemptive patent covering every type of motor-driven vehicle. A couple of years later, another person obtains a patent on an internal combustion engine.

In such a situation, the second patentee, the one who actually invented the internal combustion engine that would make the car run, cannot make or sell such a vehicle unless he gets permission from the dominant patentee. Conversely, because the second patentee happens to have the only practical means of powering the vehicle, the patentee of the vehicle itself cannot make or sell a motor-driven vehicle with this internal combustion engine without infringing on the engine patentee.

Each patent holder needs to cooperate with the other to make a car. Because such cruxes are common, companies and inventors often must collaborate in order to produce anything at all. Indeed, hardly a single sophisticated product would be possible without an elaborate network of collaborative cross-licensing deals with other inventors and manufacturers.

This is becoming increasingly true because systems of all kinds are becoming too complex to exist without the intellectual property of others.

A patent is a powerful tool, but it may not be the best way to secure the competitive advantage companies need. A patent gives an inventor a monopoly for 20 years from date of application. But to earn these exclusive rights on your technology, you must also make an enabling disclosure to all competitors. In short, your secret new technology is no longer a secret.

You can take violators to court, but the cost can be enormous. Court battles have hampered the launch of many promising products or services. Legal property rights are only as good as your ability to defend them. Defense of intellectual property takes time, energy, focus, and financial resources that often can be better deployed elsewhere.

Also, some patents take two to seven years or more to obtain. You may spend thousands to patent an invention and millions to assemble an intellectual property portfolio only to realize that several years have gone by—an Ice Age in a marketplace that measures cycles of innovation in nanoseconds.

This is the paradox of patents. You get a patent in order to lock out would-be competitors. But by the time you get one on a newfangled rose, the blush may already be gone.

The longer it takes to bring an invention from concept to consumers, the greater the chance that enthusiasm among researchers and developers will wane. Creative energy propels ideas along and carries new products or services to the marketplace. Inspiration fuels innovation. For these reasons, inventors may be better off keeping quiet about their inventions as they race to bring fully developed products and services to the marketplace ahead of competitors. To patent or not to patent is a difficult decision to make unless you can articulate the end game. In the case where the invention is being developed for future technology transfer; it is essential that objective feedback from the marketplace be considered prior to embarking on a long and expensive foray to assemble intellectual property rights.

NUTS AND BOLTS OF GETTING A PATENT

If you chose to apply for a patent, you'll need to know what can be patented and what it involves.

What Can Be Patented?

An invention can be patented only if it fits within one of the following classifications or conditions:

- It must involve a *process*, which can be taken to mean art, method, or mode of operation. It may include a novel use of a known process, machine, manufacture, or composition of matter. This means a patentable process may involve the use of old steps that are used in a new way to create a fresh way of making or doing something.
- It must be some sort of new *machine*, which applies to both hand-operated and automated devices. This also means engines, apparatus, or any number of devices that do something or produce some effect when activated. A patentable machine may crank out smoothies or mathematical computations.
- It must involve a novel *composition of matter*. This pertains to mixtures of ingredients, chemicals, or physical elements that produce a defined effect. A new mélange of chemicals used as a medicine is an example.
- Or it must involve a seemingly nebulous term, *manufacture*. This term is often used as a kind of all-purpose way of defining any number of inventions that don't fall under the other categories. This can include such difficult-to-define products as building structures and designs, sound recordings, and even genetically engineered organisms. Another category might include software. Still, some types of software are unpatentable, such as those that involve the invention of a mathematical algorithm.

As new technologies are created, questions about what can and can't be patented arise almost daily. In particular, debate is growing over genetically engineered inventions and to what extent they are patentable. For example, can the manipulation of genes to create a clone of a human being be patented?

Provisional Patent Applications

Starting June 8, 1995, the U.S. Patent and Trademark Office (USPTO) provides the option to inventors of filing a provisional application for a patent. This short-form application is designed to be a lower-cost first patent filing in the United States and to give U.S. applicants parity with foreign applicants under the General Agreement on Tariffs and Trade (GATT) Uruguay Round Agreements.

The provisional application allows filing without a formal patent claim, oath, declaration, or any prior art statement. It is a tool to establish an early effective filing date in a nonprovisional patent application filed under 35 U.S.C. §111(a), and it also allows the filer to use the term "Patent Pending."

A provisional application for a patent is in effect for 12 months from the date it is filed, and this time period cannot be extended. If you file a provisional application, you must then file a corresponding nonprovisional application for patent sometime during the 12-month pendency period to benefit from the earlier filing date of the provisional application. The non-provisional application must contain or be amended to contain a specific reference to the provisional application.

Once a provisional application is filed, an inventor may convert the provisional application to a nonprovisional application by filing a grantable petition requesting such a conversion within 12 months of the provisional application filing date. This procedure is in lieu of filing a nonprovisional application.

However, converting a provisional application to a nonprovisional application (versus filing a nonprovisional application claiming the benefit of the provisional application) will have a negative impact on the patent term. The term of a patent issuing from a nonprovisional application resulting from the conversion of a provisional application will be measured from the original filing date of the provisional application.

Although a claim is not required in a provisional application, the description in the provisional application must adequately support the subject matter claimed in the later filed nonprovisional application to benefit from the earlier filing date of the provisional application.

In addition, the inventor should disclose how the invention is constructed and to be used to enable any person skilled in the art to which the invention pertains to make and use the invention. The provisional disclosure should also include the best method for executing and applying the invention. The provisional application can be filed up to one year following the date of first sale, offer for sale, public use, or publication of the invention.

In summary, the provisional application provides simplified filing with a lower initial investment with one full year to assess the invention's commercial potential before committing to the higher cost and effort of filing a nonprovisional patent application.

For additional information on patents and provisional applications, contact the USPTO's Internet site at *http://www.uspto.gov/.*

Defusing Patent Time Bombs

While most work in getting a patent involves timely filing of paperwork and crafting of precise descriptive boilerplate, lesser-known pitfalls exist that can wreck even the most scrupulously built patent application. One of the most pernicious is "prior art."

Say you are an inventor who has created a nifty new widget. You decide a patent is the right way to go, so you begin jumping through the application hoops, filing the appropriate papers and hiring an intellectual property lawyer.

An upcoming conference gives you an opportunity to gently gloat about the scientific merits of your invention. Since you are well within the one-year grace period by which you must file your patent application after publicly disclosing the nature of your invention, you feel safe in your disclosure.

Think again. While you are correct in thinking you can publish to your heart's content on the airwaves and the Internet about your invention, there is nothing to bar folks outside the United States from snatching your invention and using it themselves, now that it's in the public domain.

In effect, you may have just given your invention away free to the very global market you hoped to tap. For scientists at universities and federal laboratories this presents an ongoing dilemma regarding the dissemination of scientific knowledge in publications and at conferences versus the desire to protect intellectual capital. This is a deeper dichotomy than it first appears to be. History has shown that when intellectual property rights are abrogated, so is the investment that is often necessary to manifest these rights into technological improvements.

LEVERAGING INTELLECTUAL CAPITAL

Traditional accounting methods may balance the books, but they reveal nothing about Microsoft's most valuable asset: intellectual capital.

Intellectual capital is a company's collective brainpower and experience that can be used to create wealth. Indeed, the chief assets of most companies are its clever employees. Working together, they use their knowledge, experience, and tools to provide a product or service that differentiate the company in the marketplace.

Companies that recognize the value of intellectual capital almost always share a common approach—they use the collective smarts and know-how of their employees, vendors, and customers to create superior (and usually more profitable) products. They understand that brains plus inspiration equals success in the form of profits—*virtual alchemy.*

Today, companies increasingly understand that they must leverage their intellectual capital to outmaneuver competitors in the marketplace. And they must understand something else: intellectual capital is more than the sum of employee capabilities. Intellectual capital is a company's entire

Figure 9.1
Corporate Assets Modified after the New Organizational Wealth (Karl Erik Svelby)

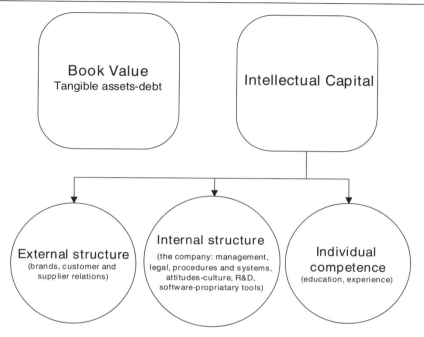

Source: Gross, Reischl, and Abercrombie 2000

network of contacts, from old college buddies to subcontractors to customers to family members. In short, it is everyone who can partner with companies in a symbiotic sharing of services.

But intellectual capital isn't simply what goes down the elevator at 6 o'clock every workday. And neither is it simply a chorus of employees plus vendor staff plus clients. Rather, it is the energy, experience, and degrees of positive collective purpose of all these folks, leavened with a high tolerance for the ambiguity of new ideas as well as the intuitive firings of neurons. All of that combined is what adds up to intellectual capital. Creating and using intellectual capital means being able to work fast together. This doesn't mean you and your employees need to aspire to some sort of perpetual frenzy. Rather, it means competing effectively in a knowledge economy—thinking, acting, and changing direction as quickly as ideas occur.

That's because ideas and intellectual capital can have short shelf lives. A super new idea worth millions today may be stale bread as early as tomorrow.

THE KNOWLEDGE ECONOMY REVOLUTION HAS ALREADY BEGUN

Okay, so maybe you missed out on a plum opportunity to buy a future technology leader at a low price because you couldn't read between the lines of traditional financial reports to perceive hidden values. You weren't the only one. We see the new New Economy as one where companies of all types use intellectual capital to increase the value of their enterprises.

And high-tech companies aren't the only ones that are out in front. Curiously, many of the big, traditional manufacturing outfits are pioneering new ways to harness knowledge for profit. Indeed, the majority of stock value for companies like home products behemoth Procter & Gamble Co. and retailing giant Wal-Mart Stores, Inc., comes from structural intellectual capital.

You could say that trying to create intellectual capital is a lot like trying to cull would-be super students and slackers from a pile of college entrance applications. Safe, traditional bets will be on the straight-A kid with the long list of extracurriculars. But an intuitive hunch on a candidate with middling SATs and an oddball array of hobbies could mean the difference between an alumnus who is a bright corporate grinder or an unconventional industry leader.

Just as students bring different talents to a college campus, so do the various parts of a business and its wider network contribute to a company's intellectual capital.

HUMAN CAPITAL

Employees aren't the fodder they once were considered—cheap, replaceable cost-generators who toted, fetched, and turned raw materials into cars and other tangible goods. Today, people are quite literally the flesh and bones of a company—or, rather, the brains. Their collective know-how, experience, and even institutional memory are what make a modern enterprise possible.

Plenty of chief executive officers pay lip service to the notion that people are a company's greatest assets. This isn't just another mantra du jour. Human capital is the most important part of a business built on brains.

Indeed, a company isn't a place where people go to pull levers and drill holes; it's a kind of conceptual rallying point for encouraging dynamic

Figure 9.2
Intellectual Capital

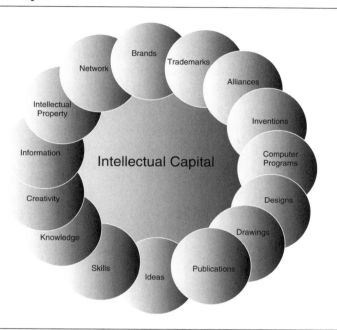

Source: Gross, Reischl, and Abercrombie 2000

thinking. Human brains, not brawn, are now the engines that drive the economy; attracting and nurturing the talents of this human capital is paramount. Successful knowledge companies constantly work to harness, and not choke, the talents of employees and managers toward collective learning and improvement.

If a company isn't downright tireless about tapping the creativity and innovation of its employees, it will die. And managers must be catalysts—they must unleash creativity rather than corral it.

Curiously, while humans are a company's most valuable assets, they are assets that cannot be owned. Cash and machines may be owned; folks cannot. But, as Patrick H. Sullivan points out in his book, *Profiting from Intellectual Capital,* the company does own its intellectual assets:

> While the firm does not own its human capital, it does own the intellectual assets. Human capital, employees and stakeholders, may break their relationships with the firm at any time. Employees retire, are laid off, are terminated, resign, or just leave. Whatever be their knowledge or know-how,

regardless of whether they brought it with them when hired or learned it during their employ, it departs with them when they go. But any bits of their knowledge that have become codified remain with and are the property of the firm. Codified bits of knowledge add to the firm's storehouse and stock of intellectual capital. In addition, once committed to media, an idea can be shared with many others, can be discussed, improved, and expanded. It can easily be communicated to decision makers and actions or decisions made on its basis. In short, a codified bit of knowledge, an intellectual asset, can be leveraged by the firm. And, leveraged intellectual assets are what knowledge companies seek to develop.

Careers are built differently today than they were just a few short years ago. Employees once boasted of being IBM people, of bleeding blue. Today, companies may come and go in the blink of an eye. Having a career no longer means being tethered to a single company. Successful companies collaborate with other outfits and workers when it makes sense for each. Successful knowledge workers increasingly associate themselves with their profession. Currently, dedication to one's field has in many instances replaced loyalty to a specific company.

STRUCTURAL CAPITAL

You could say that structural capital is what hangs around the office once human capital has gone home for the night. Structural capital describes many things of varying degrees of physical solidity, all produced in some fashion by human capital.

First, it includes the legal framework for ownership, inventions and their patents, and publications and motifs protected by copyrights and trademarks. It also includes the culture and reputation of a business—its fabric, if you will. The signature way a company does business, its processes and systems for getting things done, also are part of its structural capital.

A company's structures include the way it deals with clients, partners, and even competitors. In turn, all of these factors contribute to structural capital. While codified, structural capital is in many ways as mutable as the human capital that made it.

CUSTOMER CAPITAL

Arguably the least tangible type of capital, customer capital is basically a highfalutin way of describing something that has kept companies and clients together for eons: goodwill. A company may be chock full of talented folks, cutting edge patents, and universal name recognition, but without a strong and loyal customer base, it's nowhere.

There are practical reasons for wanting to nurture long-term relationships with clients, and making more money ranks pretty high on the list. Companies spend lots of money courting clients; keeping them typically costs less. Plus, as client needs grow, so does your potential income. As you learn new skills from your client, you can use that knowledge to further relationships with other clients or to snag new ones. A happy client will tout your talents to other potential customers.

For example, let's say your steelmaking company is helping design a stronger, lighter-weight truck frame for a vehicle manufacturer. Chances are, both companies will gain plenty: your company will gather knowledge about improved methods for making and molding metals, while your client will learn novel vehicle construction processes. In this way, you both learn things you can apply to other clients, be they makers of steel or cars, synthetics or canoes.

The more you learn about the business of others, the better you will be in courting and keeping fresh clients of all types. You both become smarter, more versatile, and potentially more mutually profitable clients for each other.

Goodwill, or customer capital, is the glue that keeps a network together and growing. The strength and scope of a company's network overtakes traditional hard assets in importance as we move into a knowledge-based economy—and customer capital will become a precious commodity.

MEASURING INTELLECTUAL CAPITAL

How do you measure how much (if any) intellectual capital your company has? Intellectual capital doesn't exist on traditional balance books. There's no decoder ring, no x-ray glasses to pierce the secrets of these documents.

You will need to examine a combination of orthodox account ledgers and other, tougher-to-measure factors to tease out intellectual capital figures. Even then, you'll be taking an educated guess. Measuring the intellectual capital of a successful company brimming with it is a bit like trying to gaze on an electron. No matter how high you crank the microscope, you will only see the evidence of its existence.

Companies that successfully employ and expand their intellectual capital reap profits. Another outfit with numerically equal measures of intellectual capital may earn a lot less.

Figure 9.3
Creation of Intellectual Capital

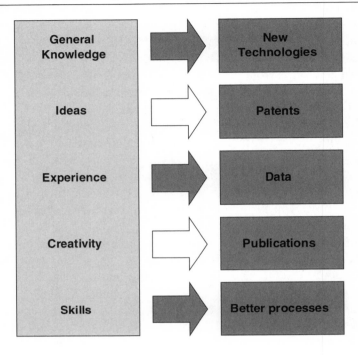

Source: Gross, Reischl, and Abercrombie 2000

The fruits of inspiration are obvious; the quality of inspiration isn't. Intellectual capital can be described as the difference between market capitalization (the total monetary value of a company's stock right now) and its book value (what's left over if you sold off all your company's assets).

Julie L. Davis and Suzanne S. Harrison, in their book, *Edison in the Boardroom,* see intellectual capital as a company's "hidden value":

It involves the firm's knowledge, know-how, relationships, innovations, and structure. It comprises both the firm's tacit and codified knowledge. It is the engine behind a firm's ability to create new products, business processes, and business forms. In addition, intellectual capital can increase exponentially. We notice that companies today are upgrading their products by adding information and capability to them. For example, we often see companies providing more intelligence in the same amount of product volume, or providing the same amount of intelligence in a smaller amount of product volume. Examples of products containing more and more information per unit of volume are telephones, computers, appliances, children's toys, credit cards with embedded chips, bar codes on retail products, and office copiers that self-diagnose their own operating problems—to name just a few.

Even a recent downward adjustment in marketplace valuations of public companies, a look at the market capitalization of the companies that make up the NASDAQ 100 is testimony to the awakening of companies to the importance of intellectual capital and its place in the determination of corporate value. While economies once were driven by wars or even weather, the global market runs on big ideas. In the next chapter we discuss less subjective methods for evaluating a companies' intellectual capital portfolio using bibliometrics and patent citation analysis.

Chapter 10

MEASURING INTELLECTUAL CAPITAL: BIBLIOMETRICS

The more original a discovery, the more obvious it seems afterward.

—Arthur Koestler, *The Act of Creation*

Eliezer Geisler (2000) has identified seven factors that have made a significant contribution to the development of U.S. science and technology:

1. The growth of research universities
2. Rapid expansion of federal R&D laboratories
3. Establishment of technology corridors near major research universities and federal laboratories
4. The GI Bill
5. Civilian utilization of military technology developed for use in World War II
6. Tradition of large public works projects, for example, the Hoover Dam
7. Growth of federal agencies with specific missions and/or regulatory agendas

The tremendous increase in the development of science and technology in the United States has in large part resulted from significant public sector support. It is not simply a matter of the allocation of government funding, but rather application of resources to an already fertile soil for innovation. Diversity is the foundation of innovation. Cultural, religious, ethnic, and philosophical diversity fosters a climate that encourages questioning of values, aspirations, and goals. Earnest questioning leads to enhanced knowledge and innovation.

Ultimately there are multiple approaches. Many, many paths lead to success and fulfillment. Whether the focus is the solution to a stubborn scientific problem or the resolution of marketplace inefficiency through a superior product or service, the collective basis for innovative leaps is the spiritual aspiration we as individuals and collectively as a society evolve: our ideals, thoughts, and manifestations.

All life forms on the earth are evolving together. Evolution in the realm of ideas creates scientific innovation. Sometimes these innovations are paradigm-shifting, as they disrupt our current systems of thought and action. Although initially difficult to embrace, these disruptive technological innovations have the potential to greatly enhance the quality of life and human productivity.

This is so because the evolution of thought transmitted into practice creates a more cohesive level of thought and action. These thoughts ultimately reflect and reinforce a state of coherency between our thought, actions, and the results of practicing both. Thought is not only creative, it is the most fluid expression of our free will and therefore our most precious natural resource.

Fiber optics transmitting coherent laser light containing enormous amounts of information during Web-based communications is highly analogous to the underlying proposition that all life is inextricably interwoven. Intellectual capital is our collective contribution to the evolutionary force that propels all life forward. On a practical level, the issue is not whether we should use public funds to develop a technologic infrastructure, but how we can best utilize the national treasure we have created. The question behind the question is: How do we build linkage between federal laboratory innovation and the marketplace?

The immediate answer seems to be the use of equity exchange to facilitate technology transfers. A range of metrics for science and technology has been developed to better understand the veracity and long-term value of such investments (table 10.1).

YOU CAN ONLY MANAGE WHAT YOU CAN MEASURE

The investments are primarily expenditures, and the financial metrics of performance are returns on these expenditures—return of equity, return on assets, time to break-even, cost reduction per unit, and so forth. The intro-

Table 10.1
Measures of Science and Technology

Investments in research and development
Financial & business metrics
Bibliometrics and citation analysis
Introduction to the market of new products, services and even business

Table 10.2
Competitive Patent Analysis: Some Key Questions

Who are our competitors?
How does our patent portfolio composition rate?
Is our technology expanding or contracting?
Where are competitors seeking foreign patents?
What is our current technology focus?

(Modified after presentation by Mogee Research & Analysis Associates, 2001)

duction of new products and services requires the assessment of financial performance, and straightforwardly quantified. Where art meets science in the measurement of science and technology is the area of bibliometrics and patent citation analysis.

Bibliometrics, or literally *knowledge measure,* consists of quantifying the number of scientific reports, articles, proceedings, papers, abstracts, presentations, and other extractable physical measures of research outcomes across companies, disciplines, and/or industries.

Patents themselves offer an indirect measure of the level of effort and amount of investment organizations are making in a particular technology sector. These measures typically consist of the number of patents issued, basic science citations per patent, other patents cited per patent, and how recently the patent has been issued.

Patent analysis is a valuable tool for intellectual property analysis and management. Specifically, this involves the analysis of large data sets of patents, with appropriate clustering to indicate invention linkages, for the purpose of uncovering patterns of technological development activities.

Alone, patent analysis is a qualitative tool for determining the extent of technological development. For a more complete competitive analysis it is necessary to augment the patent analysis with other such business inputs as corporate or government investments and such outputs as economic productivity, market share, and return on equity.

Table 10.3
Benefits of Bibliometrics

Structure	Flexible: Can be applied to companies, groups, institutions, and countries.
	Low cost and contains high face validity.
Measurement	Few assumptions required for the direct counting of publications.
Representation	Citation analysis can identify individuals, companies, institutions, etc. that have made a significant impact on science and technology. Method allows for the identifications of needs, trends and for the performance of competitive analyses.

Bibliometrics are objective measurements of published outputs of science and technology. In bibliometrics, quantity is measured by the number of publications that appear in journals of science and technology. The quality of these technological developments is measured by the number of citations that appear for a given article or patent. In general, bibliometric measures can be used to track the development of science and technology or the relative strengths and weaknesses of a specific company or organization in a particular scientific discipline. However accurate the counts are, they are still rough estimates of scientific progress, because far more is not counted, such as the relative marketplace utility or the acceptance or strength of a particular technology.

Of the more than eight thousand scientific journals, approximately two thousand publish 95 percent of all cited articles.

Bibliometrics has demonstrated robustness as a tool for the evaluation of science and technology. This is true in spite of such weaknesses as coverage of scientific articles only; the exclusion of reports, letters, and other communications; the insensitivity to stage of technology development; the lack of an objective quality standard other than publishing; and the self-selecting phenomena that takes place in every professional association. Nevertheless, the benefits (table 10.3) clearly favor the use of bibliometrics for the assessment of progress at both the corporate and governmental level in the development of science and technology.

PATENT CITATION ANALYSIS IS A GOOD INDICATOR OF A FLUID TECHNOLOGY FOCUS

As intellectual capital plays an important role in determining the value of companies' competitive analyses, bibliometrics and patent analysis will

Figure 10.1
Sample Patent Citation Analysis

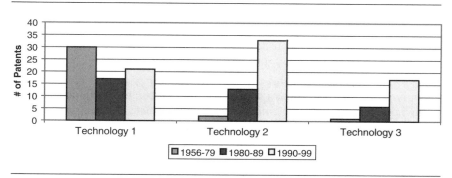

(Modified after Mogee Research and Analysis Associates 2001)

Figure 10.2
**Number of Citations on U.S. Patents to Scientific and Technical Articles:
1987–98**

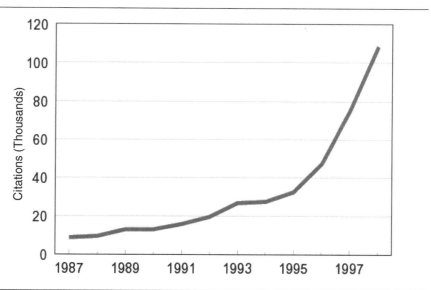

Source: National Science Board 2000

become more common in the internal and external evaluation of a company's competitive position. Mogee Research and Analysis associates uses detailed patent citation analysis to present corporate trends in technology migration (figure 10.1).

NATIONALLY, THE GROWTH OF INTELLECTUAL CAPITAL IS BASED UPON THE GROWTH OF SCIENCE AND TECHNOLOGY

Since the National Science Foundation began using patent citation analysis in 1972, the techniques have become quite exacting in spite of the difficulty of tracking disparate families of patents across enterprises. The current trend is clear (figure 10.2). As developments in science and technology continue, the amount of intellectual capital available for companies to leverage will increase. This points to both the importance of federal funding for basic research and the need for companies to build relationships with government laboratories and university research centers to enhance their intellectual capital, while controlling costs, in a rapidly changing technological landscape.

Chapter 11

"THERE IS PLENTY OF ROOM AT THE BOTTOM": U.S. GOVERNMENT LABORATORY RESEARCH AND THE NANOTECHNOLOGY REVOLUTION

Physical concepts are free creations of the human mind and are not, however it may seem, uniquely determined by the external world.

—Albert Einstein, 1938

Nanotechnology concerns itself with the very small. Nano is the prefix for one billionth (10^{-9}). Therefore, one nanometer is a billionth of a meter. About ten hydrogen atoms side by side is a nanometer wide. A DNA molecule is a bit less than 2.5 nanometers wide. Viruses are 10–100 nanometers in length.

Nanotechnology is the science of constructing complex "machines" on an atomic scale. It is a field of manufacturing somewhere between Michelangelo's approach to sculpture (removing the unwanted pieces) and the process of cell division by which all living things grow.

THE MEEK SHALL INHERIT THE EARTH

The strategic National Nanotechnology Initiative serves as an excellent example of how federally funded research can lead to the development of new industries and provide ongoing basic research sustenance to strengthen corporate product development efforts.

(After the title of a lecture presented by Dr. Richard Feynman at the American Physical Society meeting, California Institute of Technology, 1959)

Not only does nanotechnology focus on the small, but also on the swift. Atoms can move incredibly quickly, up to about 7,000 miles per hour in the atmosphere. After being struck by a photon, the molecule responsible for vision goes from bent to straight in about 200×10^{-15} seconds—that's 200 femto seconds (Crandall 1996).

The diminutive size of nano particles, combined with their supersonic interactions, results in a probabilistic flora that explores almost all possible interactions among these particles. Life forces seek to control these interactions to enhance the organization and survival of living systems. This aspect that partially defines life may help describe what is replicated with nanotechnology assembler systems.

Nanotechnology presents an unusual terrain, one where classical distinctions between animate and inanimate may be permanently blurred, and an area where the normal human illusion of control over matter and energy could launch a sense of hubris so large as to eradicate sensibility.

Nanotechnology is big, very big. Over a long period of time, it will likely change life, commerce, and the global community in which we live. It reminds me of a recapitulation of a primary movement within a symphony, one where the original theme is revisited with much stronger emphasis than the last visit due to what it picked up during the sojourn. The trip in this case is that of being a natural philosopher and evolving into a specialist and yet again becoming a natural philosopher. Only this time, the tools are much, much better while coupled with a more exact, yet still superficial understanding of matter, energy, and life.

THREE FORMS OF CARBON

The nice thing about rules, even the ones meant to be broken, is that they define a specific reference frame. The laws of physics and the laws of the State of Florida are not inextricably interwoven. They can and do coexist and live separate, independent lives in their specific reference frames. The science of nanotechnology has the potential to bridge every human discipline, from scientific inquiry to spiritual discovery. For example, the ethical issues that will be raised concerning the use of nanotechnology will make the current stem cell research conundrum simplistic by comparison. However, on the other side of this problematic baggage is potentially the greatest single technological revolution in the history of mankind, and it's just getting underway.

In 1985, a new form of a pure carbon molecule containing 60 carbon atoms arranged in the shape of a soccer ball was discovered (figure 11.1).

Figure 11.1
C$_{60}$ Buckminsterfullerene

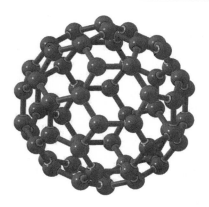

This third form of carbon, the prior two being graphite and diamonds, is known as buckminsterfullerene or buckyballs for short (after R. Buckminster Fuller, whose geodesic domes bear a resemblance to C$_{60}$) and may prove to become a basic building block of many different nanotechnology structures. Rice University professors Richard Smalley and Robert F. Curl, Jr., and University of Sussex professor Sir Harold W. Kroto were awarded the Nobel Prize in 1996 for this discovery.

Fittingly, Smalley has founded Carbon Nanotechnologies to produce buckminsterfullerene. Carbon Nanotechnologies produces carbon nanotubes, a really thin pipe made of a rolled-up sheet of carbon atoms just one atom thick. These nanotubes are the strongest known fibers, about 60 times stronger than steel for the same weight. Additionally, by adjusting the orientation of the carbon atoms in the lattice, these tubes can be made to conduct or superconduct. The cost of tubes of C$_{60}$ cost $15 per gram or $6,810 per pound in 2002.

Breakthrough sciences like nanotechnology have the potential to enhance productivity and thereby create marketplace value and wealth. This is the primary reason why it so vitally important to have long-term sponsored research funding for basic science initiatives. In the case of nanotechnology, the federal government under the Clinton administration had approved a $422 million budget in 2001. This was a 56 percent increase over the prior year. The following table indicates the breakdown by agency for nanotechnology funding for the proposed budget for FY 2002.

Table 11.1
Summary of Federal Nanotechnology Investment in FY 2002 Budget
Request (in million of dollars)

Department/Agency	FY 2000 NNI Budget	FY 2001 NNI Budget	FY 2002 Budget Request
Department of Defense	$70	$110	$133.0
Department of Energy	58	93	97.0
Department of Justice	—	—	1.4
Environmental Protection Agency	—	—	5.0
National Aeronautics and Space Administration	5	20	46.0
National Institutes of Health	32	39	45.0
National Institute of Standards and Technology	8	10	17.5
National Science Foundation	97	150	174.0
Total	$270	$422	$518.9

* FY 2002 entry for DoD is subject to change as a result of the Defense Strategy Review.
** Figures are not available for four departments that participate in the federal nanotechnology investment starting with January 2001: Department of State (DOS), Department of Transportation (DOT), Department of Treasury (DOTreas), and U.S. Department of Agriculture (USDA). National Nanotechnology Initiative is abbreviated NNI.

In addition, a significant effort is underway to explore synergies between research efforts ongoing in the different government agencies.

POETRY IS WHAT YOU FIND BETWEEN AGENCIES

According to Dr. M. C. Roco of the National Science Foundation the coordination will identify the most promising research directions; fund complementary/synergistic fields of research that are critical for the advancement of the nanoscience and engineering field; develop a balanced infrastructure (portfolio of programs, development of new specific tools, instrumentation, simulation infrastructure, standards for nanoscale); correlate funding activities for centers and networks of excellence; share the high costs of R&D activities; develop a broad workforce trained in the many aspects necessary to nanotechnology; study the diverse, complex implications for society, such as the effect of nanomaterial manufacturing on the environment and the effect of nanodevices on health; and avoid unnecessary duplication of efforts.

THE BUSINESS OF NANOTECHNOLOGY

Nanobusiness is off and running, although it is still very early. A rapidly growing number of companies are developing nanotechnology products and services.

Venture capital firms have recently funded five nanotechnology firms with more than $70 million (figure 11.2), and we believe this is just the beginning.

To facilitate contacting firms working in this fertile new area of technology development, we present without recommendation the following

Table 11.2
Proposed Nanotechnology Intergovernmental Agency Collaborative Activities

Agency	DOD	DOE	DOJ	EPA	NASA	NIH	NIST	NSF
Fundamental research	X	X		X	X		X	
Nanostructured materials	X	X		X	X	X	X	X
Molecular electronics	X			X		X	X	
Spin electronics	X				X			X
Lab-on-a-chip (nanocomponents)	X	X	X		X	X	X	X
Biosensors, bioinformatics		X		X	X		X	
Bioengineering	X	X				X		X
Quantum computing	X	X			X		X	X
Measurements and standards for tools	X	X		X		X	X	X
Nanoscale theory, modeling, simulation	X	X			X			X
Environmental monitoring	X		X	X			X	
Nanorobotics		X			X			X
Unmanned missions	X				X			
International collaboration	X	X	X	X	X	X	X	X
Nanofabrication user facilities		X	X	X	X	X	X	

Source: National Nanotechnology Investment in the FY 2002 Budget Request by the President. M.C. Roco, NSF Chair, National Science and Technology Council's Subcommittee on Nanoscale Science, Engineering, and Technology (NSET). Extras from AAAS Report XXVI, Washington, D.C., July 2001, pp. 225–233. Available at www.nano.gov.

Figure 11.2
Recent Venture Capital Funding for Nanotechnology Firms

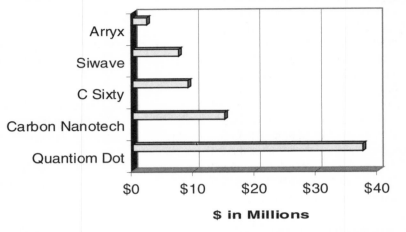

Source: Ross 2001

list of companies in the nano sciences with a brief description of their products and services (Nanotechnology Database, sponsored by the National Science Foundation, Loyola College, Maryland).

Argonide Nanometals Corporation

Argonide's nanometals group is an active participant in the U.S. National Nanotechnology Initiative. Its focus is the production of novel nanometal powders and certain ceramics as well as their applications for catalysis, nanodevices, nanoelectronics, nanosensors, powder metallurgy, corrosion- and wear-resistant coatings, and as additives to lubricants. In addition to Argonide's in-house R&D efforts, its nanometals focus involves a CRADA with DOE, employing a large group of scientists in Tomsk, Russia. Several U.S. national laboratories (Los Alamos, National Renewable Energy, and Allied Signal's Kansas City Operations) are also contributors to this nano effort.

Atomasoft

Molecular nanotechnology requires technological advances in three areas: nanomanipulation, mechanochemistry, and system design. Atomasoft works to enhance system design.

The mission of Atomasoft is to develop, in collaboration with other organizations as much as possible, software and design for nanotechnology. Molecular manufacturing hopes to impact all aspects of our lives. Nanocomputers and their software will also play a key role in the development of molecular manufacturing. In view of the crucial importance of various types of software, Atomasoft will focus its efforts on building a community able to create software and design. It will encourage the development of software and design for nanotechnology and nanotechnology-related processes. It will open discussion and provide tools to create and publish software and design on its Web site and also provide information about nanotechnology. Later Atomasoft will create software for simulations, to test and search for bugs in nanometer-scale devices. It will research how to design nanomachines faster and how to create new applications with these nanomachines. Its goal is to provide tools for the development of nanotechnology.

California Molecular Electronics Corporation (CALMEC)

CALMEC is a new company dedicated to the advancement and commercial development of the field of molecular electronics. The company is developing important intellectual property in this emerging field with an aim to accelerate its advancement from concept to reality. Included in the company's patent portfolio is the chiropticene switch, the first practical molecular switch with applications in many fields, including computation, telecommunications, and imaging.

DEAL International Inc.

DEAL manufactures carbon nanotubes (bucky tubes) for research and commercial requirements. It currently manufactures multiwalled carbon nanotubes and is in the process of making single-walled carbon nanotubes. DEAL also has capabilities to do research and development of devices using carbon nanotubes in the fuel cell and other research programs.

IBM

IBM research teams are hard at work on projects on the tiniest scale, exploring the manipulation of materials—and even data—at the atomic level. Nanotechnology is bringing new advances for fields such as computer storage technology.

Keweenaw Nanoscience Center

Keweenaw Nanoscience Center specializes in the development of quantum optics and nanotechnology for applications in life sciences and the electronics industry.

M.B.N. Srl

M.B.N. developed a proprietary process for producing mechanomade powders by high-energy milling. This process is highly flexible and allows the production of nanophased materials by a combination of reaction milling, mechanical alloying, and high-energy mixing. Mechanomade materials range from high-speed steels to copper and intermetallic alloys, from ceramics to metal matrix nanocomposites and metal flakes.

Molecular Manufacturing Enterprises Incorporated (MMEI)

MMEI was founded to help accelerate advancements in the field of molecular nanotechnology. Molecular nanotechnology involves manipulating structures with atomic precision. By working at a molecular level in a directed fashion, tremendous advantages are possible over any manufacturing methods currently available.

Nanogen, Inc.

Formed in 1993, Nanogen has developed technology that integrates advanced microelectronics and molecular biology on proprietary semiconductor microchips. The technology has broad commercial applications in biomedical research, medical diagnostics, genomic research, genetic testing, and drug discovery. It also is potentially applicable to environmental, industrial, and agricultural analyses. Nanogen's technology uses active microelectronics to move and concentrate charged molecules to designated test sites on the semiconductor microchip. The ability to concentrate and move molecules electronically provides unique advantages of flexibility, speed, accuracy, and efficiency.

NanoLab, Inc.

NanoLab develops devices based on carbon nanotubes. It grows aligned carbon nanotubes on various substrates and manufactures bulk nanomaterial, with control over diameter and length. Current products fabricated from aligned carbon nanotubes on substrates include field emission arrays, supercapacitors, Scanning, Tunneling, Microscopy (STM) tips, and infrared detectors. Other products are in development.

NanoLogic, Inc.

NanoLogic focuses on the integration of nanotechnology into computers to create extreme performance processors in novel logical architectures and develop new applications of nanoelectronics for the consumer market.

Nanomat, Inc.

Nanomat, Inc. is a high-technology company that provides the following services to its clients:

- Synthesis, consolidation, and processing of a wide variety of nanocrystalline materials, or nanomaterials, and nanotechnologies (technologies employing nanostructures) for structural, nonstructural, microelectronic, and biomedical applications.
- Consultation on nanomaterials and nanotechnologies.
- Consultation on various conventional materials synthesis, processing, and applications.
- Consultation on process and product development efforts.
- Technical assistance to start-up and established corporations.
- Technical and business proposal preparation and evaluation.

NanoPac, Inc.

NanoPac is commercializing a process to produce bulk, sintered ceramic materials with a nanoscale grain size. Such materials have exhibited significant improvements in wear resistance, toughness, lowered coefficient of friction, and improved surface finish. Among the materials produced to date are single-phase alumina, titania, silicon nitride, and zirconia. Also, NanoPac has extended its method to produce ceramic-ceramic composites in which both phases retain the nanoscale in fully dense bulk ceramics. Potential uses for its materials are engine components, cutting tools, impact plates, and medical implants, among others.

Nanophase Technologies Corporation

The origin of Nanophase can be traced back to research performed during the 1980s at Argonne National Laboratory, a DOE facility. Interested in studying the properties of nanocrystalline materials, researchers at Argonne conceived a unique process to fabricate them. This process, commonly referred to today as gas phase condensation, could produce small quantities of materials with unique characteristics. Besides their sizes being measured in nanometers, the particles were of high purity, had no residual surface contaminants, were spherical, and were nonporous. Convinced that these materials were commercially important and that gas phase condensation could be scaled to produce them in large quantities at reasonable cost, Argonne scientist Dr. Richard Siegel founded Nanophase in 1989.

NanoPowders Industries (NPI)

NPI is a young company in the field of precious metal powders and flakes. NPI produces silver powder and other special alloy powders for electronic components.

Nanotechnology Development Corporation (NTDC)

NTDC is a technology company formed to rapidly exploit the advances being made in the field of digital matter control.

Nanoscale Materials Inc. (NMI)

NMI was founded in 1995 to develop and commercialize reactive nanoparticles and related technologies. These reactive nanoparticles are extremely small particles of matter having extraordinary physical and chemical properties that hold promise for meeting a wide range of needs in both civilian and military markets.

INT Media Group (INTM)

INTM has launched NanotechPlanet.com—the first Web site devoted to in-depth coverage of the nanotechnology industry. NanotechPlanet.com was created to serve the emerging nanotechnology business community. NanotechPlanet.com offers weekly features, news, and financial briefs updates, interviews with executives from leading nanotechnology companies at all stages of development, a free e-mail newsletter, and an ever-growing database compiled to serve nanotechnology professionals and investors.

nanoTITAN, Inc.

nanoTITAN's mission is to be the premier provider of software, information, and services to the nanotechnology community and to assume a central role in the evolution of nanotechnology from research and development to profitable application. The company is developing nanoML, an XML-based markup language for the description of nanodevices, and offers both open source and premium scientific software libraries and applications. Services include modeling and simulation, studies and analyses, and custom visualization.

Powdermet Inc.

Powdermet designs, develops, and manufactures nanoengineered particulates using fluidized bed vapor plating technology. These nanoengineered materials are composed of micron and submicron core particles with 30–200 nm metal and ceramic coating applied to their surfaces to modify wear, friction, optical, and/or electronic properties, as well as enhance processability and control the final material microstructure. Powdermet currently produces, in bulk, more than 30 nanoengineered particle materials at costs comparable to current raw materials, primarily for the metal-cutting tool-and-die and spray deposition markets.

UHV Technologies, Inc.

UHV Technologies is an advanced materials R&D, thin film coatings/equipment manufacturing company, with emphasis on development of thin film cathodes (nanocrystalline diamond/carbon, nanotubes, aluminum gallium nitride, and ferroelectric cathodes) and their applications.

Xerox Palo Alto Research Center (PARC)

PARC performs pioneering research that covers a broad spectrum of research fields, ranging from electronic materials and device research through computer-based systems and software, to research into work practices and technologies in use. The center's mission is to pursue those technologies that relate to Xerox's current and emerging businesses. PARC has contributed to user interfaces, electronic components, embedded software, and architectures for each new line of Xerox copiers, printers, and systems reprographics products.

Zyvex

Zyvex's goal is to build one of the key pieces of molecular nanotechnology: the assembler. The term assembler is fuzzy and should be more clearly defined. In Zyvex's context, nanomanufacturing plant might be a better definition. This is a system of unspecified size (possibly quite large), capable of manufacturing bulk materials or arbitrary structures with atomic precision, getting nearly every atom in the desired place. It probably performs its task by doing mechanochemistry, which is a chemical reaction helped over its normal reaction barriers by mechanical force. Another possibility is positional electrochemistry, which overcomes the reaction barriers by careful use of electric charge.

CONCLUSION

It's almost as if the essence of America's very best technology has been hidden away in the garage, out of sight and mind, just waiting to be discovered.

While some people have called for more and more research in the areas of health care, aerospace, the military, and other disciplines, whole stockpiles of important research discoveries have been left to gather dust on the shelf. Even worse, other nations better prepared to take advantage of all this important American research have been able to benefit and bring products to market.

Thankfully, it is beginning to change, and American entrepreneurs are finally in a position to make good use of all the hard work that America's research laboratories have been putting forth.

Not surprisingly, the richness of this research results directly from the richness of the diverse American culture and experience and from our nation's basic confidence in individual initiative and problem solving. Some of the world's best problem solving takes place in more than 600 laboratories run by the federal government.

Taken together, these labs form a powerful research machine that works every day in virtually every scientific field. Ideas pour out of these labs in a torrent of creativity and innovation.

While the labs have provided a massive flow of ideas for many years, it took some far-reaching legislation during the 1980s to harness all that energy and inspire the transference to the marketplace.

The Stevenson-Wydler Technology Innovation Act, the Bayh-Dole University and Small Business Patent Procedures Act, the National Cooperative Research Act, the Federal Technology Transfer Act, and the National Competitiveness Technology Transfer Act offered the much-needed tools for extracting the true value from all these important "idea factories."

Understanding this legislation—and understanding how it can be used to its best advantage—is an important component for directing the best federal laboratory ideas to the marketplace. If brainpower is the engine of the New Economy, then the opportunities offered by technology-transfer legislation is certainly the transmission.

This book is a very basic roadmap. It describes the route that connects those idea-rich federal laboratories with the companies that can turn those ideas into products and services that the market wants and needs.

Entrepreneurs who can follow this route have the opportunity to harness the power of some of the world's most powerful ideas while minimizing invention risk.

Appendix I

OVERVIEW OF SIGNIFICANT TECHNOLOGY TRANSFER LEGISLATION

Stevenson-Wydler Technology Innovation Act of 1980 (Public Law 96–480)

- Focused on dissemination of information.
- Required federal laboratories to take an active role in technical cooperation.
- Established Offices of Research and Technology Application at major federal laboratories.

Bayh-Dole Act of 1980 (Public Law 96–517)

- Permitted universities, not for profits, and small businesses to obtain title to inventions developed with governmental support.
- Allowed government-owned, government-operated (GOGO) laboratories to grant exclusive licenses to patents.

Small Business Innovation Development Act of 1982 (Public Law 97–219)

- Required agencies to provide special funds for small business R&D connected to the agencies' missions.

Cooperative Research Act of 1984 (Public Law 98–462)

- Eliminated treble damage aspect of antitrust concerns for companies wishing to pool research resources and engage in joint, precompetitive R&D.

Prepared by the Federal Laboratory Consortium for Technology Transfer

- Resulted in consortia: Semiconductor Research Corporation (SRC) and Microelectronics and Computer Technology Corporation (MCC), among others.

Trademark Clarification Act of 1984 (Public Law 98–620)
- Permitted decisions to be made at the laboratory level in government-owned, contractor-operated (GOCO) laboratories as to the awarding of licenses for patents.
- Permitted contractors to receive patent royalties for use in R&D, awards, or for education.
- Permitted private companies, regardless of size, to obtain exclusive licenses.
- Permitted laboratories run by universities and nonprofit institutions to retain title to inventions within limitations.

Japanese Technical Literature Act of 1986 (Public Law 99–502)
- Improved the availability of Japanese science and engineering literature in the United States.

Federal Technology Transfer Act of 1986 (Public Law 99–502)
- Made technology transfer a responsibility of all federal laboratory scientists and engineers
- Mandated that technology transfer responsibility be considered in laboratory employee performance evaluations.
- Established principle of royalty sharing for federal inventors (15 percent minimum) and set up a reward system for other innovators.
- Legislated a charter for Federal Laboratory Consortium (FLC) for Technology Transfer and provided a funding mechanism for that organization to carry out its work
- Provided specific requirements, incentives, and authorities for the federal laboratories.
- Empowered each agency to give the director of GOGO laboratories authority to enter into cooperative R&D agreements (CRADAs) and negotiate licensing agreements with streamlined headquarters review.
- Allowed laboratories to make advance agreements with large and small companies on title and license to inventions resulting CRADAS with government laboratories.
- Allowed directors of GOGO laboratories to negotiate licensing agreements for inventions made at their laboratories.

- Provided for exchanging GOGO laboratory personnel, services, and equipment with their research partners.
- Made it possible to grant and waive rights to GOGO laboratory inventions and intellectual property.
- Allowed current and former federal employees to participate in commercial development, to the extent there is no conflict of interest.

Malcom Baldrige National Quality Improvement Act of 1987 (Public Law 100–107)

- Established categories and criteria for the Malcom Baldrige National Quality Award.

Executive Orders 12591 and 12618 (1987): Facilitating Access to Science and Technology.

- Promoted access to science and technology.

Omnibus Trade and Competitiveness Act of 1988 (Public Law 100–418)

- Placed emphasis on the need for public/private cooperation for assuring full use of results of research.
- Established centers for transferring manufacturing technology.
- Established industrial extension services within states and an information clearinghouse on successful state and local technology programs.
- Changed the name of the National Bureau of Standards to the National Institute of Standards and Technology and broadened its technology transfer role.
- Extended royalty payment requirements to nongovernment employees of federal laboratories.
- Authorized training technology transfer centers administered by the Department of Education.

National Institute of Standards and Technology Authorization Act for FY 1989 (Public Law 100–519)

- Established a Technology Administration within the Department of Commerce.
- Permitted contractual consideration for rights to intellectual property other than patents in CRADAs.
- Included software development contributors as eligible for awards.
- Clarified the rights of guest worker inventors regarding royalties.

Water Resources Development Act of 1988 (Public Law 100–676)

- Authorized Army Corps of Engineers laboratories and research centers to enter intoCRADAs.
- Allowed the corps to fund up to 50 percent of the cost of cooperative projects.

National Competitiveness Technology Transfer Act of 1989 (Public Law 101–189) (included as section 313 et seq. of DoD Authorization Act for FY 1990)

- Granted COCO federal laboratories opportunities to enter into CRADAs and other activities with universities and private industry, in essentially the same ways as highlighted under the Federal Technology Transfer Act of 1986.
- Allowed information and innovations brought into, and created through, CRADAs to be protected from disclosure.
- Provided a technology transfer mission for the nuclear weapons laboratories.

Defense Authorization Act for FY 1991 (Public Law 101–510)

- Established model programs for national defense laboratories to demonstrate successful relationships between federal government, state and local governments, and small business.
- Provided for a federal laboratory to enter into a contract or memorandum of understanding with a partnership intermediary to perform services related to cooperative or joint activities with small business.
- Provided for development and implementation of a National Defense Manufacturing Technology Plan.

Intermodal Surface Transportation Efficiency Act of 1991 (Public Law 102–240)

- Authorized the Department of Transportation to provide not more than 50 percent of the cost of CRADAs for highway research and development.
- Encouraged innovative solutions to highway problems and stimulated the marketing of new technologies on a cost-shared basis of more than 50 percent if there is substantial public interest or benefit.

American Technology Preeminence Act of 1991 (Public Law 102–245)

- Extended FLC mandate, removed FLC responsibility for conducting a grant program, and required the inclusion of the results of an independent annual audit in the FLC annual report to Congress and the president.

- Included intellectual property as potential contributions under CRADAs.
- Required the secretary of commerce to report on the advisability of authorizing a new form of CRADA that permits federal contributions of funds.
- Allowed laboratory directors to give excess equipment to educational institutions and nonprofit organizations as a gift.

Small Business Technology Transfer Act of 1992 (Public Law 102–564)

- Established a three-year pilot program, the Small Business Technology Transfer (STTR) program, at DoD, DOE, HHS, NASA, and National Science Foundation (NSF).
- Directed the Small Business Administration (SBA) to oversee and coordinate the implementation of the STTR program.
- Designed the STTR similar to the Small Business Innovation Research (SBIR) program.
- Required each of the five agencies to fund cooperative R&D projects involving a small company and researcher at a university, federally funded research and development center, or nonprofit research institution.

National Department of Defense Authorization Act for 1993 (Public Law 102–25)

- Facilitated and encouraged technology transfer to small businesses.

National Defense Authorization Act for FY 1993 (Public Law 102–484)

- Extended the streamlining for small business technology transfer procedures for nonfederal laboratory contractors.
- Directed DOE to issue guidelines to facilitate technology transfer to small businesses.
- Extended the potential for CRADAs to some DoD-funded Federally Funded Research and Development Centers (FFRDCs) not owned by the government.

National Department of Defense Authorization Act for 1994 (Public Law 103–160)

- Broadened the definition of a laboratory to include weapons production facilities of the DOE.

Source: Technology Innovation. Chapter 63 United States Code Annotated Title 15, Commerce and Trade, Sections 3701–3715. Prepared for the Federal Laboratory Consortium for Technology Transfer. St. Paul, Minn.: West Publishing, 1994.

Appendix II

BAYH-DOLE ACT

PUBLIC LAW 96-517-DEC. 12, 1980

Public Law 96–517
96th Congress
  An Act
  To amend the patent and trademark laws.

Be it enacted by the Senate and House of Representatives of the United States of America in Congress assembled. That title 35 of the United States Code, entitled "Patents," is amended by adding after chapter 29 the following new chapter 30:

CHAPTER 30—PRIOR ART CITATIONS TO OFFICE AND REEXAMINATION OF PATENTS

  Sec.

301. Citation of prior art.

302. Request for reexamination.

303. Determination of issue by Commissioner.

304. Reexamination order by Commissioner.

305. Conduct of reexamination proceedings.

306. Appeal.

307. Certificate of patentability, unpatentability, and claim cancellation.

§ 301. Citation of Prior Art

Any person at any time may cite to the Office in writing prior art consisting of patents or printed publications which that person believes to have a bearing on the patentability of any claim of a particular patent. If the person explains in writing the pertinency and manner of applying such prior art to at least one claim of the patent, the citation of such prior art and the explanation thereof will become a part of the official file of the patent. At the written request of the person citing the prior art, his or her identity will be excluded from the patent file and kept confidential.

§ 302. Request for Reexamination

Any person at any time may file a request for reexamination by the Office of any claim of a patent on the basis of any prior art cited under the provisions of section 301 of this title. The request must be in writing and must be accompanied by payment of a reexamination fee established by the Commissioner of Patents pursuant to the provisions of section 41 of this title. The request must set forth the pertinency and manner of applying cited prior art to every claim for which reexamination is requested. Unless the requesting person is the owner of the patent, the Commissioner promptly will send a copy of the request to the owner of record of the patent.

§ 303. Determination of Issue by Commissioner

(a) Within three months following the filing of a request for reexamination under the provisions of section 302 of this title, the Commissioner will determine whether a substantial new question of patentability affecting any claim of the patent concerned is raised by the request, with or without consideration of other patents or printed publications. On his own initiative, and any time, the Commissioner may determine whether a substantial new question of patentability is raised by patents and publications discovered by him or cited under the provisions of section 301 of this title.

(b) A record of the Commissioner's determination under subsection (a) of this section will be placed in the official file of the patent, and a copy promptly will be given or mailed to the owner of record of the patent and to the person requesting reexamination, if any.

(c) A determination by the Commissioner pursuant to subsection (a) of this section that no substantial new question of patentability has been raised will be final and nonappealable. Upon such a determination, the Commissioner may refund a portion of the reexamination fee required under section 302 of this title.

§ 304. Reexamination Order by Commissioner

If, in a determination made under the provisions of subsection 303(a) of this title, the Commissioner finds that a substantial new question of patentability affecting any claim of a patent is raised, the determination will include an order for reexamination of the patent for resolution of the question. The patent owner will be given a reasonable period, not less than two months from the date a copy of the determination is given or mailed to him, within which he may file a statement on such question, including any amendment to his patent and new claim or claims he may wish to propose, for consideration in the reexamination. If the patent owner files such a statement, he promptly will serve a copy of it on the person who has requested reexamination under the provisions of section 302 of this title. Within a period of two months from the date of service, that person may file and have considered in the reexamination a reply to any statement filed by the patent owner. That person promptly will serve on the patent owner a copy of any reply filed.

§ 305. Conduct of Reexamination Proceedings

After the times for filing the statement and reply provided for by section 304 of this title have expired, reexamination will be conducted according to the procedures established for initial examination under the provisions of sections 132 and 133 of this title. In any reexamination proceeding under this chapter, the patent owner will be permitted to propose any amendment to his patent and a new claim or claims thereto, in order to distinguish the invention as claimed from the prior art cited under the provisions of section 301 of this title, or in response to a decision adverse to the patentability of a claim of a patent. No proposed amended or new claim enlarging the scope of a claim of the patent will be permitted in a reexamination proceeding under this chapter. All reexamination proceedings under this section, including any appeal to the Board of Patent Appeals and Interferences, will be conducted with special dispatch within the Office.

§ 306. Appeal

The patent owner involved in a reexamination proceeding under this chapter may appeal under the provisions of section 134 of this title, and may seek court review under the provisions of sections 141 to 145 of this title, with respect to any decision adverse to the patentability of any original or proposed amended or new claim of the patent.

§ 307. Certificate of Patentability, Unpatentability, and Claim Cancellation

(a) In a reexamination proceeding under this chapter, when the time for appeal has expired or any appeal proceeding has terminated, the Commissioner will issue and publish a certificate canceling any claim of the patent finally determined to be unpatentable, confirming any claim of the patent determined to be patentable, and incorporating in the patent any proposed amended or new claim determined to be patentable.

(b) Any proposed amended or new claim determined to be patentable and incorporated into a patent following a reexamination proceeding will have the same effect as that specified in section 252 of this title for reissued patents on the right of any person who made, purchased, or used within the United States, or imported into the United States, anything patented by such proposed amended or new claim, or who made substantial preparation for the same, prior to issuance of a certificate under the provisions of subsection (a) of this section.

CHAPTER 4—PATENT FEES; FUNDING; SEARCH SYSTEMS

§ 41. Patent Fees; Patent and Trademark Search Systems

(a) The Commissioner shall charge the following fees:

   (1)

      (A) On filing each application for an original patent, except in design or plant cases, $760.

      (B) In addition, on filing or on presentation at any other time, $78 for each claim in independent form which is in excess of 3, $18 for each claim (whether independent or dependent) which is in excess of 20, and $260 for each application containing a multiple dependent claim.

      (C) On filing each provisional application for an original patent, $150.

   (2) For issuing each original or reissue patent, except in design or plant cases, $1,210.

   (3) In design and plant cases—

      (A) on filing each design application, $310;

      (B) on filing each plant application, $480;

(C) on issuing each design patent, $430; and

(D) on issuing each plant patent, $580.

(4)

(A) On filing each application for the reissue of a patent, $760.

(B) In addition, on filing or on presentation at any other time, $78 for each claim in independent form which is in excess of the number of independent claims of the original patent, and $18 for each claim (whether independent or dependent) which is in excess of 20 and also in excess of the number of claims of the original patent.

(5) On filing each disclaimer, $110.

(6)

(A) On filing an appeal from the examiner to the Board of Patent Appeals and Interferences, $300.

(B) In addition, on filing a brief in support of the appeal, $300, and on requesting an oral hearing in the appeal before the Board of Patent Appeals and Interferences, $260.

(7) On filing each petition for the revival of an unintentionally abandoned application for a patent or for the unintentionally delayed payment of the fee for issuing each patent, $1,210, unless the petition is filed under section 133 or 151 of this title, in which case the fee shall be $110.

(8) For petitions for 1-month extensions of time to take actions required by the Commissioner in an application—

(A) on filing a first petition, $110;

(B) on filing a second petition, $270; and

(C) on filing a third petition or subsequent petition, $490.

(9) Basic national fee for an international application where the Patent and Trademark Office was the International Preliminary Examining Authority and the International Searching Authority, $670.

(10) Basic national fee for an international application where the Patent and Trademark Office was the International Searching Authority but not the International Preliminary Examining Authority, $760.

(11) Basic national fee for an international application where the Patent and Trademark Office was neither the International Searching Authority nor the International Preliminary Examining Authority, $970.

(12) Basic national fee for an international application where the international preliminary examination fee has been paid to the Patent

and Trademark Office, and the international preliminary examination report states that the provisions of Article 33(2), (3), and (4) of the Patent Cooperation Treaty have been satisfied for all claims in the application entering the national stage, $96.

(13) For filing or later presentation of each independent claim in the national stage of an international application in excess of 3, $78.

(14) For filing or later presentation of each claim (whether independent or dependent) in a national stage of an international application in excess of 20, $18.

(15) For each national stage of an international application containing a multiple dependent claim, $260.

For the purpose of computing fees, a multiple dependent claim referred to in section 112 of this title or any claim depending therefrom shall be considered as separate dependent claims in accordance with the number of claims to which reference is made. Errors in payment of the additional fees may be rectified in accordance with regulations of the Commissioner.

(b) The Commissioner shall charge the following fees for maintaining in force all patents based on applications filed on or after December 12, 1980:

(1) 3 years and 6 months after grant, $940.

(2) 7 years and 6 months after grant, $1,900.

(3) 11 years and 6 months after grant, $2,910.

Unless payment of the applicable maintenance fee is received in the Patent and Trademark Office on or before the date the fee is due or within a grace period of 6 months thereafter, the patent will expire as of the end of such grace period. The Commissioner may require the payment of a surcharge as a condition of accepting within such 6-month grace period the payment of an applicable maintenance fee. No fee may be established for maintaining a design or plant patent in force.

(c)

(1) The Commissioner may accept the payment of any maintenance fee required by subsection (b) of this section which is made within twenty-four months after the six-month grace period if the delay is shown to the satisfaction of the Commissioner to have been unintentional, or at any time after the six-month grace period if the delay is shown to the satisfaction of the Commissioner to have been unavoidable. The Commissioner may require the payment of a surcharge as a condition of accepting payment of any maintenance fee after the six-month grace period. If the Commissioner accepts payment of a maintenance fee after the six-month grace period, the patent shall be considered as not having expired at the end of the grace period.

(2) A patent, the term of which has been maintained as a result of the acceptance of a payment of a maintenance fee under this subsection, shall not abridge or affect the right of any person or that person's successors in business who made, purchased, offered to sell, or used anything protected by the patent within the United States, or imported anything protected by the patent into the United States after the 6-month grace period but prior to the acceptance of a maintenance fee under this subsection, to continue the use of, to offer for sale, or to sell to others to be used, offered for sale, or sold, the specific thing so made, purchased, offered for sale, used, or imported. The court before which such matter is in question may provide for the continued manufacture, use, offer for sale, or sale of the thing made, purchased, offered for sale, or used within the United States, or imported into the United States, as specified, or for the manufacture, use, offer for sale, or sale in the United States of which substantial preparation was made after the 6-month grace period but before the acceptance of a maintenance fee under this subsection, and the court may also provide for the continued practice of any process that is practiced, or for the practice of which substantial preparation was made, after the 6-month grace period but before the acceptance of a maintenance fee under this subsection, to the extent and under such terms as the court deems equitable for the protection of investments made or business commenced after the 6-month grace period but before the acceptance of a maintenance fee under this subsection.

(d) The Commissioner shall establish fees for all other processing, services, or materials relating to patents not specified in this section to recover the estimated average cost to the Office of such processing, services, or materials, except that the Commissioner shall charge the following fees for the following services:

(1) For recording a document affecting title, $40 per property.

(2) For each photocopy, $0.25 per page.

(3) For each black and white copy of a patent, $3.

The yearly fee for providing a library specified in section 13 of this title with uncertified printed copies of the specifications and drawings for all patents in that year shall be $50.

(e) The Commissioner may waive the payment of any fee for any service or material related to patents in connection with an occasional or incidental request made by a department or agency of the Government, or any officer thereof. The Commissioner may provide any applicant issued a notice under section 132 of this title with a copy of the specifications and drawings for all patents referred to in that notice without charge.

(f) The fees established in subsections (a) and (b) of this section may be adjusted by the Commissioner on October 1, 1992, and every year thereafter, to reflect any fluctuations occurring during the previous 12 months in the Consumer Price Index, as determined by the Secretary of Labor. Changes of less than 1 per centum may be ignored.

(g) No fee established by the Commissioner under this section shall take effect until at least 30 days after notice of the fee has been published in the Federal Register and in the Official Gazette of the Patent and Trademark Office.

(h)

   (1) Fees charged under subsection (a) or (b) shall be reduced by 50 percent with respect to their application to any small business concern as defined under section 3 of the Small Business Act, and to any independent inventor or nonprofit organization as defined in regulations issued by the Commissioner of Patents and Trademarks.

   (2) With respect to its application to any entity described in paragraph (1), any surcharge or fee charged under subsection (c) or (d) shall not be higher than the surcharge or fee required of any other entity under the same or substantially similar circumstances.

(i)

   (1) The Commissioner shall maintain, for use by the public, paper or microform collections of United States patents, foreign patent documents, and United States trademark registrations arranged to permit search for and retrieval of information. The Commissioner may not impose fees directly for the use of such collections, or for the use of the public patent or trademark search rooms or libraries.

   (2) The Commissioner shall provide for the full deployment of the automated search systems of the Patent and Trademark Office so that such systems are available for use by the public, and shall assure full access by the public to, and dissemination of, patent and trademark information, using a variety of automated methods, including electronic bulletin boards and remote access by users to mass storage and retrieval systems.

   (3) The Commissioner may establish reasonable fees for access by the public to the automated search systems of the Patent and Trademark Office. If such fees are established, a limited amount of free access shall be made available to users of the systems for purposes of education and training. The Commissioner may waive the payment by an individual of fees authorized by this subsection upon a showing of need or hardship, and if such a waiver is in the public interest.

   (4) The Commissioner shall submit to the Congress an annual report on the automated search systems of the Patent and Trademark Office and the access by the public to such systems. The Commissioner

shall also publish such report in the *Federal Register*. The Commissioner shall provide an opportunity for the submission of comments by interested persons on each such report.

§ 42. Patent and Trademark Office Funding

(a) All fees for services performed by or materials furnished by the Patent and Trademark Office will be payable to the Commissioner.

(b) All fees paid to the Commissioner and all appropriations for defraying the costs of the activities of the Patent and Trademark Office will be credited to the Patent and Trademark Office Appropriation Account in the Treasury of the United States.

(c) To the extent and in the amounts provided in advance in appropriations Acts, fees authorized in this title or any other Act to be charged or established by the Commissioner shall be collected by and shall be available to the Commissioner to carry out the activities of the Patent and Trademark Office. Fees available to the Commissioner under section 31 of the Trademark Act of 1946 may be used only for the processing of trademark registrations and for other activities, services, and materials relating to trademarks and to cover a proportionate share of the administrative costs of the Patent and Trademark Office.

(d) The Commissioner may refund any fee paid by mistake or any amount paid in excess of that required.

(e) Secretary of Commerce shall, on the day each year on which the President submits the annual budget to the Congress, provide to the Committees on the Judiciary of the Senate and the House of Representatives -

   (1) a list of patent and trademark fee collections by the Patent and Trademark Office during the preceding fiscal year;

   (2) a list of activities of the Patent and Trademark Office during the preceding fiscal year which were supported by patent fee expenditures, trademark fee expenditures, and appropriations;

   (3) budget plans for significant programs, projects, and activities of the Office, including out-year funding estimates;

   (4) any proposed disposition of surplus fees by the Office; and

   (5) such other information as the committees consider necessary.

CHAPTER 37—NATIONAL STAGE

§ 376. Fees

(a) The required payment of the international fee and the handling fee, which amounts are specified in the Regulations, shall be paid in United

States currency. The Patent and Trademark Office shall charge a national fee as provided in section 41(a), and may also charge the following fees:

(1) A transmittal fee (see section 361(d));

(2) A search fee (see section 361(d));

(3) A supplemental search fee (to be paid when required);

(4) A preliminary examination fee and any additional fees (see section 362(b)).

(5) Such other fees as established by the Commissioner.

(b) The amounts of fees specified in subsection (a) of this section, except the international fee and the handling fee, shall be prescribed by the Commissioner. He may refund any sum paid by mistake or in excess of the fees so specified, or if required under the treaty and the Regulations. The Commissioner may also refund any part of the search fee, the national fee, the preliminary examination fee, and any additional fees, where he determines such refund to be warranted.

CHAPTER 18—PATENT RIGHTS IN INVENTIONS MADE WITH FEDERAL ASSISTANCE

Sec.

200. Policy and objective.

201. Definitions.

202. Disposition of rights.

203. March-in rights.

204. Preference for United States industry.

205. Confidentiality.

206. Uniform clauses and regulations.

207. Domestic and foreign protection of federally owned inventions.

208. Regulations governing Federal licensing.

209. Restrictions on licensing of federally owned inventions.

210. Precedence of chapter.

211. Relationship to antitrust laws.

§ 200. Policy and Objective

It is the policy and objective of the Congress to use the patent system to promote the utilization of inventions arising from federally supported research or development; to encourage maximum participation of small business firms in federally supported research and development efforts; to promote collaboration between commercial concerns and nonprofit organizations, including universities; to ensure that inventions made by nonprofit organizations and small business firms are used in a manner to promote free competition and enterprise; to promote the commercialization and public availability of inventions made in the United States by United States industry and labor; to ensure that the Government obtains sufficient rights in federally supported inventions to meet the needs of the Government and protect the public against nonuse or unreasonable use of inventions; and to minimize the costs of administering policies in this area.

§ 201. Definitions

As used in this chapter -
(a) The term "Federal agency" means any executive agency as defined in section 105 of title 5, United States Code, and the military departments as defined by section 102 of title 5, United States Code.

(b) The term "funding agreement" means any contract, grant, or cooperative agreement entered into between any Federal agency, other than the Tennessee Valley Authority, and any contractor for the performance of experimental, developmental, or research work funded in whole or in part by the Federal Government. Such term includes any assignment, substitution of parties, or subcontract of any type entered into for the performance of experimental, developmental, or research work under a funding agreement as herein defined.

(c) The term "contractor" means any person, small business firm, or nonprofit organization that is a party to a funding agreement.

(d) The term "invention" means any invention or discovery which is or may be patentable or otherwise protectable under this title or any novel variety of plant which is or may be protectable under the Plant Variety Protection Act (7 U.S.C. 2321 et seq.).

(e) The term "subject invention" means any invention of the contractor conceived or first actually reduced to practice in the performance of work under a funding agreement: Provided, That in the case of a variety of plant, the date of determination (as defined in section 41(d) of the Plant Variety Protection Act (7 U.S.C. 2401(d))) must also occur during the period of contract performance.

(f) The term "practical application" means to manufacture in the case of a composition or product, to practice in the case of a process or method, or to operate in the case of a machine or system; and, in each case, under such conditions as to establish that the invention is being utilized and that its benefits are to the extent permitted by law or Government regulations available to the public on reasonable terms.

(g) The term "made" when used in relation to any invention means the conception or first actual reduction to practice of such invention.

(h) The term "small business firm" means a small business concern as defined at section 2 of Public Law 85–536 (15 U.S.C.632) and implementing regulations of the Administrator of the Small Business Administration.

(i) The term "nonprofit organization" means universities and other institutions of higher education or an organization of the type described in section 501(c)(3) of the Internal Revenue Code of 1986 (26 U.S.C. 501(c)) and exempt from taxation under section 501(a) of the Internal Revenue Code (26 U.S.C. 501(a)) or any nonprofit scientific or educational organization qualified under a State nonprofit organization statute.

§ 202. Disposition of Rights

(a) Each nonprofit organization or small business firm may, within a reasonable time after disclosure as required by paragraph (c)(1) of this section, elect to retain title to any subject invention: Provided, however, That a funding agreement may provide otherwise.

(i) when the contractor is not located in the United States or does not have a place of business located in the United States or is subject to the control of a foreign government,

(ii) in exceptional circumstances when it is determined by the agency that restriction or elimination of the right to retain title to any subject invention will better promote the policy and objectives of this chapter,

(iii) when it is determined by a Government authority which is authorized by statute or Executive order to conduct foreign intelligence or counter-intelligence activities that the restriction or elimination of the right to retain title to any subject invention is necessary to protect the security of such activities, or

(iv) when the funding agreement includes the operation of a Government-owned, contractor-operated facility of the Department of Energy primarily dedicated to that Department's naval nuclear propulsion or weapons related programs and all funding agreement limitations under this subparagraph on the contractor's right to elect title to a subject invention are limited to inventions occurring under the above two programs of the Department of Energy. (FOOTNOTE 2) The rights of the nonprofit organization or small business firm shall be subject to the provisions of paragraph (c) of this section and the other provisions of this chapter. So in original.

(b)

(1) The rights of the Government under subsection (a) shall not be exercised by a Federal agency unless it first determines that at least one of the conditions identified in clauses (i) through (iv) of subsection (a) exists. Except in the case of subsection (a)(iii), the agency shall file with the Secretary of Commerce, within thirty days after the award of the applicable funding agreement, a copy of such determination. In the case of a determination under subsection (a)(ii), the statement shall include an analysis justifying the determination. In the case of determinations applicable to funding agreements with small business firms, copies shall also be sent to the Chief Counsel for Advocacy of the Small Business Administration. If the Secretary of Commerce believes that any individual determination or pattern of determinations is contrary to the policies and objectives of this chapter or otherwise not in conformance with this chapter, the Secretary shall so advise the head of the agency concerned and the Administrator of the Office of Federal Procurement Policy, and recommend corrective actions.

(2) Whenever the Administrator of the Office of Federal Procurement Policy has determined that one or more Federal agencies are utilizing the authority of clause (i) or (ii) of subsection (a) of this section in a manner that is contrary to the policies and objectives of this chapter, the Administrator is authorized to issue regulations describing classes of situations in which agencies may not exercise the authorities of those clauses.

(3) At least once every 5 years, the Comptroller General shall transmit a report to the Committees on the Judiciary of the Senate and House of Representatives on the manner in which this chapter is being implemented by the agencies and on such other aspects of Government patent policies and practices with respect to federally funded inventions as the Comptroller General believes appropriate.

(4) If the contractor believes that a determination is contrary to the policies and objectives of this chapter or constitutes an abuse of discretion by the agency, the determination shall be subject to the last paragraph of section 203(2).

(c) Each funding agreement with a small business firm or nonprofit organization shall contain appropriate provisions to effectuate the following:

(1) That the contractor disclose each subject invention to the Federal agency within a reasonable time after it becomes known to contrac-

tor personnel responsible for the administration of patent matters, and that the Federal Government may receive title to any subject invention not disclosed to it within such time.

(2) That the contractor make a written election within two years after disclosure to the Federal agency (or such additional time as may be approved by the Federal agency) whether the contractor will retain title to a subject invention: Provided, That in any case where publication, on sale, or public use, has initiated the one year statutory period in which valid patent protection can still be obtained in the United States, the period for election may be shortened by the Federal agency to a date that is not more than sixty days prior to the end of the statutory period: And provided further, That the Federal Government may receive title to any subject invention in which the contractor does not elect to retain rights or fails to elect rights within such times.

(3) That a contractor electing rights in a subject invention agrees to file a patent application prior to any statutory bar date that may occur under this title due to publication, on sale, or public use, and shall thereafter file corresponding patent applications in other countries in which it wishes to retain title within reasonable times, and that the Federal Government may receive title to any subject inventions in the United States or other countries in which the contractor has not filed patent applications on the subject invention within such times.

(4) With respect to any invention in which the contractor elects rights, the Federal agency shall have a nonexclusive, nontransferrable, irrevocable, paid-up license to practice or have practiced for or on behalf of the United States any subject invention throughout the world: Provided, That the funding agreement may provide for such additional rights; including the right to assign or have assigned foreign patent rights in the subject invention, as are determined by the agency as necessary for meeting the obligations of the United States under any treaty, international agreement, arrangement of cooperation, memorandum of understanding, or similar arrangement, including military agreement relating to weapons development and production.

(5) The right of the Federal agency to require periodic reporting on the utilization or efforts at obtaining utilization that are being made by the contractor or his licensees or assignees: Provided, That any such information as well as any information on utilization or efforts at obtaining utilization obtained as part of a proceeding under section 203 of this chapter shall be treated by the Federal agency as commercial and financial information obtained from a person and privileged and confidential and not subject to disclosure under section 552 of title 5 of the United States Code.

(6) An obligation on the part of the contractor, in the event a United States patent application is filed by or on its behalf or by any assignee of the contractor, to include within the specification of such application and any patent issuing thereon, a statement specifying that the invention was made with Government support and that the Government has certain rights in the invention.

(7) In the case of a nonprofit organization,

    (A) a prohibition upon the assignment of rights to a subject invention in the United States without the approval of the Federal agency, except where such assignment is made to an organization which has as one of its primary functions the management of inventions (provided that such assignee shall be subject to the same provisions as the contractor);

    (B) a requirement that the contractor share royalties with the inventor;

    (C) except with respect to a funding agreement for the operation of a Government-owned-contractor-operated facility, a requirement that the balance of any royalties or income earned by the contractor with respect to subject inventions, after payment of expenses (including payments to inventors) incidental to the administration of subject inventions, be utilized for the support of scientific research or education;

    (D) a requirement that, except where it proves infeasible after a reasonable inquiry, in the licensing of subject inventions shall be given to small business firms; and

    (E) with respect to a funding agreement for the operation of a Government-owned-contractor-operated facility, requirements

        (i) that after payment of patenting costs, licensing costs, payments to inventors, and other expenses incidental to the administration of subject inventions, 100 percent of the balance of any royalties or income earned and retained by the contractor during any fiscal year up to an amount equal to 5 percent of the annual budget of the facility, shall be used by the contractor for scientific research, development, and education consistent with the research and development mission and objectives of the facility, including activities that increase the licensing potential of other inventions of the facility; provided that if said balance exceeds 5 percent of the annual budget of the facility, that 75 percent of such excess shall be paid to the Treasury of the United States and the remaining 25 percent shall be used for the same purposes as described above in this clause (D); and

      (ii) that, to the extent it provides the most effective technology transfer, the licensing of subject inventions shall be administered by contractor employees on location at the facility.

    (8) The requirements of sections 203 and 204 of this chapter.

(d) If a contractor does not elect to retain title to a subject invention in cases subject to this section, the Federal agency may consider and after consultation with the contractor grant requests for retention of rights by the inventor subject to the provisions of this Act and regulations promulgated hereunder.

(e) In any case when a Federal employee is a coinventor of any invention made under a funding agreement with a nonprofit organization or small business firm, the Federal agency employing such coinventor is authorized to transfer or assign whatever rights it may acquire in the subject invention from its employee to the contractor subject to the conditions set forth in this chapter.

(f)

    (1) No funding agreement with a small business firm or nonprofit organization shall contain a provision allowing a Federal agency to require the licensing to third parties of inventions owned by the contractor that are not subject inventions unless such provision has been approved by the head of the agency and a written justification has been signed by the head of the agency. Any such provision shall clearly state whether the licensing may be required in connection with the practice of a subject invention, a specifically identified work object, or both. The head of the agency may not delegate the authority to approve provisions or sign justifications required by this paragraph.

    (2) A Federal agency shall not require the licensing of third parties under any such provision unless the head of the agency determines that the use of the invention by others is necessary for the practice of a subject invention or for the use of a work object of the funding agreement and that such action is necessary to achieve the practical application of the subject invention or work object. Any such determination shall be on the record after an opportunity for an agency hearing. Any action commenced for judicial review of such determination shall be brought within sixty days after notification of such determination.

§ 203. March-in Rights

With respect to any subject invention in which a small business firm or nonprofit organization has acquired title under this chapter, the Federal agency under whose funding agreement the subject invention was made shall have the right, in accordance with such procedures as are provided in regulations promulgated hereunder, to require the contractor, an assignee or exclusive licensee of a subject invention to grant a nonexclusive, partially exclusive, or exclusive license in any field of use to a responsible applicant or applicants, upon terms that are reasonable under the circumstances, and if the contractor, assignee, or exclusive licensee refuses such request, to grant such a license itself, if the Federal agency determines that such—

(a) action is necessary because the contractor or assignee has not taken, or is not expected to take within a reasonable time, effective steps to achieve practical application of the subject invention in such field of use;

(b) action is necessary to alleviate health or safety needs which are not reasonably satisfied by the contractor, assignee, or their licensees;

(c) action is necessary to meet requirements for public use specified by Federal regulations and such requirements are not reasonably satisfied by the contractor, assignee, or licensees; or

(d) action is necessary because the agreement required by section 204 has not been obtained or waived or because a licensee of the exclusive right to use or sell any subject invention in the United States is in breach of its agreement obtained pursuant to section 204.

(1) A determination pursuant to this section or section 202(b)(4) shall not be subject to the Contract Disputes Act (41 U.S.C. Sec. 601 et seq.). An administrative appeals procedure shall be established by regulations promulgated in accordance with section 206. Additionally, any contractor, inventor, assignee, or exclusive licensee adversely affected by a determination under this section may, at any time within sixty days after the determination is issued, file a petition in the United States Court of Federal Claims, which shall have jurisdiction to determine the appeal on the record and to affirm, reverse, remand or modify, ", (FOOTNOTE 2) as appropriate, the determination of the Federal agency. In cases described in paragraphs (a) and (c), the agency's determination shall be held in abeyance pending the exhaustion of appeals or petitions filed under the preceding sentence.

§ 204. Preference for United States industry

Notwithstanding any other provision of this chapter, no small business firm or nonprofit organization which receives title to any subject invention and no assignee of any such small business firm or nonprofit organization shall grant to any person the exclusive right to use or sell any subject invention in the United States unless such person agrees that any products embodying the subject invention or produced through the use of the subject invention will be manufactured substantially in the United States. However, in individual cases, the requirement for such an agreement may be waived by the Federal agency under whose funding agreement the invention was made upon a showing by the small business firm, nonprofit organization, or assignee that reasonable but unsuccessful efforts have been made to grant licenses on similar terms to potential licensees that would be likely to manufacture substantially in the United States or that under the circumstances domestic manufacture is not commercially feasible.

§ 205. Confidentiality

Federal agencies are authorized to withhold from disclosure to the public information disclosing any invention in which the Federal Government owns or may own a right, title, or interest (including a nonexclusive license) for a reasonable time in order for a patent application to be filed. Furthermore, Federal agencies shall not be required to release copies of any document which is part of an application for patent filed with the United States Patent and Trademark Office or with any foreign patent office.

§ 206. Uniform Clauses and Regulations

The Secretary of Commerce may issue regulations which may be made applicable to Federal agencies implementing the provisions of sections 202 through 204 of this chapter and shall establish standard funding agreement provisions required under this chapter. The regulations and the standard funding agreement shall be subject to public comment before their issuance.

§ 207. Domestic and Foreign Protection of Federally Owned Inventions

(a)   Each Federal agency is authorized to -

(1) apply for, obtain, and maintain patents or other forms of protection in the United States and in foreign countries on inventions in which the Federal Government owns a right, title, or interest;

(2) grant nonexclusive, exclusive, or partially exclusive licenses under federally owned patent applications, patents, or other

forms of protection obtained, royalty-free or for royalties or other consideration, and on such terms and conditions, including the grant to the licensee of the right of enforcement pursuant to the provisions of chapter 29 of this title as determined appropriate in the public interest;

(3) undertake all other suitable and necessary steps to protect and administer rights to federally owned inventions on behalf of the Federal Government either directly or through contract; and

(4) transfer custody and administration, in whole or in part, to another Federal agency, of the right, title, or interest in any federally owned invention.

(b)   For the purpose of assuring the effective management of Government-owned inventions, the Secretary of Commerce is authorized to -

(1) assist Federal agency efforts to promote the licensing and utilization of Government-owned inventions;

(2) assist Federal agencies in seeking protection and maintaining inventions in foreign countries, including the payment of fees and costs connected therewith; and

(3) consult with and advise Federal agencies as to areas of science and technology research and development with potential for commercial utilization.

§ 208. Regulations Governing Federal Licensing

The Secretary of Commerce is authorized to promulgate regulations specifying the terms and conditions upon which any federally owned invention, other than inventions owned by the Tennessee Valley Authority, may be licensed on a nonexclusive, partially exclusive, or exclusive basis.

§ 209. Restrictions on Licensing of Federally Owned Inventions

(a) No Federal agency shall grant any license under a patent or patent application on a federally owned invention unless the person requesting the license has supplied the agency with a plan for development and/or marketing of the invention, except that any such plan may be treated by the Federal agency as commercial and financial information obtained from a person and privileged and confidential and not subject to disclosure under section 552 of title 5 of the United States Code.

(b) A Federal agency shall normally grant the right to use or sell any federally owned invention in the United States only to a licensee that agrees that any products embodying the invention or produced through the use of the invention will be manufactured substantially in the United States.

(c)

(1) Each Federal agency may grant exclusive or partially exclusive licenses in any invention covered by a federally owned domestic patent or patent application only if, after public notice and opportunity for filing written objections, it is determined that—

(A) the interests of the Federal Government and the public will best be served by the proposed license, in view of the applicant's intentions, plans, and ability to bring the invention to practical application or otherwise promote the invention's utilization by the public;

(B) the desired practical application has not been achieved, or is not likely expeditiously to be achieved, under any nonexclusive license which has been granted, or which may be granted, on the invention;

(C) exclusive or partially exclusive licensing is a reasonable and necessary incentive to call forth the investment of risk capital and expenditures to bring the invention to practical application or otherwise promote the invention's utilization by the public; and

(D) the proposed terms and scope of exclusivity are not greater than reasonably necessary to provide the incentive for bringing the invention to practical application or otherwise promote the invention's utilization by the public.

(2) A Federal agency shall not grant such exclusive or partially exclusive license under paragraph (1) of this subsection if it determines that the grant of such license will tend substantially to lessen competition or result in undue concentration in any section of the country in any line of commerce to which the technology to be licensed relates, or to create or maintain other situations inconsistent with the antitrust laws.

(3) First preference in the exclusive or partially exclusive licensing of federally owned inventions shall go to small business firms submitting plans that are determined by the agency to be within the capabilities of the firms and equally likely, if executed, to bring the invention to practical application as any plans submitted by applicants that are not small business firms.

(d) After consideration of whether the interests of the Federal Government or United States industry in foreign commerce will be enhanced, any Federal agency may grant exclusive or partially exclusive licenses in any invention covered by a foreign patent application or patent, after public notice and opportunity for filing written objections, except that a Federal agency shall not grant such exclusive or partially exclusive license if it determines that the grant of such license will tend substantially to lessen competition or result in undue concentration in any section of the United States in any line of commerce to which the technology to be licensed relates, or to create or maintain other situations inconsistent with antitrust laws.

(e) The Federal agency shall maintain a record of determinations to grant exclusive or partially exclusive licenses.

(f) Any grant of a license shall contain such terms and conditions as the Federal agency determines appropriate for the protection of the interests of the Federal Government and the public, including provisions for the following:

(1) periodic reporting on the utilization or efforts at obtaining utilization that are being made by the licensee with particular reference to the plan submitted: Provided, That any such information may be treated by the Federal agency as commercial and financial information obtained from a person and privileged and confidential and not subject to disclosure under section 552 of title 5 of the United States Code;

(2) the right of the Federal agency to terminate such license in whole or in part if it determines that the licensee is not executing the plan submitted with its request for a license and the licensee cannot otherwise demonstrate to the satisfaction of the Federal agency that it has taken or can be expected to take within a reasonable time, effective steps to achieve practical application of the invention;

(3) the right of the Federal agency to terminate such license in whole or in part if the licensee is in breach of an agreement obtained pursuant to paragraph (b) of this section; and

(4) the right of the Federal agency to terminate the license in whole or in part if the agency determines that such action is necessary to meet requirements for public use specified by Federal regulations issued after the date of the license and such requirements are not reasonably satisfied by the licensee.

§ 210. Precedence of Chapter

(a) This chapter shall take precedence over any other Act which would require a disposition of rights in subject inventions of small business firms or nonprofit organizations contractors in a manner that is inconsistent with this chapter, including but not necessarily limited to the following:

(1) section 10(a) of the Act of June 29, 1935, as added by title I of the Act of August 14, 1946 (7 U.S.C. 427i(a); 60 Stat. 1085);

(2) section 205(a) of the Act of August 14, 1946 (7 U.S.C. 1624(a); 60 Stat. 1090);

(3) section 501(c) of the Federal Mine Safety and Health Act of 1977 (30 U.S.C. 951(c); 83 Stat. 742);

(4) section 30168(e) of title 49;

(5) section 12 of the National Science Foundation Act of 1950 (42 U.S.C. 1871(a); 82 Stat. 360); (FOOTNOTE 1) See References in Text note below.

(6) section 152 of the Atomic Energy Act of 1954 (42 U.S.C.2182; 68 Stat. 943);

(7) section 305 of the National Aeronautics and Space Act of 1958 (42 U.S.C.2457);

(8) section 6 of the Coal Research Development Act of 1960 (30 U.S.C.666; 74 Stat. 337);

(9) section 4 of the Helium Act Amendments of 1960 (50 U.S.C.167b; 74 Stat. 920);

(10) section 32 of the Arms Control and Disarmament Act of 1961 (22 U.S.C.2572; 75 Stat. 634);

(11) section 9 of the Federal Nonnuclear Energy Research and Development Act of 1974 (42 U.S.C.5901; 88 Stat. 1878);

(12) section 5(d) of the Consumer Product Safety Act (15 U.S.C. 2054(d); 86 Stat. 1211);

(13) section 3 of the Act of April 5, 1944 (30 U.S.C.323; 58 Stat. 191);

(14) section 8001(c)(3) of the Solid Waste Disposal Act (42 U.S.C. 6981(c); 90 Stat. 2829);

(15) section 219 of the Foreign Assistance Act of 1961 (22 U.S.C.2179; 83 Stat. 806);

(16) section 427(b) of the Federal Mine Health and Safety Act of 1977 (30 U.S.C. 937(b); 86 Stat. 155);

(17) section 306(d) of the Surface Mining and Reclamation Act of 1977 (30 U.S.C. 1226(d); 91 Stat. 455);

(18) section 21(d) of the Federal Fire Prevention and Control Act of 1974 (15 U.S.C. 2218(d); 88 Stat. 1548);

(19) section 6(b) of the Solar Photovoltaic Energy Research Development and Demonstration Act of 1978 (42 U.S.C. 5585(b); 92 Stat. 2516);

(20) section 12 of the Native Latex Commercialization and Economic Development Act of 1978 (7 U.S.C. 178(j); 92 Stat. 2533); and

(21) section 408 of the Water Resources and Development Act of 1978 (42 U.S.C.7879; 92 Stat. 1360).

The Act creating this chapter shall be construed to take precedence over any future Act unless that Act specifically cites this Act and provides that it shall take precedence over this Act.

(b) Nothing in this chapter is intended to alter the effect of the laws cited in paragraph (a) of this section or any other laws with respect to the disposition of rights in inventions made in the performance of funding agreements with persons other than nonprofit organizations or small business firms.

(c) Nothing in this chapter is intended to limit the authority of agencies to agree to the disposition of rights in inventions made in the performance of work under funding agreements with persons other than nonprofit organizations or small business firms in accordance with the Statement of Government Patent Policy issued on February 18, 1983, agency regulations, or other applicable regulations or to otherwise limit the authority of agencies to allow such persons to retain ownership of inventions except that all funding agreements, including those with other than small business firms and nonprofit organizations, shall include the requirements established in paragraph 202(c)(4) and section 203 of this title.. Any disposition of rights in inventions made in accordance with the Statement or implementing regulations, including any disposition occurring before enactment of this section, are hereby authorized. So in original.

(d) Nothing in this chapter shall be construed to require the disclosure of intelligence sources or methods or to otherwise affect the authority granted to the Director of Central Intelligence by statute or Executive order for the protection of intelligence sources or methods.

(e) The provisions of the Stevenson-Wydler Technology Innovation Act of 1980 shall take precedence over the provisions of this chapter to the extent that they permit or require a disposition of rights in subject inventions which is inconsistent with this chapter.

§ 211. Relationship to Antitrust Laws

Nothing in this chapter shall be deemed to convey to any person immunity from civil or criminal liability, or to create any defenses to actions, under any antitrust law.

TITLE 17—COPYRIGHTS

Sec.

117. Limitations on exclusive rights: Computer programs.

§ 117. Limitations on Exclusive Rights: Computer Programs

(a) Making of Additional Copy or Adaptation by Owner of Copy. -

Notwithstanding the provisions of section 106, it is not an infringement for the owner of a copy of a computer program to make or authorize the making of another copy or adaptation of that computer program provided:

> (1) that such a new copy or adaptation is created as an essential step in the utilization of the computer program in conjunction with a machine and that it is used in no other manner, or
>
> (2) that such new copy or adaptation is for archival purposes only and that all archival copies are destroyed in the event that continued possession of the computer program should cease to be rightful.

(b) Lease, Sale, or Other Transfer of Additional Copy or Adaptation. -

Any exact copies prepared in accordance with the provisions of this section may be leased, sold, or otherwise transferred, along with the copy from which such copies were prepared, only as part of the lease, sale, or other transfer of all rights in the program. Adaptations so prepared may be transferred only with the authorization of the copyright owner.

(c) Machine Maintenance or Repair. -

Notwithstanding the provisions of section 106, it is not an infringement for the owner or lessee of a machine to make or authorize the making of a copy of a computer program if such copy is made solely by virtue of the activation of a machine that lawfully contains an authorized copy of the computer program, for purposes only of maintenance or repair of that machine, if—

> (1) such new copy is used in no other manner and is destroyed immediately after the maintenance or repair is completed; and
>
> (2) with respect to any computer program or part thereof that is not necessary for that machine to be activated, such program or part thereof is not accessed or used other than to make such new copy by virtue of the activation of the machine.

(d) Definitions. -

For purposes of this section -

(1) the "maintenance" of a machine is the servicing of the machine in order to make it work in accordance with its original specifications and any changes to those specifications authorized for that machine; and

(2) the "repair" of a machine is the restoring of the machine to the state of working in accordance with its original specifications and any changes to those specifications authorized for that machine.

Appendix III

STEVENSON-WYDLER TECHNOLOGY INNOVATION ACT OF 1980

- United States Code
  - TITLE 15—COMMERCE AND TRADE
    - CHAPTER 63—TECHNOLOGY INNOVATION

CHAPTER 63—TECHNOLOGY INNOVATION

- § 3701. Findings.
- § 3702. Purpose.
- § 3703. Definitions.
- § 3704. Commerce and technological innovation.

  - (a) Establishment.
  - (b) Under Secretary and Assistant Secretary.
  - (c) Duties.
  - (d) Japanese technical literature.
  - (e) Omitted.
  - (f) Experimental Program to Stimulate Competitive Technology.

- § 3704a. Clearinghouse for State and Local Initiatives on Productivity, Technology, and Innovation.

  - (a) Establishment.
  - (b) Responsibilities.

- (c) Terms.
- (d) Chairman and Vice Chairman.
- (e) Executive Director and employees.
- (f) Funding.
- (g) Contributions.
- (h) Annual report.

Sec. 3701. Findings

The Congress finds and declares that:

- (1) Technology and industrial innovation are central to the economic, environmental, and social well-being of citizens of the United States.
- (2) Technology and industrial innovation offer an improved standard of living, increased public and private sector productivity, creation of new industries and employment opportunities, improved public services, and enhanced competitiveness of United States products in world markets.
- (3) Many new discoveries and advances in science occur in universities and Federal laboratories, while the application of this new knowledge to commercial and useful public purposes depends largely upon actions by business and labor. Cooperation among academia, Federal laboratories, labor, and industry, in such forms as technology transfer, personnel exchange, joint research projects, and others, should be renewed, expanded, and strengthened.
- (4) Small businesses have performed an important role in advancing industrial and technological innovation.
- (5) Industrial and technological innovation in the United States may be lagging when compared to historical patterns and other industrialized nations.
- (6) Increased industrial and technological innovation would reduce trade deficits, stabilize the dollar, increase productivity gains, increase employment, and stabilize prices.
- (7) Government antitrust, economic, trade, patent, procurement, regulatory, research and development, and tax policies have significant impacts upon industrial innovation and development of technology, but there is insufficient knowledge of their effects in particular sectors of the economy.
- (8) No comprehensive national policy exists to enhance technological innovation for commercial and public purposes. There is a need for such a policy, including a strong national policy supporting domestic technology transfer and utilization of the science and technology resources of the Federal Government.
- (9) It is in the national interest to promote the adaptation of technological innovations to State and local government uses. Technological innovations

can improve services, reduce their costs, and increase productivity in State and local governments.

- (10) The Federal laboratories and other performers of federally funded research and development frequently provide scientific and technological developments of potential use to State and local governments and private industry. These developments, which include inventions, computer software, and training technologies, should be made accessible to those governments and industry. There is a need to provide means of access and to give adequate personnel and funding support to these means.
- (11) The Nation should give fuller recognition to individuals and companies which have made outstanding contributions to the promotion of technology or technological manpower for the improvement of the economic, environmental, or social well-being of the United States.

Sec. 3702. Purpose

It is the purpose of this chapter to improve the economic, environmental, and social well-being of the United States by—

- (1) establishing organizations in the executive branch to study and stimulate technology;
- (2) promoting technology development through the establishment of cooperative research centers;
- (3) stimulating improved utilization of federally funded technology developments, including inventions, software, and training technologies, by State and local governments and the private sector;
- (4) providing encouragement for the development of technology through the recognition of individuals and companies which have made outstanding contributions in technology; and
- (5) encouraging the exchange of scientific and technical personnel among academia, industry, and Federal laboratories.

Sec. 3703. Definitions

As used in this chapter, unless the context otherwise requires, the term—

- (1) "Office" means the Office of Technology Policy established under section 3704 of this title.
- (2) "Secretary" means the Secretary of Commerce.
- (3) "Under Secretary" means the Under Secretary of Commerce for Technology appointed under section 3704(b)(1) of this title.

- (4) "Centers" means the Cooperative Research Centers established under section 3705 [1] or section 3707

- (5) "Nonprofit institution" means an organization owned and operated exclusively for scientific or educational purposes, no part of the net earnings of which inures to the benefit of any private shareholder or individual.

- (6) "Federal laboratory" means any laboratory, any federally funded research and development center, or any center established under section 3705 [1] or section 3707 [1] of this title that is owned, leased, or otherwise used by a Federal agency and funded by the Federal Government, whether operated by the Government or by a contractor.

- (7) "Supporting agency" means either the Department of Commerce or the National Science Foundation, as appropriate.

- (8) "Federal agency" means any executive agency as defined in section 105 of title 5 and the military departments as defined in section 102 of such title, as well as any agency of the legislative branch of the Federal Government.

- (9) "Invention" means any invention or discovery which is or may be patentable or otherwise protected under title 35 or any novel variety of plant which is or may be protectable under the Plant Variety Protection Act (7 U.S.C. 2321 et seq.).

- (10) "Made" when used in conjunction with any invention means the conception or first actual reduction to practice of such invention.

- (11) "Small business firm" means a small business concern as defined in section 632 of this title and implementing regulations of the Administrator of the Small Business Administration.

- (12) "Training technology" means computer software and related materials which are developed by a Federal agency to train employees of such agency, including but not limited to software for computer-based instructional systems and for interactive video disc systems.

- (13) "Clearinghouse" means the Clearinghouse for State and Local Initiatives on Productivity, Technology, and Innovation established by section 3704a of this title.

Sec. 3704. Commerce and Technological Innovation

- (a) Establishment

There is established in the Department of Commerce a Technology Administration, which shall operate in accordance with the provisions, findings, and purposes of this chapter. The Technology Administration shall include—

  - (1) the National Institute of Standards and Technology;

- (2) the National Technical Information Service; and
- (3) a policy analysis office, which shall be known as the Office of Technology Policy.

- (b) Under Secretary and Assistant Secretary

  The President shall appoint, by and with the advice and consent of the Senate, to the extent provided for in appropriations Acts—

  - (1) an Under Secretary of Commerce for Technology, who shall be compensated at the rate provided for level III of the Executive Schedule in section 5314 of title 5; and
  - (2) an Assistant Secretary of Commerce for Technology Policy, who shall serve as policy analyst for the Under Secretary.

- (c) Duties

  The Secretary, through the Under Secretary, as appropriate, shall—

  - (1) manage the Technology Administration and supervise its agencies, programs, and activities;
  - (2) conduct technology policy analyses to improve United States industrial productivity, technology, and innovation, and cooperate with United States industry in the improvement of its productivity, technology, and ability to compete successfully in world markets;
  - (3) carry out any functions formerly assigned to the Office of Productivity, Technology, and Innovation;
  - (4) assist in the implementation of the Metric Conversion Act of 1975 (15 U.S.C. 205a et seq.);
  - (5) determine the relationships of technological developments and international technology transfers to the output, employment, productivity, and world trade performance of United States and foreign industrial sectors;
  - (6) determine the influence of economic, labor and other conditions, industrial structure and management, and government policies on technological developments in particular industrial sectors worldwide;
  - (7) identify technological needs, problems, and opportunities within and across industrial sectors that, if addressed, could make a significant contribution to the economy of the United States;
  - (8) assess whether the capital, technical and other resources being allocated to domestic industrial sectors which are likely to generate new technologies are adequate to meet private and social demands for goods and services and to promote productivity and economic growth;
  - (9) propose and support studies and policy experiments, in cooperation with other Federal agencies, to determine the effectiveness of

measures with the potential of advancing United States technological innovation;

- (10) provide that cooperative efforts to stimulate industrial innovation be undertaken between the Under Secretary and other officials in the Department of Commerce responsible for such areas as trade and economic assistance;

- (11) encourage and assist the creation of centers and other joint initiatives by State of [1] local governments, regional organizations, private businesses, institutions of higher education, nonprofit organizations, or Federal laboratories to encourage technology transfer, to stimulate innovation, and to promote an appropriate climate for investment in technology-related industries;

- (12) propose and encourage cooperative research involving appropriate Federal entities, State or local governments, regional organizations, colleges or universities, nonprofit organizations, or private industry to promote the common use of resources, to improve training programs and curricula, to stimulate interest in high technology careers, and to encourage the effective dissemination of technology skills within the wider community;

- (13) serve as a focal point for discussions among United States companies on topics of interest to industry and labor, including discussions regarding manufacturing and discussions regarding emerging technologies;

- (14) consider government measures with the potential of advancing United States technological innovation and exploiting innovations of foreign origin; and

- (15) publish the results of studies and policy experiments.

- (d) Japanese technical literature

  - (1) In addition to the duties specified in subsection (c) of this section, the Secretary and the Under Secretary shall establish, and through the National Technical Information Service and with the cooperation of such other offices within the Department of Commerce as the Secretary considers appropriate, maintain a program (including an office in Japan) which shall, on a continuing basis—

    - (A) monitor Japanese technical activities and developments;

    - (B) consult with businesses, professional societies, and libraries in the United States regarding their needs for information on Japanese developments in technology and engineering;

    - (C) acquire and translate selected Japanese technical reports and documents that may be of value to agencies and departments of the

Federal Government, and to businesses and researchers in the United States; and

- (D) coordinate with other agencies and departments of the Federal Government to identify significant gaps and avoid duplication in efforts by the Federal Government to acquire, translate, index, and disseminate Japanese technical information. Activities undertaken pursuant to subparagraph (C) of this paragraph shall only be performed on a cost-reimbursable basis. Translations referred to in such subparagraph shall be performed only to the extent that they are not otherwise available from sources within the private sector in the United States.

- (2) Beginning in 1986, the Secretary shall prepare annual reports regarding important Japanese scientific discoveries and technical innovations in such areas as computers, semiconductors, biotechnology, and robotics and manufacturing. In preparing such reports, the Secretary shall consult with professional societies and businesses in the United States. The Secretary may, to the extent provided in advance by appropriation Acts, contract with private organizations to acquire and translate Japanese scientific and technical information relevant to the preparation of such reports.

- (3) The Secretary also shall encourage professional societies and private businesses in the United States to increase their efforts to acquire, screen, translate, and disseminate Japanese technical literature.

- (4) In addition, the Secretary shall compile, publish, and disseminate an annual directory which lists—

  - (A) all programs and services in the United States that collect, abstract, translate, and distribute Japanese scientific and technical information; and

  - (B) all translations of Japanese technical documents performed by agencies and departments of the Federal Government in the preceding 12 months that are available to the public.

- (5) The Secretary shall transmit to the Congress, within 1 year after August 14, 1986, a report on the activities of the Federal Government to collect, abstract, translate, and distribute declassified Japanese scientific and technical information.

- (e) Omitted

- (f) Experimental Program to Stimulate Competitive Technology

  - (1) In general

The Secretary, acting through the Under Secretary, shall establish for fiscal year 1999 a program to be known as the Experimental Program to

Stimulate Competitive Technology (referred to in this subsection as the "program"). The purpose of the program shall be to strengthen the technological competitiveness of those States that have historically received less Federal research and development funds than those received by a majority of the States.

- (2) Arrangements

  In carrying out the program, the Secretary, acting through the Under Secretary, shall—

  - (A) enter into such arrangements as may be necessary to provide for the coordination of the program through the State committees established under the Experimental Program to Stimulate Competitive Research of the National Science Foundation; and
  - (B) cooperate with—
    - (i) any State science and technology council established under the program under subparagraph (A); and
    - (ii) representatives of small business firms and other appropriate technology-based businesses.

- (3) Grants and cooperative agreements

  In carrying out the program, the Secretary, acting through the Under Secretary, may make grants or enter into cooperative agreements to provide for—

  - (A) technology research and development;
  - (B) technology transfer from university research;
  - (C) technology deployment and diffusion; and
  - (D) the strengthening of technological capabilities through consortia comprised of—
    - (i) technology-based small business firms;
    - (ii) industries and emerging companies;
    - (iii) universities; and
    - (iv) State and local development agencies and entities.

- (4) Requirements for making awards
  - (A) In general

  In making awards under this subsection, the Secretary, acting through the Under Secretary, shall ensure that the awards are awarded on a competitive basis that includes a review of the merits of the activities that are the subject of the award.

  - (B) Matching requirement

The non-Federal share of the activities (other than planning activities) carried out under an award under this subsection shall be not less than 25 percent of the cost of those activities.

- (5) Criteria for States

The Secretary, acting through the Under Secretary, shall establish criteria for achievement by each State that participates in the program. Upon the achievement of all such criteria, a State shall cease to be eligible to participate in the program.

- (6) Coordination

To the extent practicable, in carrying out this subsection, the Secretary, acting through the Under Secretary, shall coordinate the program with other programs of the Department of Commerce.

- (7) Report
  - (A) In general

Not later than 90 days after October 30, 1998, the Under Secretary shall prepare and submit a report that meets the requirements of this paragraph to the Secretary. Upon receipt of the report, the Secretary shall transmit a copy of the report to the Committee on Commerce, Science, and Transportation of the Senate and the Committee on Science of the House of Representatives.

  - (B) Requirements for report

The report prepared under this paragraph shall contain with respect to the program—

- (i) a description of the structure and procedures of the program;
- (ii) a management plan for the program;
- (iii) a description of the merit-based review process to be used in the program;
- (iv) milestones for the evaluation of activities to be assisted under the program in fiscal year 1999;
- (v) an assessment of the eligibility of each State that participates in the Experimental Program to Stimulate Competitive Research of the National Science Foundation to participate in the program under this subsection; and
- (vi) the evaluation criteria with respect to which the overall management and effectiveness of the program will be evaluated.

Footnote

[1] So in original. Probably should be "or."

Sec. 3704a. Clearinghouse for State and Local Initiatives on Productivity, Technology, and Innovation

- (a) Establishment

  There is established within the Office of Productivity, Technology, and Innovation a Clearinghouse for State and Local Initiatives on Productivity, Technology, and Innovation. The Clearinghouse shall serve as a central repository of information on initiatives by State and local governments to enhance the competitiveness of American business through the stimulation of productivity, technology, and innovation and Federal efforts to assist State and local governments to enhance competitiveness.

- (b) Responsibilities

  The Clearinghouse may—

  - (1) establish relationships with State and local governments, and regional and multistate organizations of such governments, which carry out such initiatives;

  - (2) collect information on the nature, extent, and effects of such initiatives, particularly information useful to the Congress, Federal agencies, State and local governments, regional and multistate organizations of such governments, businesses, and the public throughout the United States;

  - (3) disseminate information collected under paragraph (2) through reports, directories, handbooks, conferences, and seminars;

  - (4) provide technical assistance and advice to such governments with respect to such initiatives, including assistance in determining sources of assistance from Federal agencies which may be available to support such initiatives;

  - (5) study ways in which Federal agencies, including Federal laboratories, are able to use their existing policies and programs to assist State and local governments, and regional and multistate organizations of such governments, to enhance the competitiveness of American business;

  - (6) make periodic recommendations to the Secretary, and to other Federal agencies upon their request, concerning modifications in Federal policies and programs which would improve Federal assistance to State and local technology and business assistance programs;

  - (7) develop methodologies to evaluate State and local programs, and, when requested, advise State and local governments, and regional and multistate organizations of such governments, as to which programs are most effective in enhancing the competitiveness of American business through the stimulation of productivity, technology, and innovation; and

- (8) make use of, and disseminate, the nationwide study of State industrial extension programs conducted by the Secretary.

- (c) Contracts

In carrying out subsection (b) of this section, the Secretary may enter into contracts for the purpose of collecting information on the nature, extent, and effects of initiatives.

- (d) Triennial report

The Secretary shall prepare and transmit to the Congress once each 3 years a report on initiatives by State and local governments to enhance the competitiveness of American businesses through the stimulation of productivity, technology, and innovation. The report shall include recommendations to the President, the Congress, and to Federal agencies on the appropriate Federal role in stimulating State and local efforts in this area. The first of these reports shall be transmitted to the Congress before January 1, 1989.

Sec. 3704b. National Technical Information Service

- (a) Powers
  - (1) The Secretary of Commerce, acting through the Director of the National Technical Information Service (hereafter in this section referred to as the "Director") is authorized to do the following:
    - (A) Enter into such contracts, cooperative agreements, joint ventures, and other transactions, in accordance with all relevant provisions of Federal law applicable to such contracts and agreements, and under reasonable terms and conditions, as may be necessary in the conduct of the business of the National Technical Information Service (hereafter in this section referred to as the "Service").
    - (B) In addition to the authority regarding fees contained in section 2 of the Act entitled "An Act to provide for the dissemination of technological, scientific, and engineering information to American business and industry, and for other purposes" enacted September 9, 1950 (15 U.S.C. 1152), retain and, subject to appropriations Acts, utilize its net revenues to the extent necessary to implement the plan submitted under subsection (f)(3)(D) of this section.
    - (C) Enter into contracts for the performance of part or all of the functions performed by the Promotion Division of the Service prior to October 24, 1988. The details of any such contract, and a statement of its effect on the operations and personnel of the Service, shall be

provided to the appropriate committees of the Congress 30 days in advance of the execution of such contract.

- (D) Employ such personnel as may be necessary to conduct the business of the Service.

- (E) For the period of October 1, 1991, through September 30, 1992, only, retain and use all earned and unearned monies heretofore or hereafter received, including receipts, revenues, and advanced payments and deposits, to fund all obligations and expenses, including inventories and capital equipment. An increase or decrease in the personnel of the Service shall not affect or be affected by any ceilings on the number or grade of personnel.

- (2) The functions and activities of the Service specified in subsection (e)(1) through (6) of this section are permanent Federal functions to be carried out by the Secretary through the Service and its employees, and shall not be transferred from the Service, by contract or otherwise, to the private sector on a permanent or temporary basis without express approval of the Congress. Functions or activities—

  - (A) for the procurement of supplies, materials, and equipment by the Service;

  - (B) referred to in paragraph (1)(C); or

  - (C) to be performed through joint ventures or cooperative agreements which do not result in a reduction in the Federal workforce of the affected programs of the service, [1]

- (3) For the purposes of this subsection, the term "net revenues" means the excess of revenues and receipts from any source, other than royalties and other income described in section 3710c(a)(4) [2] of this title, over operating expenses.

- (4) Omitted.

- (b) Director of the Service

The management of the Service shall be vested in a Director who shall report to the Under Secretary of Commerce for Technology and the Secretary of Commerce.

- (c) Advisory Board

  - (1) There is established the Advisory Board of the National Technical Information Service, which shall be composed of a chairman and four other members appointed by the Secretary.

  - (2) In appointing members of the Advisory Board the Secretary shall solicit recommendations from the major users and beneficiaries of the Service's activities and shall select individuals experienced in providing or utilizing technical information.

- (3) The Advisory Board shall review the general policies and operations of the Service, including policies in connection with fees and charges for its services, and shall advise the Secretary and the Director with respect thereto.
- (4) The Advisory Board shall meet at the call of the Secretary, but not less often than once each six months.

- (d) Audits

The Secretary of Commerce shall provide for annual independent audits of the Service's financial statements beginning with fiscal year 1988, to be conducted in accordance with generally accepted accounting principles.

- (e) Functions

The Secretary of Commerce, acting through the Service, shall—

  - (1) establish and maintain a permanent repository of nonclassified scientific, technical, and engineering information;
  - (2) cooperate and coordinate its operations with other Government scientific, technical, and engineering information programs;
  - (3) make selected bibliographic information products available in a timely manner to depository libraries as part of the Depository Library Program of the Government Printing Office;
  - (4) in conjunction with the private sector as appropriate, collect, translate into English, and disseminate unclassified foreign scientific, technical, and engineering information;
  - (5) implement new methods or media for the dissemination of scientific, technical, and engineering information, including producing and disseminating information products in electronic format; and
  - (6) carry out the functions and activities of the Secretary under the Act entitled "An Act to provide for the dissemination of technological, scientific, and engineering information to American business and industry, and for other purposes" enacted September 9, 1950 (15 U.S.C. 1151 et seq.), and the functions and activities of the Secretary performed through the National Technical Information Service as of October 24, 1988, under this chapter.

- (f) Notification of Congress
  - (1) The Secretary of Commerce and the Director shall keep the appropriate committees of Congress fully and currently informed about all activities related to the carrying out of the functions of the Service, including changes in fee policies.
  - (2) Within 90 days after October 24, 1988, the Secretary of Commerce shall submit to the Congress a report on the current fee structure of the Service, including an explanation of the basis for the fees, taking into

consideration all applicable costs, and the adequacy of the fees, along with reasons for the declining sales at the Service of scientific, technical, and engineering publications. Such report shall explain any actions planned or taken to increase such sales at reasonable fees.

- (3) The Secretary shall submit an annual report to the Congress which shall—
  - (A) summarize the operations of the Service during the preceding year, including financial details and staff levels broken down by major activities;
  - (B) detail the operating plan of the Service, including specific expense and staff needs, for the upcoming year;
  - (C) set forth details of modernization progress made in the preceding year;
  - (D) describe the long-term modernization plans of the Service; and
  - (E) include the results of the most recent annual audit carried out under subsection (d) of this section.
- (4) The Secretary shall also give the Congress detailed advance notice of not less than 30 calendar days of—
  - (A) any proposed reduction-in-force;
  - (B) any joint venture or cooperative agreement which involves a financial incentive to the joint venturer or contractor; and
  - (C) any change in the operating plan submitted under paragraph (3)(B) which would result in a variation from such plan with respect to expense levels of more than 10 percent.

Footnotes

[1] So in original. Probably should be capitalized. Shall not be considered functions or activities for purposes of this paragraph.

[2] See References in Text note below.

Sec. 3704b-1. Recovery of Operating Costs through Fee Collections

Operating costs for the National Technical Information Service associated with the acquisition, processing, storage, bibliographic control, and archiving of information and documents shall be recovered primarily through the collection of fees.

Sec. 3704b-2. Transfer of Federal Scientific and Technical Information

- (a) Transfer

    The head of each Federal executive department or agency shall transfer in a timely manner to the National Technical Information Service unclassified scientific, technical, and engineering information which results from federally funded research and development activities for dissemination to the private sector, academia, State and local governments, and Federal agencies. Only information which would otherwise be available for public dissemination shall be transferred under this subsection. Such information shall include technical reports and information, computer software, application assessments generated pursuant to section 3710(c) of this title, and information regarding training technology and other federally owned or originated technologies. The Secretary shall issue regulations within one year after February 14, 1992, outlining procedures for the ongoing transfer of such information to the National Technical Information Service.

- (b) Annual report to Congress

    As part of the annual report required under section 3704b(f)(3) of this title, the Secretary shall report to Congress on the status of efforts under this section to ensure access to Federal scientific and technical information by the public. Such report shall include—

    - (1) an evaluation of the comprehensiveness of transfers of information by each Federal executive department or agency under subsection (a) of this section;

    - (2) a description of the use of Federal scientific and technical information;

    - (3) plans for improving public access to Federal scientific and technical information; and

    - (4) recommendations for legislation necessary to improve public access to Federal scientific and technical information.

Sec. 3705. Cooperative Research Centers

- (a) Establishment

    The Secretary shall provide assistance for the establishment of Cooperative Research Centers. Such Centers shall be affiliated with any university, or other nonprofit institution, or group thereof, that applies for and is awarded a grant or enters into a cooperative agreement under this section. The objective of the Centers is to enhance technological innovation through—

- (1) the participation of individuals from industry and universities in cooperative technological innovation activities;
- (2) the development of the generic research base, important for technological advance and innovative activity, in which individual firms have little incentive to invest, but which may have significant economic or strategic importance, such as manufacturing technology;
- (3) the education and training of individuals in the technological innovation process;
- (4) the improvement of mechanisms for the dissemination of scientific, engineering, and technical information among universities and industry;
- (5) the utilization of the capability and expertise, where appropriate, that exists in Federal laboratories; and
- (6) the development of continuing financial support from other mission agencies, from State and local government, and from industry and universities through, among other means, fees, licenses, and royalties.
- (b) Activities

The activities of the Centers shall include, but need not be limited to—

- (1) research supportive of technological and industrial innovation including cooperative industry-university research;
- (2) assistance to individuals and small businesses in the generation, evaluation, and development of technological ideas supportive of industrial innovation and new business ventures;
- (3) technical assistance and advisory services to industry, particularly small businesses; and
- (4) curriculum development, training, and instruction in invention, entrepreneurship, and industrial innovation. Each Center need not undertake all of the activities under this subsection.
- (c) Requirements

Prior to establishing a Center, the Secretary shall find that—

- (1) consideration has been given to the potential contribution of the activities proposed under the Center to productivity, employment, and economic competitiveness of the United States;
- (2) a high likelihood exists of continuing participation, advice, financial support, and other contributions from the private sector;
- (3) the host university or other nonprofit institution has a plan for the management and evaluation of the activities proposed within the particular Center, including:
    - (A) the agreement between the parties as to the allocation of patent rights on a nonexclusive, partially exclusive, or exclusive license

basis to and inventions conceived or made under the auspices of the Center; and

- • (B) the consideration of means to place the Center, to the maximum extent feasible, on a self-sustaining basis;
- • (4) suitable consideration has been given to the university's or other nonprofit institution's capabilities and geographical location; and
- • (5) consideration has been given to any effects upon competition of the activities proposed under the Center.
- • (d) Planning grants

The Secretary is authorized to make available nonrenewable planning grants to universities or nonprofit institutions for the purpose of developing a plan required under subsection (c)(3) of this section.

- • (e) Research and development utilization

In the promotion of technology from research and development efforts by Centers under this section, chapter 18 of title 35 shall apply to the extent not inconsistent with this section.

Sec. 3706. Grants and Cooperative Agreements

- • (a) In general

The Secretary may make grants and enter into cooperative agreements according to the provisions of this section in order to assist any activity consistent with this chapter, including activities performed by individuals. The total amount of any such grant or cooperative agreement may not exceed 75 percent of the total cost of the program.

- • (b) Eligibility and procedure

Any person or institution may apply to the Secretary for a grant or cooperative agreement available under this section. Application shall be made in such form and manner, and with such content and other submissions, as the Assistant Secretary shall prescribe. The Secretary shall act upon each such application within 90 days after the date on which all required information is received.

- • (c) Terms and conditions
  - • (1) Any grant made, or cooperative agreement entered into, under this section shall be subject to the limitations and provisions set forth in paragraph (2) of this subsection, and to such other terms, conditions, and requirements as the Secretary deems necessary or appropriate.
  - • (2) Any person who receives or utilizes any proceeds of any grant made or cooperative agreement entered into under this section shall keep such records as the Secretary shall by regulation prescribe as being

necessary and appropriate to facilitate effective audit and evaluation, including records which fully disclose the amount and disposition by such recipient of such proceeds, the total cost of the program or project in connection with which such proceeds were used, and the amount, if any, of such costs which was provided through other sources.

Sec. 3707. National Science Foundation Cooperative Research Centers

* (a) Establishment and provisions

The National Science Foundation shall provide assistance for the establishment of Cooperative Research Centers. Such Centers shall be affiliated with a university, or other nonprofit institution, or a group thereof. The objective of the Centers is to enhance technological innovation as provided in section 3705(a) of this title through the conduct of activities as provided in section 3705(b) of this title.

* (b) Planning grants

The National Science Foundation is authorized to make available nonrenewable planning grants to universities or nonprofit institutions for the purpose of developing the plan, as described under section 3705(c)(3) of this title.

* (c) Terms and conditions

Grants, contracts, and cooperative agreements entered into by the National Science Foundation in execution of the powers and duties of the National Science Foundation under this chapter shall be governed by the National Science Foundation Act of 1950 (42 U.S.C. 1861 et seq.) and other pertinent Acts.

Sec. 3708. Administrative Arrangements

* (a) Coordination

The Secretary and the National Science Foundation shall, on a continuing basis, obtain the advice and cooperation of departments and agencies whose missions contribute to or are affected by the programs established under this chapter, including the development of an agenda for research and policy experimentation. These departments and agencies shall include but not be limited to the Departments of Defense, Energy, Education, Health and Human Services, Housing and Urban Development, the Environmental Protection Agency, National Aeronautics and Space Administration, Small Business Administration, Council of Economic

Advisers, Council on Environmental Quality, and Office of Science and Technology Policy.

- (b) Cooperation

  It is the sense of the Congress that departments and agencies, including the Federal laboratories, whose missions are affected by, or could contribute to, the programs established under this chapter, should, within the limits of budgetary authorizations and appropriations, support or participate in activities or projects authorized by this chapter.

- (c) Administrative authorization

  - (1) Departments and agencies described in subsection (b) of this section are authorized to participate in, contribute to, and serve as resources for the Centers and for any other activities authorized under this chapter.

  - (2) The Secretary and the National Science Foundation are authorized to receive moneys and to receive other forms of assistance from other departments or agencies to support activities of the Centers and any other activities authorized under this chapter.

- (d) Cooperative efforts

  The Secretary and the National Science Foundation shall, on a continuing basis, provide each other the opportunity to comment on any proposed program of activity under section 3705, 3707, 3710, 3710d, 3711a, or 3712 of this title before funds are committed to such program in order to mount complementary efforts and avoid duplication.

Sec. 3710. Utilization of Federal Technology

- (a) Policy

  - (1) It is the continuing responsibility of the Federal Government to ensure the full use of the results of the Nation's Federal investment in research and development. To this end the Federal Government shall strive where appropriate to transfer federally owned or originated technology to State and local governments and to the private sector.

  - (2) Technology transfer, consistent with mission responsibilities, is a responsibility of each laboratory science and engineering professional.

  - (3) Each laboratory director shall ensure that efforts to transfer technology are considered positively in laboratory job descriptions, employee promotion policies, and evaluation of the job performance of scientists and engineers in the laboratory.

- (b) Establishment of Research and Technology Applications Offices

Each Federal laboratory shall establish an Office of Research and Technology Applications. Laboratories having existing organizational structures which perform the functions of this section may elect to combine the Office of Research and Technology Applications within the existing organization. The staffing and funding levels for these offices shall be determined between each Federal laboratory and the Federal agency operating or directing the laboratory, except that (1) each laboratory having 200 or more full-time equivalent scientific, engineering, and related technical positions shall provide one or more full-time equivalent positions as staff for its Office of Research and Technology Applications, and (2) each Federal agency which operates or directs one or more Federal laboratories shall make available sufficient funding, either as a separate line item or from the agency's research and development budget, to support the technology transfer function at the agency and at its laboratories, including support of the Offices of Research and Technology Applications. Furthermore, individuals filling positions in an Office of Research and Technology Applications shall be included in the overall laboratory/agency management development program so as to ensure that highly competent technical managers are full participants in the technology transfer process. The agency head shall submit to Congress at the time the President submits the budget to Congress an explanation of the agency's technology transfer program for the preceding year and the agency's plans for conducting its technology transfer function for the upcoming year, including plans for securing intellectual property rights in laboratory innovations with commercial promise and plans for managing such innovations so as to benefit the competitiveness of United States industry.

- (c) Functions of Research and Technology Applications Offices

It shall be the function of each Office of Research and Technology Applications—

- (1) to prepare application assessments for selected research and development projects in which that laboratory is engaged and which in the opinion of the laboratory may have potential commercial applications;

- (2) to provide and disseminate information on federally owned or originated products, processes, and services having potential application to State and local governments and to private industry;

- (3) to cooperate with and assist the National Technical Information Service, the Federal Laboratory Consortium for Technology Transfer, and other organizations which link the research and development resources of that laboratory and the Federal Government as a whole to potential users in State and local government and private industry;

- (4) to provide technical assistance to State and local government officials; and

- (5) to participate, where feasible, in regional, State, and local programs designed to facilitate or stimulate the transfer of technology for the benefit of the region, State, or local jurisdiction in which the Federal laboratory is located. Agencies which have established organizational structures outside their Federal laboratories which have as their principal purpose the transfer of federally owned or originated technology to State and local government and to the private sector may elect to perform the functions of this subsection in such organizational structures. No Office of Research and Technology Applications or other organizational structures performing the functions of this subsection shall substantially compete with similar services available in the private sector.

- (d) Dissemination of technical information

  The National Technical Information Service shall—

  - (1) serve as a central clearinghouse for the collection, dissemination and transfer of information on federally owned or originated technologies having potential application to State and local governments and to private industry;

  - (2) utilize the expertise and services of the National Science Foundation and the Federal Laboratory Consortium for Technology Transfer, particularly in dealing with State and local governments;

  - (3) receive requests for technical assistance from State and local governments, respond to such requests with published information available to the Service, and refer such requests to the Federal Laboratory Consortium for Technology Transfer to the extent that such requests require a response involving more than the published information available to the Service;

  - (4) provide funding, at the discretion of the Secretary, for Federal laboratories to provide the assistance specified in subsection (c)(3) of this section;

  - (5) use appropriate technology transfer mechanisms such as personnel exchanges and computer-based systems; and

  - (6) maintain a permanent archival repository and clearinghouse for the collection and dissemination of nonclassified scientific, technical, and engineering information.

- (e) Establishment of Federal Laboratory Consortium for Technology Transfer

  - (1) There is hereby established the Federal Laboratory Consortium for Technology Transfer (hereinafter referred to as the "Consortium") which, in cooperation with Federal Laboratories [1] and the private sector, shall—

    - (A) develop and (with the consent of the Federal laboratory concerned) administer techniques, training courses, and materials concerning technology transfer to increase the awareness of Federal laboratory employees regarding the commercial potential of laboratory technology and innovations;

- (B) furnish advice and assistance requested by Federal agencies and laboratories for use in their technology transfer programs (including the planning of seminars for small business and other industry);

- (C) provide a clearinghouse for requests, received at the laboratory level, for technical assistance from States and units of local governments, businesses, industrial development organizations, not-for-profit organizations including universities, Federal agencies and laboratories, and other persons, and—

  - (i) to the extent that such requests can be responded to with published information available to the National Technical Information Service, refer such requests to that Service, and

  - (ii) otherwise refer these requests to the appropriate Federal laboratories and agencies;

- (D) facilitate communication and coordination between Offices of Research and Technology Applications of Federal laboratories;

- (E) utilize (with the consent of the agency involved) the expertise and services of the National Science Foundation, the Department of Commerce, the National Aeronautics and Space Administration, and other Federal agencies, as necessary;

- (F) with the consent of any Federal laboratory, facilitate the use by such laboratory of appropriate technology transfer mechanisms such as personnel exchanges and computer-based systems;

- (G) with the consent of any Federal laboratory, assist such laboratory to establish programs using technical volunteers to provide technical assistance to communities related to such laboratory;

- (H) facilitate communication and cooperation between Offices of Research and Technology Applications of Federal laboratories and regional, State, and local technology transfer organizations;

- (I) when requested, assist colleges or universities, businesses, non-profit organizations, State or local governments, or regional organizations to establish programs to stimulate research and to encourage technology transfer in such areas as technology program development, curriculum design, long-term research planning, personnel needs projections, and productivity assessments;

- (J) seek advice in each Federal laboratory consortium region from representatives of State and local governments, large and small business, universities, and other appropriate persons on the effectiveness of the program (and any such advice shall be provided at no expense to the Government); and

- (K) work with the Director of the National Institute on Disability and Rehabilitation Research to compile a compendium of current and projected Federal Laboratory technologies and projects that have or will have an intended or recognized impact on the available range of assistive technology for individuals with disabilities (as defined in section 3002 of title 29), including technologies and projects that incorporate the principles of universal design (as defined in section 3002 of title 29), as appropriate.

- (2) The membership of the Consortium shall consist of the Federal laboratories described in clause (1) of subsection (b) of this section and such other laboratories as may choose to join the Consortium. The representatives to the Consortium shall include a senior staff member of each Federal laboratory which is a member of the Consortium and a senior representative appointed from each Federal agency with one or more member laboratories.

- (3) The representatives to the Consortium shall elect a Chairman of the Consortium.

- (4) The Director of the National Institute of Standards and Technology shall provide the Consortium, on a reimbursable basis, with administrative services, such as office space, personnel, and support services of the Institute, as requested by the Consortium and approved by such Director.

- (5) Each Federal laboratory or agency shall transfer technology directly to users or representatives of users, and shall not transfer technology directly to the Consortium. Each Federal laboratory shall conduct and transfer technology only in accordance with the practices and policies of the Federal agency which owns, leases, or otherwise uses such Federal laboratory.

- (6) Not later than one year after October 20, 1986, and every year thereafter, the Chairman of the Consortium shall submit a report to the President, to the appropriate authorization and appropriation committees of both Houses of the Congress, and to each agency with respect to which a transfer of funding is made (for the fiscal year or years involved) under paragraph (7), concerning the activities of the Consortium and the expenditures made by it under this subsection during the year for which the report is made. Such report shall include an annual independent audit of the financial statements of the Consortium, conducted in accordance with generally accepted accounting principles.

- (7)
  - (A) Subject to subparagraph (B), an amount equal to 0.008 percent of the budget of each Federal agency from any Federal source, including related overhead, that is to be utilized by or on behalf of the laboratories of such agency for a fiscal year referred to in subparagraph (B)(ii) shall be transferred by such agency to the National Institute of Standards and Technology at the beginning of the fiscal year involved. Amounts so transferred shall be provided by the Institute to the Consortium for the purpose of carrying out activities of the Consortium under this subsection.
  - (B) A transfer shall be made by any Federal agency under subparagraph (A), for any fiscal year, only if the amount so transferred by that agency (as determined under such subparagraph) would exceed $10,000.
  - (C) The heads of Federal agencies and their designees, and the directors of Federal laboratories, may provide such additional support for operations of the Consortium as they deem appropriate.
- (f) Repealed. Pub. L. 104–66, title III, Sec. 3001(f), Dec. 21, 1995, 109 Stat. 734
- (g) Functions of Secretary
  - (1) The Secretary, through the Under Secretary, and in consultation with other Federal agencies, may—
    - (A) make available to interested agencies the expertise of the Department of Commerce regarding the commercial potential of inventions and methods and options for commercialization which are available to the Federal laboratories, including research and development limited partnerships;
    - (B) develop and disseminate to appropriate agency and laboratory personnel model provisions for use on a voluntary basis in cooperative research and development arrangements; and
    - (C) furnish advice and assistance, upon request, to Federal agencies concerning their cooperative research and development programs and projects.
  - (2) Two years after October 20, 1986, and every two years thereafter, the Secretary shall submit a summary report to the President and the Congress on the use by the agencies and the Secretary of the authorities specified in this chapter. Other Federal agencies shall cooperate in the report's preparation.
  - (3) Not later than one year after October 20, 1986, the Secretary shall submit to the President and the Congress a report regarding—

- (A) any copyright provisions or other types of barriers which tend to restrict or limit the transfer of federally funded computer software to the private sector and to State and local governments, and agencies of such State and local governments; and

- (B) the feasibility and cost of compiling and maintaining a current and comprehensive inventory of all federally funded training software.

- (h) Repealed. Pub. L. 100–519, title II, Sec. 212(a)(4), Oct. 24, 1988, 102 Stat. 2595

- (i) Research equipment

  The Director of a laboratory, or the head of any Federal agency or department, may loan, lease, or give research equipment that is excess to the needs of the laboratory, agency, or department to an educational institution or nonprofit organization for the conduct of technical and scientific education and research activities. Title of ownership shall transfer with a gift under the [2] section.

Footnotes

[1] So in original. Probably should not be capitalized.

[2] So in original. Probably should be "this."

Sec. 3710a. Cooperative Research and Development Agreements

- (a) General authority

  Each Federal agency may permit the director of any of its Government-operated Federal laboratories, and, to the extent provided in an agency-approved joint work statement, the director of any of its Government-owned, contractor-operated laboratories—

  - (1) to enter into cooperative research and development agreements on behalf of such agency (subject to subsection (c) of this section) with other Federal agencies; units of State or local government; industrial organizations (including corporations, partnerships, and limited partnerships, and industrial development organizations); public and private foundations; nonprofit organizations (including universities); or other persons (including licensees of inventions owned by the Federal agency); and

  - (2) to negotiate licensing agreements under section 207 of title 35, or under other authorities (in the case of a Government-owned, contractor-operated laboratory, subject to subsection (c) of this section) for inventions made or other intellectual property developed at the laboratory and other inventions or other intellectual property that may be voluntarily assigned to the Government.

- (b) Enumerated authority

  - (1) Under an agreement entered into pursuant to subsection (a)(1) of this section, the laboratory may grant, or agree to grant in advance, to a collaborating party patent licenses or assignments, or options thereto, in any invention made in whole or in part by a laboratory employee under the agreement, for reasonable compensation when appropriate. The laboratory shall ensure, through such agreement, that the collaborating party has the option to choose an exclusive license for a prenegotiated field of use for any such invention under the agreement or, if there is more than one collaborating party, that the collaborating parties are offered the option to hold licensing rights that collectively encompass the rights that would be held under such an exclusive license by one party. In consideration for the Government's contribution under the agreement, grants under this paragraph shall be subject to the following explicit conditions:

    - (A) A nonexclusive, nontransferable, irrevocable, paid-up license from the collaborating party to the laboratory to practice the invention or have the invention practiced throughout the world by or on behalf of the Government. In the exercise of such license, the Government shall not publicly disclose trade secrets or commercial or financial information that is privileged or confidential within the meaning of section 552(b)(4) of title 5 or which would be considered as such if it had been obtained from a non-Federal party.

    - (B) If a laboratory assigns title or grants an exclusive license to such an invention, the Government shall retain the right—

      - (i) to require the collaborating party to grant to a responsible applicant a nonexclusive, partially exclusive, or exclusive license to use the invention in the applicant's licensed field of use, on terms that are reasonable under the circumstances; or

      - (ii) if the collaborating party fails to grant such a license, to grant the license itself.

    - (C) The Government may exercise its right retained under subparagraph (B) only in exceptional circumstances and only if the Government determines that—

      - (i) the action is necessary to meet health or safety needs that are not reasonably satisfied by the collaborating party;

- (ii) the action is necessary to meet requirements for public use specified by Federal regulations, and such requirements are not reasonably satisfied by the collaborating party; or
- (iii) the collaborating party has failed to comply with an agreement containing provisions described in subsection (c)(4)(B) of this section.

  This determination is subject to administrative appeal and judicial review under section 203(2) of title 35.

- (2) Under agreements entered into pursuant to subsection (a)(1) of this section, the laboratory shall ensure that a collaborating party may retain title to any invention made solely by its employee in exchange for normally granting the Government a nonexclusive, nontransferable, irrevocable, paid-up license to practice the invention or have the invention practiced throughout the world by or on behalf of the Government for research or other Government purposes.

- (3) Under an agreement entered into pursuant to subsection (a)(1) of this section, a laboratory may—

  - (A) accept, retain, and use funds, personnel, services, and property from a collaborating party and provide personnel, services, and property to a collaborating party;
  - (B) use funds received from a collaborating party in accordance with subparagraph (A) to hire personnel to carry out the agreement who will not be subject to full-time-equivalent restrictions of the agency;
  - (C) to the extent consistent with any applicable agency requirements or standards of conduct, permit an employee or former employee of the laboratory to participate in an effort to commercialize an invention made by the employee or former employee while in the employment or service of the Government; and
  - (D) waive, subject to reservation by the Government of a nonexclusive, irrevocable, paid-up license to practice the invention or have the invention practiced throughout the world by or on behalf of the Government, in advance, in whole or in part, any right of ownership which the Federal Government may have to any subject invention made under the agreement by a collaborating party or employee of a collaborating party.

- (4) A collaborating party in an exclusive license in any invention made under an agreement entered into pursuant to subsection (a)(1) of this section shall have the right of enforcement under chapter 29 of title 35.

- (5) A Government-owned, contractor-operated laboratory that enters into a cooperative research and development agreement pursuant to subsection (a)(1) of this section may use or obligate royalties or other income accruing to the laboratory under such agreement with respect to any invention only—

- (A) for payments to inventors;
- (B) for purposes described in clauses (i), (ii), (iii), and (iv) of section 3710c(a)(1)(B) of this title; and
- (C) for scientific research and development consistent with the research and development missions and objectives of the laboratory.

- (c) Contract considerations
  - (1) A Federal agency may issue regulations on suitable procedures for implementing the provisions of this section; however, implementation of this section shall not be delayed until issuance of such regulations.
  - (2) The agency in permitting a Federal laboratory to enter into agreements under this section shall be guided by the purposes of this chapter.
  - (3)
    - (A) Any agency using the authority given it under subsection (a) of this section shall review standards of conduct for its employees for resolving potential conflicts of interest to make sure they adequately establish guidelines for situations likely to arise through the use of this authority, including but not limited to cases where present or former employees or their partners negotiate licenses or assignments of titles to inventions or negotiate cooperative research and development agreements with Federal agencies (including the agency with which the employee involved is or was formerly employed).
    - (B) If, in implementing subparagraph (A), an agency is unable to resolve potential conflicts of interest within its current statutory framework, it shall propose necessary statutory changes to be forwarded to its authorizing committees in Congress.
  - (4) The laboratory director in deciding what cooperative research and development agreements to enter into shall—
    - (A) give special consideration to small business firms, and consortia involving small business firms; and
    - (B) give preference to business units located in the United States which agree that products embodying inventions made under the cooperative research and development agreement or produced through the use of such inventions will be manufactured substantially in the United States and, in the case of any industrial organization or other person subject to the control of a foreign company or government, as appropriate, take into consideration whether or not such foreign government permits United States agencies, organizations, or

other persons to enter into cooperative research and development agreements and licensing agreements.

- (5)

  - (A) If the head of the agency or his designee desires an opportunity to disapprove or require the modification of any such agreement presented by the director of a Government-operated laboratory, the agreement shall provide a 30-day period within which such action must be taken beginning on the date the agreement is presented to him or her by the head of the laboratory concerned.

  - (B) In any case in which the head of an agency or his designee disapproves or requires the modification of an agreement presented by the director of a Government-operated laboratory under this section, the head of the agency or such designee shall transmit a written explanation of such disapproval or modification to the head of the laboratory concerned.

  - (C)

    - (i) Except as provided in subparagraph (D), any agency which has contracted with a non-Federal entity to operate a laboratory shall review and approve, request specific modifications to, or disapprove a joint work statement that is submitted by the director of such laboratory within 90 days after such submission. In any case where an agency has requested specific modifications to a joint work statement, the agency shall approve or disapprove any resubmission of such joint work statement within 30 days after such resubmission, or 90 days after the original submission, whichever occurs later. No agreement may be entered into by a Government-owned, contractor-operated laboratory under this section before both approval of the agreement under clause (iv) and approval under this clause of a joint work statement.

    - (ii) In any case in which an agency which has contracted with a non-Federal entity to operate a laboratory disapproves or requests the modification of a joint work statement submitted under this section, the agency shall promptly transmit a written explanation of such disapproval or modification to the director of the laboratory concerned.

    - (iii) Any agency which has contracted with a non-Federal entity to operate a laboratory or laboratories shall develop and provide to such laboratory or laboratories one or more model cooperative research and development agreements, for the purposes of standardizing practices and procedures, resolving common legal issues, and enabling review of cooperative research and development agreements to be carried out in a routine and prompt manner.

- (iv) An agency which has contracted with a non-Federal entity to operate a laboratory shall review each agreement under this section. Within 30 days after the presentation, by the director of the laboratory, of such agreement, the agency shall, on the basis of such review, approve or request specific modification to such agreement. Such agreement shall not take effect before approval under this clause.

- (v) If an agency fails to complete a review under clause (iv) within the 30-day period specified therein, the agency shall submit to the Congress, within 10 days after the end of that 30-day period, a report on the reasons for such failure. The agency shall, at the end of each successive 30-day period thereafter during which such failure continues, submit to the Congress another report on the reasons for the continuing failure. Nothing in this clause relieves the agency of the requirement to complete a review under clause (iv).

- (vi) In any case in which an agency which has contracted with a non-Federal entity to operate a laboratory requests the modification of an agreement presented under this section, the agency shall promptly transmit a written explanation of such modification to the director of the laboratory concerned.

- (D)

  - (i) Any non-Federal entity that operates a laboratory pursuant to a contract with a Federal agency shall submit to the agency any cooperative research and development agreement that the entity proposes to enter into with a small business firm and the joint work statement required with respect to that agreement.

  - (ii) A Federal agency that receives a proposed agreement and joint work statement under clause (i) shall review and approve, request specific modifications to, or disapprove the proposed agreement and joint work statement within 30 days after such submission. No agreement may be entered into by a Government-owned, contractor-operated laboratory under this section before both approval of the agreement and approval of a joint work statement under this clause.

  - (iii) In any case in which an agency which has contracted with an entity referred to in clause (i) disapproves or requests the modification of a cooperative research and development agreement or joint work statement submitted under that clause, the agency shall transmit a written explanation of such disapproval or modification to the head of the laboratory concerned.

- (6) Each agency shall maintain a record of all agreements entered into under this section.

- (7)

  - (A) No trade secrets or commercial or financial information that is privileged or confidential, under the meaning of section 552(b)(4) of title 5, which is obtained in the conduct of research or as a result of activities under this chapter from a non-Federal party participating in a cooperative research and development agreement shall be disclosed.

  - (B) The director, or in the case of a contractor-operated laboratory, the agency, for a period of up to 5 years after development of information that results from research and development activities conducted under this chapter and that would be a trade secret or commercial or financial information that is privileged or confidential if the information had been obtained from a non-Federal party participating in a cooperative research and development agreement, may provide appropriate protections against the dissemination of such information, including exemption from subchapter II of chapter 5 of title 5.

- (d) Definitions

  As used in this section -

  - (1) the term "cooperative research and development agreement" means any agreement between one or more Federal laboratories and one or more non-Federal parties under which the Government, through its laboratories, provides personnel, services, facilities, equipment, intellectual property, or other resources with or without reimbursement (but not funds to non-Federal parties) and the non-Federal parties provide funds, personnel, services, facilities, equipment, intellectual property, or other resources toward the conduct of specified research or development efforts which are consistent with the missions of the laboratory; except that such term does not include a procurement contract or cooperative agreement as those terms are used in sections 6303, 6304, and 6305 of title 31;

  - (2) the term "laboratory" means—

    - (A) a facility or group of facilities owned, leased, or otherwise used by a Federal agency, a substantial purpose of which is the performance of research, development, or engineering by employees of the Federal Government;

    - (B) a group of Government-owned, contractor-operated facilities (including a weapon production facility of the Department of Energy) under a common contract, when a substantial purpose of the contract is the performance of research and development, or the production, maintenance, testing, or dismantlement of a nuclear weapon or its components, for the Federal Government; and

    - (C) a Government-owned, contractor-operated facility (including a weapon production facility of the Department of Energy) that is not under a common contract described in subparagraph (B), and the primary purpose of which is the performance of research and development, or the production, maintenance, testing, or dismantlement of a nuclear weapon or its components, for the Federal Government, but such term does not include any facility covered by Executive Order No. 12344, dated February 1, 1982, pertaining to the naval nuclear propulsion program;

- (3) the term "joint work statement" means a proposal prepared for a Federal agency by the director of a Government-owned, contractor-operated laboratory describing the purpose and scope of a proposed cooperative research and development agreement, and assigning rights and responsibilities among the agency, the laboratory, and any other party or parties to the proposed agreement; and

- (4) the term "weapon production facility of the Department of Energy" means a facility under the control or jurisdiction of the Secretary of Energy that is operated for national security purposes and is engaged in the production, maintenance, testing, or dismantlement of a nuclear weapon or its components.

- (e) Determination of laboratory missions

For purposes of this section, an agency shall make separate determinations of the mission or missions of each of its laboratories.

- (f) Relationship to other laws

Nothing in this section is intended to limit or diminish existing authorities of any agency.

- (g) Principles

In implementing this section, each agency which has contracted with a non-Federal entity to operate a laboratory shall be guided by the following principles:

- (1) The implementation shall advance program missions at the laboratory, including any national security mission.

- (2) Classified information and unclassified sensitive information protected by law, regulation, or Executive order shall be appropriately safeguarded.

Sec. 3710b. Rewards for scientific, engineering, and technical personnel of Federal agencies

The head of each Federal agency that is making expenditures at a rate of more than $50,000,000 per fiscal year for research and development in its Government-operated laboratories shall use the appropriate statutory authority to develop and implement a cash awards program to reward its scientific, engineering, and technical personnel for—

- (1) inventions, innovations, computer software, or other outstanding scientific or technological contributions of value to the United States due to commercial application or due to contributions to missions of the Federal agency or the Federal government, [1] or
- (2) exemplary activities that promote the domestic transfer of science and technology development within the Federal Government and result in utilization of such science and technology by American industry or business, universities, State or local governments, or other non-Federal parties.

Footnote

[1] So in original. Probably should be capitalized.

Sec. 3710c. Distribution of Royalties Received by Federal Agencies

- (a) In general
  - (1) Except as provided in paragraphs (2) and (4), any royalties or other payments received by a Federal agency from the licensing and assignment of inventions under agreements entered into by Federal laboratories under section 3710a of this title, and from the licensing of inventions of Federal laboratories under section 207 of title 35 or under any other provision of law, shall be retained by the laboratory which produced the invention and shall be disposed of as follows:
    - (A)
      - (i) The head of the agency or laboratory, or such individual's designee, shall pay each year the first $2,000, and thereafter at least 15 percent, of the royalties or other payments to the inventor or coinventors.
      - (ii) An agency or laboratory may provide appropriate incentives, from royalties, or other payments, to laboratory employees who are not an inventor of such inventions but who substantially increased the technical value of such inventions.
      - (iii) The agency or laboratory shall retain the royalties and other payments received from an invention until the agency or laboratory makes payments to employees of a laboratory under clause (i) or (ii).
    - (B) The balance of the royalties or other payments shall be transferred by the agency to its laboratories, with the majority share of the

royalties or other payments from any invention going to the laboratory where the invention occurred. The royalties or other payments so transferred to any laboratory may be used or obligated by that laboratory during the fiscal year in which they are received or during the succeeding fiscal year—

- (i) to reward scientific, engineering, and technical employees of the laboratory, including developers of sensitive or classified technology, regardless of whether the technology has commercial applications;
- (ii) to further scientific exchange among the laboratories of the agency;
- (iii) for education and training of employees consistent with the research and development missions and objectives of the agency or laboratory, and for other activities that increase the potential for transfer of the technology of the laboratories of the agency;
- (iv) for payment of expenses incidental to the administration and licensing of intellectual property by the agency or laboratory with respect to inventions made at that laboratory, including the fees or other costs for the services of other agencies, persons, or organizations for intellectual property management and licensing services; or
- (v) for scientific research and development consistent with the research and development missions and objectives of the laboratory.
- (C) All royalties or other payments retained by the agency or laboratory after payments have been made pursuant to subparagraphs (A) and (B) that is unobligated and unexpended at the end of the second fiscal year succeeding the fiscal year in which the royalties and other payments were received shall be paid into the Treasury.
- (2) If, after payments to inventors under paragraph (1), the royalties or other payments received by an agency in any fiscal year exceed 5 percent of the budget of the Government-operated laboratories of the agency for that year, 75 percent of such excess shall be paid to the Treasury of the United States and the remaining 25 percent may be used or obligated under paragraph (1)(B). Any funds not so used or obligated shall be paid into the Treasury of the United States.
- (3) Any payment made to an employee under this section shall be in addition to the regular pay of the employee and to any other awards made to the employee, and shall not affect the entitlement of the employee to any regular pay, annuity, or award to which he is otherwise entitled or for which he is otherwise eligible or limit the amount

thereof. Any payment made to an inventor as such shall continue after the inventor leaves the laboratory or agency. Payments made under this section shall not exceed $150,000 per year to any one person, unless the President approves a larger award (with the excess over $150,000 being treated as a Presidential award under section 4504 of title 5).

- (4) A Federal agency receiving royalties or other payments as a result of invention management services performed for another Federal agency or laboratory under section 207 of title 35, may retain such royalties or payments to the extent required to offset payments to inventors under clause (i) of paragraph (1)(A), costs and expenses incurred under clause (iv) of paragraph (1)(B), and the cost of foreign patenting and maintenance for any invention of the other agency. All royalties and other payments remaining after offsetting the payments to inventors, costs, and expenses described in the preceding sentence shall be transferred to the agency for which the services were performed, for distribution in accordance with paragraph (1)(B).

- (b) Certain assignments

  If the invention involved was one assigned to the Federal agency—

  - (1) by a contractor, grantee, or participant, or an employee of a contractor, grantee, or participant, in an agreement or other arrangement with the agency, or

  - (2) by an employee of the agency who was not working in the laboratory at the time the invention [1] was made,

- (c) Reports

  - (1) In making their annual budget submissions Federal agencies shall submit, to the appropriate authorization and appropriation committees of both Houses of the Congress, summaries of the amount of royalties or other income received and expenditures made (including inventor awards) under this section.

  - (2) The Comptroller General, five years after October 20, 1986, shall review the effectiveness of the various royalty-sharing programs established under this section and report to the appropriate committees of the House of Representatives and the Senate, in a timely manner, his findings, conclusions, and recommendations for improvements in such programs.

Footnote

[1] So in original. Probably should be "invention." The agency unit that was involved in such assignment shall be considered to be a laboratory for purposes of this section.

Sec. 3710d. Employee activities

- (a) In general

  If a Federal agency which has ownership of or the right of ownership to an invention made by a Federal employee does not intend to file for a patent application or otherwise to promote commercialization of such invention, the agency shall allow the inventor, if the inventor is a Government employee or former employee who made the invention during the course of employment with the Government, to obtain or retain title to the invention (subject to reservation by the Government of a nonexclusive, nontransferrable, irrevocable, paid-up license to practice the invention or have the invention practiced throughout the world by or on behalf of the Government). In addition, the agency may condition the inventor's right to title on the timely filing of a patent application in cases when the Government determines that it has or may have a need to practice the invention.

- (b) "Special Government employees" defined

  For purposes of this section, Federal employees include "special Government employees" as defined in section 202 of title 18.

- (c) Relationship to other laws

  Nothing in this section is intended to limit or diminish existing authorities of any agency.

Sec. 3711. National Technology Medal

- (a) Establishment

  There is hereby established a National Technology Medal, which shall be of such design and materials and bear such inscriptions as the President, on the basis of recommendations submitted by the Office of Science and Technology Policy, may prescribe.

- (b) Award

  The President shall periodically award the medal, on the basis of recommendations received from the Secretary or on the basis of such other information and evidence as he deems appropriate, to individuals or companies, which in his judgment are deserving of special recognition by reason of their outstanding contributions to the promotion of technology or technological manpower for the improvement of the economic, environmental, or social well-being of the United States.

- (c) Presentation

  The presentation of the award shall be made by the President with such ceremonies as he may deem proper.

Sec. 3711a. Malcolm Baldrige National Quality Award

- (a) Establishment

  There is hereby established the Malcolm Baldrige National Quality Award, which shall be evidenced by a medal bearing the inscriptions "Malcolm Baldrige National Quality Award" and "The Quest for Excellence." The medal shall be of such design and materials and bear such additional inscriptions as the Secretary may prescribe.

- (b) Making and presentation of award

  - (1) The President (on the basis of recommendations received from the Secretary), or the Secretary, shall periodically make the award to companies and other organizations which in the judgment of the President or the Secretary have substantially benefited the economic or social well-being of the United States through improvements in the quality of their goods or services resulting from the effective practice of quality management, and which as a consequence are deserving of special recognition.

  - (2) The presentation of the award shall be made by the President or the Secretary with such ceremonies as the President or the Secretary may deem proper.

  - (3) An organization to which an award is made under this section, and which agrees to help other American organizations improve their quality management, may publicize its receipt of such award and use the award in its advertising, but it shall be ineligible to receive another such award in the same category for a period of 5 years.

- (c) Categories in which award may be given

  - (1) Subject to paragraph (2), separate awards shall be made to qualifying organizations in each of the following categories—

    - (A) Small businesses.
    - (B) Companies or their subsidiaries.
    - (C) Companies which primarily provide services.
    - (D) Health care providers.
    - (E) Education providers.

  - (2) The Secretary may at any time expand, subdivide, or otherwise modify the list of categories within which awards may be made as initially in effect under paragraph (1), and may establish separate awards for other organizations including units of government, upon a determination that the objectives of this section would be better served thereby; except that any such expansion, subdivision, modification, or establishment shall not be effective unless and until the Secretary has submitted a detailed description thereof to the Congress and a period of 30 days has elapsed since that submission.

- (3) Not more than two awards may be made within any subcategory in any year, unless the Secretary determines that a third award is merited and can be given at no additional cost to the Federal Government (and no award shall be made within any category or subcategory if there are no qualifying enterprises in that category or subcategory).

- (d) Criteria for qualification

  - (1) An organization may qualify for an award under this section only if it—

    - (A) applies to the Director of the National Institute of Standards and Technology in writing, for the award,

    - (B) permits a rigorous evaluation of the way in which its business and other operations have contributed to improvements in the quality of goods and services, and

    - (C) meets such requirements and specifications as the Secretary, after receiving recommendations from the Board of Overseers established under paragraph (2)(B) and the Director of the National Institute of Standards and Technology, determines to be appropriate to achieve the objectives of this section. In applying the provisions of subparagraph (C) with respect to any organization, the Director of the National Institute of Standards and Technology shall rely upon an intensive evaluation by a competent board of examiners which shall review the evidence submitted by the organization and, through a site visit, verify the accuracy of the quality improvements claimed. The examination should encompass all aspects of the organization's current practice of quality management, as well as the organization's provision for quality management in its future goals. The award shall be given only to organizations which have made outstanding improvements in the quality of their goods or services (or both) and which demonstrate effective quality management through the training and involvement of all levels of personnel in quality improvement.

  - (2)

    - (A) The Director of the National Institute of Standards and Technology shall, under appropriate contractual arrangements, carry out the Director's responsibilities under subparagraphs (A) and (B) of paragraph (1) through one or more broad-based nonprofit entities which are leaders in the field of quality management and which have a history of service to society.

- (B) The Secretary shall appoint a Board of Overseers for the award, consisting of at least five persons selected for their preeminence in the field of quality management. This board shall meet annually to review the work of the contractor or contractors and make such suggestions for the improvement of the award process as they deem necessary. The Board shall report the results of the award activities to the Director of the National Institute of Standards and Technology each year, along with its recommendations for improvement of the process.

- (e) Information and technology transfer program

  The Director of the National Institute of Standards and Technology shall ensure that all program participants receive the complete results of their audits as well as detailed explanations of all suggestions for improvements. The Director shall also provide information about the awards and the successful quality improvement strategies and programs of the award-winning participants to all participants and other appropriate groups.

- (f) Funding

  The Secretary is authorized to seek and accept gifts from public and private sources to carry out the program under this section. If additional sums are needed to cover the full cost of the program, the Secretary shall impose fees upon the organizations applying for the award in amounts sufficient to provide such additional sums. The Director is authorized to use appropriated funds to carry out responsibilities under this chapter.

- (g) Report

  The Secretary shall prepare and submit to the President and the Congress, within 3 years after August 20, 1987, a report on the progress, findings, and conclusions of activities conducted pursuant to this section along with recommendations for possible modifications thereof.

Sec. 3711b. Conference on Advanced Automotive Technologies

Not later than 180 days after December 18, 1991, the Secretary of Commerce, through the Under Secretary of Commerce for Technology, in consultation with other appropriate officials, shall convene a conference of domestic motor vehicle manufacturers, parts suppliers, Federal laboratories, and motor vehicle users to explore ways in which cooperatively they can improve the competitiveness of the United States motor vehicle industry by developing new technologies which will enhance the safety and energy savings, and lessen the environmental impact of domestic motor vehicles, and the results of such conference shall be published and then submitted to the President and to the Committees on Science, Space, and Technology and Public Works and Transportation of the House of Representatives and the Committee on Commerce, Science, and Transportation of the Senate.

Sec. 3711c. Advanced Motor Vehicle Research Award

- (a) Establishment

  There is established a National Award for the Advancement of Motor Vehicle Research and Development. The award shall consist of a medal, and a cash prize if funding is available for the prize under subsection (c) of this section. The medal shall be of such design and materials and bear inscriptions as is determined by the Secretary of Transportation.

- (b) Making and presenting award

  The Secretary of Transportation shall periodically make and present the award to domestic motor vehicle manufacturers, suppliers, or Federal laboratory personnel who, in the opinion of the Secretary of Transportation, have substantially improved domestic motor vehicle research and development in safety, energy savings, or environmental impact. No person may receive the award more than once every 5 years.

- (c) Funding for award

  The Secretary of Transportation may seek and accept gifts of money from private sources for the purpose of making cash prize awards under this section. Such money may be used only for that purpose, and only such money may be used for that purpose.

Sec. 3712. Personnel Exchanges

The Secretary and the National Science Foundation, jointly, shall establish a program to foster the exchange of scientific and technical personnel among academia, industry, and Federal laboratories. Such program shall include both (1) federally supported exchanges and (2) efforts to stimulate exchanges without Federal funding.

Sec. 3713. Authorization of Appropriations

- (a)
  - (1) There is authorized to be appropriated to the Secretary for the purposes of carrying out sections 3704, 3710(g), and 3711 of this title not to exceed $3,400,000 for the fiscal year ending September 30, 1988.

- (2) Of the amount authorized under paragraph (1) of this subsection, $2,400,000 is authorized only for the Office of Productivity, Technology, and Innovation; $500,000 is authorized only for the purpose of carrying out the requirements of the Japanese technical literature program established under section 3704(d) of this title; and $500,000 is authorized only for the patent licensing activities of the National Technical Information Service.

- (b) In addition to the authorization of appropriations provided under subsection (a) of this section, there is authorized to be appropriated to the Secretary for the purposes of carrying out section 3704a of this title not to exceed $500,000 for the fiscal year ending September 30, 1988, $1,000,000 for the fiscal year ending September 30, 1989, and $1,500,000 for the fiscal year ending September 30, 1990.

- (c) Such sums as may be appropriated under subsections (a) and (b) of this section shall remain available until expended.

- (d) To enable the National Science Foundation to carry out its powers and duties under this chapter only such sums may be appropriated as the Congress may authorize by law.

Sec. 3714. Spending Authority

No payments shall be made or contracts shall be entered into pursuant to the provisions of this chapter (other than sections 3710a, 3710b, and 3710c of this title) except to such extent or in such amounts as are provided in advance in appropriation Acts.

Sec. 3715. Use of Partnership Intermediaries

- (a) Authority

  Subject to the approval of the Secretary or head of the affected department or agency, the Director of a Federal laboratory, or in the case of a federally funded research and development center that is not a laboratory (as defined in section 3710a(d)(2) of this title), the Federal employee who is the contract officer, may—

  - (1) enter into a contract or memorandum of understanding with a partnership intermediary that provides for the partnership intermediary to perform services for the Federal laboratory that increase the likelihood of success in the conduct of cooperative or joint activities of such Federal laboratory with small business firms; and

  - (2) pay the Federal costs of such contract or memorandum of understanding out of funds available for the support of the technology transfer function pursuant to section 3710(b) of this title.

- (b) Partnership progress reports

  The Secretary shall include in each triennial report required under section 3704a(d) of this title a discussion and evaluation of the activities carried out pursuant to this section during the period covered by the report.

- (c) "Partnership intermediary" defined

  For purposes of this section, the term "partnership intermediary" means an agency of a State or local government, or a nonprofit entity owned in whole or in part by, chartered by, funded in whole or in part by, or operated in whole or in part by or on behalf of a State or local government, that assists, counsels, advises, evaluates, or otherwise cooperates with small business firms that need or can make demonstrably productive use of technology-related assistance from a Federal laboratory, including State programs receiving funds under cooperative agreements entered into under section 5121(b) of the Omnibus Trade and Competitiveness Act of 1988 (15 U.S.C. 278l note).

Sec. 3716. Critical Industries

- (a) Identification of industries and development of plan

  The Secretary shall—

  - (1) identify those civilian industries in the United States that are necessary to support a robust manufacturing infrastructure and critical to the economic security of the United States; and

  - (2) list the major research and development initiatives being undertaken, and the substantial investments being made, by the Federal Government, including its research laboratories, in each of the critical industries identified under paragraph (1).

- (b) Initial report

  The Secretary shall submit a report to the Congress within 1 year after February 14, 1992, on the actions taken under subsection (a) of this section.

- (c) Annual updates

  The Secretary shall annually submit to the Congress an update of the report submitted under subsection (b) of this section. Each such update shall—

  - (1) describe the status of each identified critical industry, including the advances and declines occurring since the most recent report; and

  - (2) identify any industries that should be added to the list of critical industries.

Sec. 3717. National Quality Council

- (a) Establishment and functions

There is established a National Quality Council (hereafter in this section referred to as the "Council"). The functions of the Council shall be—

  - (1) to establish national goals and priorities for Quality performance in business, education, government, and all other sectors of the Nation;
  - (2) to encourage and support the voluntary adoption of these goals and priorities by companies, unions, professional and business associations, coalition groups, and units of government, as well as private and nonprofit organizations;
  - (3) to arouse and maintain the interest of the people of the United States in Quality performance, and to encourage the adoption and institution of Quality performance methods by all corporations, government agencies, and other organizations; and
  - (4) to conduct a White House Conference on Quality Performance in the American Workplace that would bring together in a single forum national leaders in business, labor, education, professional societies, the media, government, and politics to address Quality performance as a means of improving United States competitiveness.

- (b) Membership

The Council shall consist of not less than 17 or more than 20 members, appointed by the Secretary. Members shall include—

  - (1) at least 2 but not more than 3 representatives from manufacturing industry;
  - (2) at least 2 but not more than 3 representatives from service industry;
  - (3) at least 2 but not more than 3 representatives from national Quality not-for-profit organizations;
  - (4) two representatives from education, one with expertise in elementary and secondary education, and one with expertise in post-secondary education;
  - (5) one representative from labor;
  - (6) one representative from professional societies;
  - (7) one representative each from local and State government;
  - (8) one representative from the Federal Quality Institute;
  - (9) one representative from the National Institute of Standards and Technology;
  - (10) one representative from the Department of Defense;

- (11) one representative from a civilian Federal agency not otherwise represented on the Council, to be rotated among such agencies every 2 years; and

- (12) one representative from the Foundation for the Malcolm Baldrige National Quality Award.

- (c) Terms

The term of office of each member of the Council appointed under paragraphs (1) through (7) of subsection (b) of this section shall be 2 years, except that when making the initial appointments under such paragraphs, the Secretary shall appoint not more than 50 percent of the members to 1 year terms. No member appointed under such paragraphs shall serve on the Council for more than 2 consecutive terms.

- (d) Chairman and Vice Chairman

The Secretary shall designate one of the members initially appointed to the Council as Chairman. Thereafter, the members of the Council shall annually elect one of their number as Chairman. The members of the Council shall also annually elect one of their members as Vice Chairman. No individual shall serve as Chairman or Vice Chairman for more than 2 consecutive years.

- (e) Executive Director and employees

The Council shall appoint and fix the compensation of an Executive Director, who shall hire and fix the compensation of such additional employees as may be necessary to assist the Council in carrying out its functions. In hiring such additional employees, the Executive Director shall ensure that no individual hired has a conflict of interest with the responsibilities of the Council.

- (f) Funding

There is established in the Treasury of the United States a National Quality Performance Trust Fund, into which all funds received by the Council, through private donations or otherwise, shall be deposited. Amounts in such Trust Fund shall be available to the Council, to the extent provided in advance in appropriations Acts, for the purpose of carrying out the functions of the Council under this Act.

- (g) Contributions

The Council may not accept private donations from a single source in excess of $25,000 per year. Private donations from a single source in excess of $10,000 per year may be accepted by the Council only on approval of two-thirds of the Council.

- (h) Annual report

The Council shall annually submit to the President and the Congress a comprehensive and detailed report on—

- (1) the progress in meeting the goals and priorities established by the Council;
- (2) the Council's operations, activities, and financial condition;
- (3) contributions to the Council from non-Federal sources;
- (4) plans for the Council's operations and activities for the future; and
- (5) any other information or recommendations the Council considers appropriate.

Appendix IV

COOPERATIVE RESEARCH AND DEVELOPMENT AGREEMENTS (CRADAS) AT NATIONAL LABS

15 USC 3710A

- United States Code
  - TITLE 15—COMMERCE AND TRADE
    - CHAPTER 63—TECHNOLOGY INNOVATION

Sec. 3710a. Cooperative Research and Development Agreements

(a) General authority. Each Federal agency may permit the director of any of its Government-operated Federal laboratories, and, to the extent provided in an agency-approved joint work statement or, if permitted by the agency, in an agency-approved annual strategic plan, the director of any of its Government-owned, contractor-operated laboratories—

  (1) to enter into cooperative research and development agreements on behalf of such agency (subject to subsection (c) of this section) with other Federal agencies; units of State or local government; industrial organizations (including corporations, partnerships, and limited partnerships, and industrial development organizations); public and private foundations; nonprofit organizations (including universities); or other persons (including licensees of inventions owned by the Federal agency); and

(2) to negotiate licensing agreements under section 207 of title 35, United States Code, or under other authorities (in the case of a Government-owned, contractor-operated laboratory, subject to subsection (c) of this section) for inventions made or other intellectual property developed at the laboratory and other inventions or other intellectual property that may be voluntarily assigned to the Government.

(b) Enumerated authority.

(1) Under an agreement entered into pursuant to subsection (a)(1), the laboratory may grant, or agree to grant in advance, to a collaborating party patent licenses or assignments, or options thereto, in any invention made in whole or in part by a laboratory employee under the agreement, or, subject to section 209 of title 35, United States Code, may grant a license to an invention which is federally owned, for which a patent application was filed before the signing of the agreement, and directly within the scope of the work under the agreement, for reasonable compensation when appropriate. The laboratory shall ensure, through such agreement, that the collaborating party has the option to choose an exclusive license for a prenegotiated field of use for any such invention under the agreement or, if there is more than one collaborating party, that the collaborating parties are offered the option to hold licensing rights that collectively encompass the rights that would be held under such an exclusive license by one party. In consideration for the Government's contribution under the agreement, grants under this paragraph shall be subject to the following explicit conditions:

(A) A nonexclusive, nontransferable, irrevocable, paid-up license from the collaborating party to the laboratory to practice the invention or have the invention practiced throughout the world by or on behalf of the Government. In the exercise of such license, the Government shall not publicly disclose trade secrets or commercial or financial information that is privileged or confidential within the meaning of section 552(b)(4) of title 5, United States Code, or which would be considered as such if it had been obtained from a non-Federal party.

(B) If a laboratory assigns title or grants an exclusive license to such an invention, the Government shall retain the right—

(i) to require the collaborating party to grant to a responsible applicant a nonexclusive, partially exclusive, or exclusive license to use the invention in the applicant's licensed field of use, on terms that are reasonable under the circumstances; or

(ii) if the collaborating party fails to grant such a license, to grant the license itself.

(C) The Government may exercise its right retained under subparagraph (B) only in exceptional circumstances and only if the Government determines that—

(i) the action is necessary to meet health or safety needs that are not reasonably satisfied by the collaborating party;

(ii) the action is necessary to meet requirements for public use specified by Federal regulations, and such requirements are not reasonably satisfied by the collaborating party; or

(iii) the collaborating party has failed to comply with an agreement containing provisions described in subsection (c)(4)(B).

This determination is subject to administrative appeal and judicial review under section 203(2) of title 35, United States Code.

(2) Under agreements entered into pursuant to subsection (a)(1), the laboratory shall ensure that a collaborating party may retain title to any invention made solely by its employee in exchange for normally granting the Government a nonexclusive, nontransferable, irrevocable, paid-up license to practice the invention or have the invention practiced throughout the world by or on behalf of the Government for research or other Government purposes.

(3) Under an agreement entered into pursuant to subsection (a)(1), a laboratory may—

(A) accept, retain, and use funds, personnel, services, and property from a collaborating party and provide personnel, services, and property to a collaborating party;

(B) use funds received from a collaborating party in accordance with subparagraph (A) to hire personnel to carry out the agreement who will not be subject to full-time-equivalent restrictions of the agency;

(C) to the extent consistent with any applicable agency requirements or standards of conduct, permit an employee or former employee of the laboratory to participate in an effort to commercialize an invention made by the employee or former employee while in the employment or service of the Government; and

(D) waive, subject to reservation by the Government of a nonexclusive, irrevocable, paid-up license to practice the invention or have the invention practiced throughout the world by or on behalf of the Government, in advance, in whole or in part, any right of ownership which the Federal Government may have to any subject invention made under the agreement by a collaborating party or employee of a collaborating party.

(4) A collaborating party in an exclusive license in any invention made under an agreement entered into pursuant to subsection (a)(1) shall have the right of enforcement under chapter 29 of title 35, United States Code [35 USCS §§ 281 et seq.].

(5) A Government-owned, contractor-operated laboratory that enters into a cooperative research and development agreement pursuant to subsection (a)(1) may use or obligate royalties or other income accruing to the laboratory under such agreement with respect to any invention only—

(A) for payments to inventors;

(B) for purposes described in clauses (i), (ii), (iii), and (iv) of section 14(a)(1)(B) [15 USCS § 3710c(a)(1)(B)]; and

(C) for scientific research and development consistent with the research and development missions and objectives of the laboratory.

(6)

(A) In the case of a laboratory that is part of the National Nuclear Security Administration, a designated official of that Administration may waive any license retained by the Government under paragraph (1)(A), (2), or (3)(D), in whole or in part and according to negotiated terms and conditions, if the designated official finds that the retention of the license by the Government would substantially inhibit the commercialization of an invention that would otherwise serve an important national security mission.

(B) The authority to grant a waiver under subparagraph (A) shall expire on the date that is five years after the date of the enactment of the Floyd D. Spence National Defense Authorization Act for Fiscal Year 2001 [enacted Oct. 30, 2000]. The expiration under the preceding sentence of authority to grant a waiver under subparagraph (A) shall not affect any waiver granted under that subparagraph before the expiration of such authority.

(C) Not later than February 15 of each year, the Administrator for Nuclear Security shall submit to Congress a report on any waivers granted under this paragraph during the preceding year.

(c) Contract considerations.

    (1) A Federal agency may issue regulations on suitable procedures for implementing the provisions of this section; however, implementation of this section shall not be delayed until issuance of such regulations.

    (2) The agency in permitting a Federal laboratory to enter into agreements under this section shall be guided by the purposes of this Act.

    (3)

        (A) Any agency using the authority given it under subsection (a) shall review standards of conduct for its employees for resolving potential conflicts of interest to make sure they adequately establish guidelines for situations likely to arise through the use of this authority, including but not limited to cases where present or former employees or their partners negotiate licenses or assignments of titles to inventions or negotiate cooperative research and development agreements with Federal agencies (including the agency with which the employee involved is or was formerly employed).

        (B) If, in implementing subparagraph (A), an agency is unable to resolve potential conflicts of interest within its current statutory framework, it shall propose necessary statutory changes to be forwarded to its authorizing committees in Congress.

    (4) The laboratory director in deciding what cooperative research and development agreements to enter into shall—

        (A) give special consideration to small business firms, and consortia involving small business firms; and

        (B) give preference to business units located in the United States which agree that products embodying inventions made under the cooperative research and development agreement or produced through the use of such inventions will be manufactured substantially in the United States and, in the case of any industrial organization or other person subject to the control of a foreign company or government, as appropriate, take into consideration whether or not such foreign government permits United States agencies, organizations, or other persons to enter into cooperative research and development agreements and licensing agreements.

    (5)

        (A) If the head of the agency or his designee desires an opportunity to disapprove or require the modification of any such agreement presented by the director of a Government-operated laboratory, the agreement shall provide a 30-day period within which such action must be taken beginning on the date the agreement is presented to him or her by the head of the laboratory concerned.

(B) In any case in which the head of an agency or his designee disapproves or requires the modification of an agreement presented by the director of a Government-operated laboratory under this section, the head of the agency or such designee shall transmit a written explanation of such disapproval or modification to the head of the laboratory concerned.

(C)

(i) Any non-Federal entity that operates a laboratory pursuant to a contract with a Federal agency shall submit to the agency any cooperative research and development agreement that the entity proposes to enter into and the joint work statement if required with respect to that agreement.

(ii) A Federal agency that receives a proposed agreement and joint work statement under clause (i) shall review and approve, request specific modifications to, or disapprove the proposed agreement and joint work statement within 30 days after such submission. No agreement may be entered into by a Government-owned, contractor-operated laboratory under this section before both approval of the agreement and approval of a joint work statement under this clause.

(iii) In any case in which an agency which has contracted with an entity referred to in clause (i) disapproves or requests the modification of a cooperative research and development agreement or joint work statement submitted under that clause, the agency shall transmit a written explanation of such disapproval or modification to the head of the laboratory concerned.

(iv) Any agency that has contracted with a non-Federal entity to operate a laboratory may develop and provide to such laboratory one or more model cooperative research and development agreements for purposes of standardizing practices and procedures, resolving common legal issues, and enabling review of cooperative research and development agreements to be carried out in a routine and prompt manner.

(v) A Federal agency may waive the requirements of clause (i) or (ii) under such circumstances as the agency considers appropriate.

(6) Each agency shall maintain a record of all agreements entered into under this section.

(7)

    (A) No trade secrets or commercial or financial information that is privileged or confidential, under the meaning of section 552(b)(4) of title 5, United States Code, which is obtained in the conduct of research or as a result of activities under this Act [15 USCS §§ 3701 et seq.] from a non-Federal party participating in a cooperative research and development agreement shall be disclosed.

    (B) The director, or in the case of a contractor-operated laboratory, the agency, for a period of up to 5 years after development of information that results from research and development activities conducted under this Act [15 USCS §§ 3701 et seq.] and that would be a trade secret or commercial or financial information that is privileged or confidential if the information had been obtained from a non-Federal party participating in a cooperative research and development agreement, may provide appropriate protections against the dissemination of such information, including exemption from subchapter II of chapter 5 of title 5, United States Code [5 USCS §§ 551 et seq.].

(d) Definitions. As used in this section—

    (1) the term "cooperative research and development agreement" means any agreement between one or more Federal laboratories and one or more non-Federal parties under which the Government, through its laboratories, provides personnel, services, facilities, equipment, intellectual property, or other resources with or without reimbursement (but not funds to non-Federal parties) and the non-Federal parties provide funds, personnel, services, facilities, equipment, intellectual property, or other resources toward the conduct of specified research or development efforts which are consistent with the missions of the laboratory; except that such term does not include a procurement contract or cooperative agreement as those terms are used in sections 6303, 6304, and 6305 of title 31, United States Code;

    (2) the term "laboratory" means—

        (A) a facility or group of facilities owned, leased, or otherwise used by a Federal agency, a substantial purpose of which is the performance of research, development, or engineering by employees of the Federal Government;

(B) a group of Government-owned, contractor-operated facilities (including a weapon production facility of the Department of Energy) under a common contract, when a substantial purpose of the contract is the performance of research and development, or the production, maintenance, testing, or dismantlement of a nuclear weapon or its components, for the Federal Government; and

(C) a Government-owned, contractor-operated facility (including a weapon production facility of the Department of Energy) that is not under a common contract described in subparagraph (B), and the primary purpose of which is the performance of research and development, or the production, maintenance, testing, or dismantlement of a nuclear weapon or its components, for the Federal Government, but such term does not include any facility covered by Executive Order No. 12344 [42 USCS § 7158 note], dated February 1, 1982, pertaining to the naval nuclear propulsion program;

(3) the term "joint work statement" means a proposal prepared for a Federal agency by the director of a Government-owned, contractor-operated laboratory describing the purpose and scope of a proposed cooperative research and development agreement, and assigning rights and responsibilities among the agency, the laboratory, and any other party or parties to the proposed agreement; and

(4) the term "weapon production facility of the Department of Energy" means a facility under the control or jurisdiction of the Secretary of Energy that is operated for national security purposes and is engaged in the production, maintenance, testing, or dismantlement of a nuclear weapon or its components.

(e) Determination of laboratory missions. For purposes of this section, an agency shall make separate determinations of the mission or missions of each of its laboratories.

(f) Relationship to other laws. Nothing in this section is intended to limit or diminish existing authorities of any agency.

(g) Principles. In implementing this section, each agency which has contracted with a non-Federal entity to operate a laboratory shall be guided by the following principles:

(1) The implementation shall advance program missions at the laboratory, including any national security mission.

(2) Classified information and unclassified sensitive information protected by law, regulation, or Executive order shall be appropriately safeguarded.

ADVANCED TECHNOLOGY PROGRAM
15 USC 278N

Sec. 278n. Advanced Technology Program

- (a) Establishment; purpose; focus; guidance

There is established in the Institute an Advanced Technology Program (hereafter in this chapter referred to as the "Program") for the purpose of assisting United States businesses in creating and applying the generic technology and research results necessary to—

- (1) commercialize significant new scientific discoveries and technologies rapidly; and

- (2) refine manufacturing technologies.

The Secretary, acting through the Director, shall assure that the Program focuses on improving the competitive position of the United States and its businesses, gives preference to discoveries and to technologies that have great economic potential, and avoids providing undue advantage to specific companies. In operating the Program, the Secretary and Director shall, as appropriate, be guided by the findings and recommendations of the Biennial National Critical Technology Reports prepared pursuant to section 6683 of title 42.

- (b) Authority of Secretary; research and development; contracts and cooperative agreements; Federal laboratories; other activities with joint ventures

Under the Program established in subsection (a) of this section, and consistent with the mission and policies of the Institute, the Secretary, acting through the Director, and subject to subsections (c) and (d) of this section, may—

- (1) aid industry-led United States joint research and development ventures (hereafter in this section referred to as "joint ventures") (which may also include universities and independent research organizations), including those involving collaborative technology demonstration projects which develop and test prototype equipment and processes, through—

  - (A) provision of organizational and technical advice; and

  - (B) participation in such joint ventures by means of grants, cooperative agreements, or contracts, if the Secretary, acting through the Director, determines participation to be appropriate, which may include

    - (i) partial start-up funding,

    - (ii) provision of a minority share of the cost of such joint ventures for up to 5 years, and

- (iii) making available equipment, facilities, and personnel,

provided that emphasis is placed on areas where the Institute has scientific or technological expertise, on solving generic problems of specific industries, and on making those industries more competitive in world markets;

- (2) provide grants to and enter into contracts and cooperative agreements with United States businesses (especially small businesses), provided that emphasis is placed on applying the Institute's research, research techniques, and expertise to those organizations' research programs;

- (3) involve the Federal laboratories in the Program, where appropriate, using among other authorities the cooperative research and development agreements provided for under section 3710a of this title; and

- (4) carry out, in a manner consistent with the provisions of this section, such other cooperative research activities with joint ventures as may be authorized by law or assigned to the Program by the Secretary.

- (c) Authority of Secretary; selection criteria; monitoring use of technologies; overseas transfer; annual report to Congress; financial reporting and auditing; routine consideration of Committee advice; dissemination of research results

The Secretary, acting through the Director, is authorized to take all actions necessary and appropriate to establish and operate the Program, including—

- (1) publishing in the Federal Register draft criteria and, no later than six months after August 23, 1988, following a public comment period, final criteria, for the selection of recipients of assistance under subsection (b)(1) and (2) of this section;

- (2) monitoring how technologies developed in its research program are used, and reporting annually to the Congress on the extent of any overseas transfer of these technologies;

- (3) establishing procedures regarding financial reporting and auditing to ensure that contracts and awards are used for the purposes specified in this section, are in accordance with sound accounting practices, and are not funding existing or planned research programs that would be conducted in the same time period in the absence of financial assistance under the Program;

- (4) assuring that the advice of the Committee established under section 278 of this title is considered routinely in carrying out the responsibilities of the Institute; and

- (5) providing for appropriate dissemination of Program research results.

- (d) Contracts or awards; criteria; restrictions

When entering into contracts or making awards under subsection (b) of this section, the following shall apply:

- (1) No contract or award may be made until the research project in question has been subject to a merit review, and has, in the opinion of the reviewers appointed by the Director and the Secretary, acting through the Director, been shown to have scientific and technical merit.

- (2) In the case of joint ventures, the Program shall not make an award unless the award will facilitate the formation of a joint venture or the initiation of a new research and development project by an existing joint venture.

- (3) No Federal contract or cooperative agreement under subsection (b)(2) of this section shall exceed $2,000,000 over 3 years, or be for more than 3 years unless a full and complete explanation of such proposed award, including reasons for exceeding these limits, is submitted in writing by the Secretary to the Committee on Commerce, Science, and Transportation of the Senate and the Committee on Science, Space, and Technology of the House of Representatives. The proposed contract or cooperative agreement may be executed only after 30 calendar days on which both Houses of Congress are in session have elapsed since such submission. Federal funds made available under subsection (b)(2) of this section shall be used only for direct costs and not for indirect costs, profits, or management fees of the contractor.

- (4) In determining whether to make an award to a particular joint venture, the Program shall consider whether the members of the joint venture have made provisions for the appropriate participation of small United States businesses in such joint venture.

- (5) Section 552 of title 5 shall not apply to the following information obtained by the Federal Government on a confidential basis in connection with the activities of any business or any joint venture receiving funding under the Program—

  - (A) information on the business operation of any member of the business or joint venture; and

  - (B) trade secrets possessed by any business or any member of the joint venture.

- (6) Intellectual property owned and developed by any business or joint venture receiving funding or by any member of such a joint venture may not be disclosed by any officer or employee of the Federal Government except in accordance with a written agreement between the owner or developer and the Program.

- (7) If a business or joint venture fails before the completion of the period for which a contract or award has been made, after all allowable costs have been paid and appropriate audits conducted, the unspent balance of the Federal funds shall be returned by the recipient to the Program.

- (8) Upon dissolution of any joint venture or at the time otherwise agreed upon, the Federal Government shall be entitled to a share of the residual assets of the joint venture proportional to the Federal share of the costs of the joint venture as determined by independent audit.

- (9) A company shall be eligible to receive financial assistance under this section only if—

  - (A) the Secretary finds that the company's participation in the Program would be in the economic interest of the United States, as evidenced by investments in the United States in research, development, and manufacturing (including, for example, the manufacture of major components or subassemblies in the United States); significant contributions to employment in the United States; and agreement with respect to any technology arising from assistance provided under this section to promote the manufacture within the United States of products resulting from that technology (taking into account the goals of promoting the competitiveness of United States industry), and to procure parts and materials from competitive suppliers; and

  - (B) either—

    - (i) the company is a United States-owned company; or

    - (ii) the Secretary finds that the company is incorporated in the United States and has a parent company which is incorporated in a country which affords to United States-owned companies opportunities, comparable to those afforded to any other company, to participate in any joint venture similar to those authorized under this chapter; affords to United States-owned companies local investment opportunities comparable to those afforded to any other company; and affords adequate and effective protection for the intellectual property rights of United States-owned companies.

- (10) Grants, contracts, and cooperative assignments under this section shall be designed to support projects which are high risk and which have the potential for eventual substantial widespread commercial application. In order to receive a grant, contract, or cooperative agreement under this section, a research and development entity shall demonstrate to the Secretary the requisite ability in research and technology development and management in the project area in which the grant, contract, or cooperative agreement is being sought.

- (11)

  - (A) Title to any intellectual property arising from assistance provided under this section shall vest in a company or companies incorporated in the United States. The United States may reserve a nonexclusive, nontransferable, irrevocable paid-up license, to have practiced for or on behalf of the United States, in connection with any such intellectual property, but shall not, in the exercise of such license, publicly disclose proprietary information related to the license. Title to any such intellectual property shall not be transferred or passed, except to a company incorporated in the United States, until the expiration of the first patent obtained in connection with such intellectual property.

  - (B) For purposes of this paragraph, the term "intellectual property" means an invention patentable under title 35 or any patent on such an invention.

  - (C) Nothing in this paragraph shall be construed to prohibit the licensing to any company of intellectual property rights arising from assistance provided under this section.

- (e) Suspension for failure to satisfy eligibility criteria

  The Secretary may, within 30 days after notice to Congress, suspend a company or joint venture from continued assistance under this section if the Secretary determines that the company, the country of incorporation of the company or a parent company, or the joint venture has failed to satisfy any of the criteria set forth in subsection (d)(9) of this section, and that it is in the national interest of the United States to do so.

- (f) Coordination with other Federal technology programs

  When reviewing private sector requests for awards under the Program, and when monitoring the progress of assisted research projects, the Secretary and the Director shall, as appropriate, coordinate with the Secretary of Defense and other senior Federal officials to ensure cooperation and coordination in Federal technology programs and to avoid unnecessary duplication of effort. The Secretary and the Director are authorized to work with the Director of the Office of Science and Technology Policy, the Secretary of Defense, and other appropriate Federal officials to form interagency working groups or special project offices to coordinate Federal technology activities.

- (g) Meetings with industry sources

  In order to analyze the need for the value of joint ventures and other research projects in specific technical fields, to evaluate any proposal made by a joint venture or company requesting the Secretary's assistance, or to monitor the progress of any joint venture or any company research project which receives Federal funds under the Program, the Secretary, the Under Secretary of Commerce for Technology, and the Director may, notwithstanding any other provision of law, meet with such industry sources as they consider useful and appropriate.

- (h) Standards development

Up to 10 percent of the funds appropriated for carrying out this section may be used for standards development and technical activities by the Institute in support of the purposes of this section.

- (i) Acceptance of funds from other Federal departments and agencies

In addition to such sums as may be authorized and appropriated to the Secretary and Director to operate the Program, the Secretary and Director also may accept funds from other Federal departments and agencies for the purpose of providing Federal funds to support awards under the Program. Any Program award which is supported with funds which originally came from other Federal departments and agencies shall be selected and carried out according to the provisions of this section.

- (j) Definitions

As used in this section—

- (1) the term "joint venture" means any group of activities, including attempting to make, making, or performing a contract, by two or more persons for the purpose of—
  - (A) theoretical analysis, experimentation, or systematic study of phenomena or observable facts;
  - (B) the development or testing of basic engineering techniques;
  - (C) the extension of investigative finding or theory of a scientific or technical nature into practical application for experimental and demonstration purposes, including the experimental production and testing of models, prototypes, equipment, materials, and processes;
  - (D) the collection, exchange, and analysis of research information;
  - (E) the production of any product, process, or service; or
  - (F) any combination of the purposes specified in subparagraphs (A), (B), (C), (D), and (E), and may include the establishment and operation of facilities for the conducting of research, the conducting of such venture on a protected and proprietary basis, and the prosecuting of applications for patents and the granting of licenses for the results of such venture; and
- (2) the term "United States-owned company" means a company that has majority ownership or control by individuals who are citizens of the United States.

Appendix V

SAMPLE CRADA AGREEMENT

STEVENSON-WYDLER (15 USC 3710)

COOPERATIVE RESEARCH AND DEVELOPMENT

AGREEMENT (hereinafter "CRADA") No._____

BETWEEN

_____

under its U.S. Department of Energy Contract

No. _____ (hereinafter "Contractor")

AND

_____ (hereinafter "Participant"),

both being hereinafter jointly referred to as the "Parties"

ARTICLE I: DEFINITIONS

A. "Government" means the United States of America and agencies thereof.

B. "DOE" means the Department of Energy, an agency of the United States of America.

C. "Contracting Officer" means the DOE employee administering the Contractor's DOE contract.

D. "Generated Information" means information produced in the performance of this CRADA.

E. "Proprietary Information" means information which embodies (i) trade secrets or (ii) commercial or financial information which is privileged or confidential under the Freedom of Information Act (5 USC 552 fb)(4)), either of which is developed at private expense outside of this CRADA and which is marked as Proprietary Information.

F. "Protected CRADA Information" means Generated Information which is marked as being Protected CRADA Information by a Party to this CRADA and which would have been Proprietary Information had it been obtained from a nonfederal entity.

G. Subject Invention means any invention of the Contractor or Participant conceived or first actually reduced to practice in the performance of work under this CRADA.

H. "Intellectual Property" means patents, trademarks, copyrights, mask works, protected CRADA information, and other forms of comparable property rights protected by federal law and other foreign counterparts.

I. "Trademark" means a distinctive mark, symbol, or emblem used in commerce by a producer or manufacturer to identify and distinguish its goods or services from those of others.

J. "Mask Work" means a series of related images, however fixed or encoded, having or representing the predetermined, three-dimensional pattern of metallic, insulating, or semiconductor material present or removed from the layers of a semiconductor chip product; and in which series the relation of the images to one another is that each image has the pattern of the surface of one form of the semiconductor chip product.

K. "RD&D" means research, development, and demonstration performed by the Contractor and the Participant under this CRADA, including works performed by consultants or other contractors and subcontractors under this CRADA.

L. "Background Intellectual Property" means the Intellectual Property rights in the items identified by the Parties in Appendix D, Background Intellectual Property, which were in existence prior to or are first produced outside of this CRADA, except that in the case of inventions in those identified items, the inventions must have been conceived outside of this CRADA and not first actually reduced to practice under this CRADA to qualify as Background Intellectual Property. Licensing of Background Intellectual Property, if agreed to by the Parties, shall be the subject of separate licensing agreements between the Parties. Background Intellectual Properties are not Subject Inventions.

ARTICLE II: STATEMENT OF WORK

Appendix A, Statement of Work, is hereby incorporated into this
CRADA by reference.
OR
Appendix A is the Statement of Work.

ARTICLE III: FUNDING AND COSTS

A. The Participant's estimated contribution is $____. The Government's
   estimated contribution, which is provided through the Contractor's contract with DOE, is $____, subject to available funding.

B. Neither Party shall have an obligation to continue or complete performance of its work at a cost in excess of its estimated cost as contained in
   Article III A above, including any subsequent amendment.

C. Each Party agrees to provide at least __ days' notice to the other Party if
   the actual cost to complete performance will exceed its estimated cost.

D. [For CRADAs that include (nonfederal) funding on a funds-in basis, an
   advance payment provision will be negotiated consistent with current
   DOE policy.]

ARTICLE IV: PERSONAL PROPERTY

All tangible personal property produced under this CRADA shall
become the property of the Participant or the Government, depending
upon whose funds were used to obtain it. Such property is identified in
Appendix A, Statement of Work. Personal Property shall be disposed of as
directed by the owner at the owner's expense. All jointly funded property
shall be owned by the Government.

ARTICLE V: DISCLAIMER

THE GOVERNMENT, THE PARTICIPANT, AND THE CONTRAC-
TOR MAKE NO EXPRESS OR IMPLIED WARRANTY AS TO THE
CONDITIONS OF THE RESEARCH OR ANY INTELLECTUAL PROP-
ERTY OR PRODUCT MADE OR DEVELOPED UNDER THIS CRADA,
OR THE OWNERSHIP, MERCHANTABILITY, OR FITNESS FOR A
PARTICULAR PURPOSE OF THE RESEARCH OR RESULTING
PRODUCT. NEITHER THE GOVERNMENT, THE PARTICIPANT, NOR
THE CONTRACTOR SHALL BE LIABLE FOR SPECIAL, CONSE-
QUENTIAL, OR INCIDENTAL DAMAGES ATTRIBUTED TO SUCH

RESEARCH OR RESULTING PRODUCT, INTELLECTUAL PROP-
ERTY, OR PRODUCT MADE OR DEVELOPED UNDER THIS CRADA.

ARTICLE VI: PRODUCT LIABILITY

Except for any liability resulting from any negligent acts or omissions of
Contractor, Participant indemnifies the Government and the Contractor for
all damages, costs, and expenses, including attorney's fees, arising from personal injury or property damage occurring as a result of the making, using,
or selling of a product, process, or service by or on behalf of the Participant,
its assignees or licensees, that was derived from the work performed under
this CRADA. In respect to this Article, neither the Government nor the Contractor shall be considered assignees or licensees of the Participant as a
result of reserved Government and Contractor rights. The indemnity set
forth in this paragraph shall apply only if Participant shall have been
informed as soon and as completely as practical by the Contractor and/or the
Government of the action alleging such claim and shall have been given an
opportunity, to the maximum extent afforded by applicable laws, rules, or
regulations, to participate in and control its defense, and the Contractor
and/or Government shall have provided all reasonably available information
and reasonable assistance requested by Participant. No settlement for which
Participant would be responsible shall be made without Participant's consent unless required by final decree of a court of competent jurisdiction.

ARTICLE VII: OBLIGATIONS AS TO
PROPRIETARY INFORMATION

A. If Proprietary Information is orally disclosed to a Party, it shall be identified as such, orally, at the time of disclosure and confirmed in a written
   summary thereof within __ days as being Proprietary Information.

B. Each Party agrees to not disclose Proprietary Information provided by
   another Party to anyone other than the CRADA Participant and Contractor without written approval of the providing Party, except to Government employees who are subject to the statutory provisions against
   disclosure of confidential information set forth in the Trade Secrets Act
   (18 USC 1905).

C. All Proprietary Information shall be returned to the provider thereof at
   the conclusion of this CRADA at the provider's expense.

D. All Proprietary Information shall be protected, unless and until such Proprietary Information shall become publicly known without the fault of

the recipient, shall come into recipient's possession without breach of any of the obligations set forth herein by the recipient, or shall be independently developed by recipient's employees who did not have access to such Proprietary Information.

(The following paragraph may be included in this article if desired.)

E. In no case shall the Contractor provide Proprietary Information of Participant to any person or entity for commercial purposes, unless otherwise agreed to in writing by such Participant.

ARTICLE VIII: OBLIGATIONS AS TO PROTECTED CRADA INFORMATION

A. Each Party may designate as Protected CRADA Information, as defined in Article I, any Generated Information produced by its employees and, with the agreement of the other Party, mark any Generated Information produced by the other Party's employees. All such designated Protected CRADA Information shall be appropriately marked.

B. For a period of ____ [not to exceed five years] from the date Protected CRADA Information is produced, Parties agree not to further disclose such Information except:

(1) As necessary to perform this CRADA;

(2) As provided in Article XI [REPORTS AND ABSTRACTS];

(3) As requested by the DOE Contracting Officer to be provided to other DOE facilities for use only at those DOE facilities with the same protection in place; or as mutually agreed by the parties in advance.

C. The obligations of (B) above shall end sooner for any Protected CRADA Information that shall become publicly known without fault of either Party, shall come into a Party's possession without breach by that Party of the obligations of (B) above, or shall be independently developed by a Party's employees who did not have access to the Protected CRADA Information.

ARTICLE IX: RIGHTS IN GENERATED INFORMATION

The Parties agree that they shall have no obligations of nondisclosure or limitations on their use of, and the Government shall have unlimited rights in, all Generated Information, all Protected CRADA Information after the expiration of the period set forth in Article VIII (B) above, and information provided to the Government or Contractor under this

CRADA that is not marked as being copyrighted (subject to Article XIII) or as Protected CRADA Information (subject to Article VIII B) or Proprietary Information (subject to Article VII B), or that is an invention, disclosure of which may later be the subject of a U.S. or foreign patent application.

ARTICLE X: EXPORT CONTROL

THE PARTIES UNDERSTAND THAT MATERIALS AND INFORMATION RESULTING FROM THE PERFORMANCE OF THIS CRADA MAY BE SUBJECT TO EXPORT CONTROL LAWS AND THAT EACH PARTY IS RESPONSIBLE FOR ITS OWN COMPLIANCE WITH SUCH LAWS.

ARTICLE XI: REPORTS AND ABSTRACTS

A. The Parties agree to produce the following deliverables:

    (1)   An initial abstract suitable for public release;

    (2)   Other abstracts (final when work is complete, and others as substantial changes in scope and dollars occur);

    (3)   A final report, to include a list of subject inventions;

    (4)   A semiannual, signed financial report of the Participant's in-kind contributions to the project;

    (5)   Other topical/periodic reports where the nature of research and magnitude of dollars justify; and

    (6)   Computer software in source- and object-code format, as defined within the Statement of Work.

B. It is understood that the Contractor has the responsibility to provide the above information at the time of its completion to the DOE Office of Scientific and Technical Information.

ARTICLE XII: PREPUBLICATION REVIEW

A. The Parties agree to secure prepublication approval from each other, which shall not be unreasonably withheld or denied beyond __days.

B. The Parties agree that neither will use the name of the other Party or its employees in any promotional activity, such as advertisements, with reference to any product or service resulting from this CRADA, without prior written approval of the other Party.

ARTICLE XIII: COPYRIGHTS

A. The Parties may assert copyright in any of their Generated Information.

B. Allocation of rights to copyrights in Generated Information will be negotiated by the Parties.

C. For Generated Information, the Parties acknowledge that the Government has for itself and others acting on its behalf, a royalty-free, nonexclusive, irrevocable, worldwide copyright license to reproduce, prepare derivative works, distribute copies to the public, and perform publicly and display publicly, by or on behalf of the Government, all copyrightable works produced in the performance of this CRADA, subject to the restrictions this CRADA places on publication of Proprietary Information and Protected CRADA Information.

D. For all copyrighted computer software produced in the performance of this CRADA, the Party owning the copyright will provide the source code, an expanded abstract, the object code, and the minimum support documentation needed by a competent user to understand and use the software to DOE's Energy Science and Technology Software Center, P.O. Box 1020, Oak Ridge, TN 37831. The expanded abstract will be treated in the same manner as Generated Information in subparagraph C of this Article.

E. The Contractor and the Participant agree that, with respect to any copyrighted computer software produced in the performance of this CRADA, DOE has the right, at the end of the period set forth in paragraph B of Article VIII hereof and at the end of each two-year interval thereafter, to request the Contractor and the Participant and any assignee or exclusive licensee of the copyrighted software to grant a nonexclusive, partially exclusive, or exclusive license to a responsible applicant upon terms that are reasonable under the circumstances, provided such grant does not cause a termination of any licensee's right to use the copyrighted computer software. If the Contractor or the Participant or any assignee or exclusive licensee refuses such request, the Contractor and the Participant agree that DOE has the right to grant the license if DOE determines that the Contractor, the Participant, assignee, or licensee has not made a satisfactory demonstration that it is actively pursuing commercialization of the copyrighted computer software. Before requiring licensing under this paragraph E, DOE shall furnish the Contractor/Participant written notice of its intentions to require the Contractor/Participant to grant the stated license, and the Contractor/Participant shall be allowed 30 days (or such longer period as may be authorized by the cognizant DOE Contracting Officer for good cause shown in writing by the Contractor/Participant) after such notice to show cause why the license should not be required to be granted. The Contractor/Participant shall have the right to appeal the decision by the DOE to the grant of the stated license to the Invention Licensing Appeal Board, as set forth in paragraphs (b)-(g) of 10 CFR 781.65, "Appeals."

F. The Parties agree to place copyright and other notices, as appropriate for the protection of copyright, in human readable form onto all physical media, and in digitally encoded form in the header of machine readable information recorded on such media such that the notice will appear in human readable form when the digital data are off-loaded or the data are accessed for display or printout.

ARTICLE XIV: REPORTING INVENTIONS

A. The Parties agree to disclose to each other each and every Subject Invention that may be patentable or otherwise protectable under the Patent Act. The Parties acknowledge that the Contractor will disclose Subject Inventions to the DOE within two (2) months after the inventor first discloses the invention in writing to the person(s) responsible for patent matters of the disclosing Party.

B. These disclosures should be in such detail as to be capable of enabling one skilled in the art to make and use the invention under 35 USC 112. The disclosure shall also identify any known actual or potential statutory bars, i.e., printed publications describing the invention or the public use or sale of the invention in this country. The Parties further agree to disclose to each other any subsequent known actual or potential statutory bar that occurs for an invention disclosed but for which a patent application has not been filed. All invention disclosures shall be marked as confidential under 35 USC 205.

ARTICLE XV: TITLE TO INVENTIONS

Whereas DOE has granted rights to the Contractor:

A. [Allocation of rights will be negotiated by the Parties.]

B. The Parties acknowledge that the DOE may obtain title to each Subject Invention reported under Article XIV for which a patent application or applications are not filed and for which any issued patents are not maintained by any Party to this CRADA.

C. The Parties acknowledge that the Government retains a nonexclusive, nontransferable, irrevocable, paid-up license to practice or to have practiced for or on behalf of the United States every Subject Invention under this CRADA throughout the world.

ARTICLE XVI: FILING PATENT APPLICATIONS

A. The Parties agree that the Party initially indicated as having an ownership interest in any Subject Inventions shall have the first opportunity to file U.S. and foreign patent applications; but if such Party does not file such applications within six months after disclosure, then the other Party to this CRADA may file patent applications on such inventions, and the Party initially having ownership efforts shall fully cooperate in this effort.

B. The Parties agree that DOE has the right to file patent applications in any country if neither Party desires to file a patent application for any Subject Invention. Notification of such negative intent shall be made in writing to the DOE Contracting Officer within nine (9) months after the initial disclosure of such invention or not later than 60 days prior to the time when any statutory bar might foreclose filing of a U.S. patent application.

ARTICLE XVII: TRADEMARKS

The Parties may seek to obtain trademark/service mark protection on products or services generated under this agreement in the United States or foreign countries. [The ownership and other rights relating to this trademark shall be as mutually agreed to in writing by the Parties.] The Parties hereby acknowledge that the Government shall have the right to indicate on any similar goods or services produced by or for the Government that such goods or services were derived from and are a DOE version of the goods or services protected by such trademark/service mark with the trademark and the owner thereof being specifically identified. In addition, the Government shall have the right to use such trademark/service mark in print or communications media.

ARTICLE XVIII: MASK WORKS

The Parties may seek to obtain legal protection for mask works fixed in semiconductor products generated under this agreement, as provided by Chapter 9 of Title 17 of the United States Code. [The rights to any mask work covered by this provision shall be as mutually agreed to in writing by the Parties.] The parties hereby acknowledge that the Government or others acting on its behalf shall retain a nonexclusive, paid-up, worldwide, irrevocable, nontransferable license to reproduce, import, or distribute the covered semiconductor product by or on behalf of the Government, and to reproduce and use the mask work by or on behalf of the Government.

ARTICLE XIX: COST OF INTELLECTUAL PROPERTY PROTECTION

Each Party shall be responsible for payment of all costs relating to copyright, trademark, and mask work filing, U.S. and foreign patent application filing and prosecution, and all costs relating to maintenance fees for U.S. and foreign patents hereunder that are owned by that Party. Government/DOE laboratory funds contributed as DOE's cost share to a CRADA cannot be given to Participant for payment of Participant's costs of filing and maintaining patents or filing for copyrights, trademarks, and mask works.

ARTICLE XX: REPORTS OF INVENTION USE

Participant agrees to submit, upon request of DOE, a nonproprietary report no more frequently than annually on efforts to utilize any technology arising under the CRADA.

ARTICLE XXI: DOE MARCH-IN RIGHTS

The Parties acknowledge that the DOE has certain march-in rights to any Subject Inventions in accordance with 48 CFR 27.304–1(G).

ARTICLE XXII: U.S. COMPETITIVENESS

The Parties agree that a purpose of this CRADA is to provide substantial benefit to the U.S. economy. In exchange for the benefits received under this CRADA, the Parties therefore agree to the following:

A. Products embodying Intellectual Property developed under this CRADA shall be substantially manufactured in the United States.

B. Processes, services, and improvements thereof that are covered by Intellectual Property developed under this CRADA shall be incorporated into the Participant's manufacturing facilities in the United States either prior to or simultaneously with implementation outside the United States. Such processes, services, and improvements, when implemented outside the United States, shall not result in reduction of the use of the same processes, services, or improvements in the United States.

ARTICLE XXIII: ASSIGNMENT OF PERSONNEL

A. It is contemplated that each Party may assign personnel to the other Party's facility as part of this CRADA. Such personnel assigned by the assigning Party to participate in or observe the research to be performed under this CRADA shall not during the period of such assignments be considered employees of the receiving Party for any purposes.

B. The receiving Party shall have the right to exercise routine administrative and technical supervisory control of the occupational activities of such personnel during the assignment period and shall have the right to approve the assignment of such personnel and/or to later request their removal by the assigning Party.

C. The assigning Party shall bear any and all costs and expenses with regard to its personnel assigned to the receiving Party's facilities under this CRADA. The receiving Party shall bear facility costs of such assignments.

ARTICLE XXIV: FORCE MAJEURE

No failure or omission by Contractor or Participant in the performance of any obligation under this CRADA shall be deemed a breach of this CRADA or create any liability if the same shall arise from any cause or causes beyond the control of Contractor or Participant, including but not limited to the following, which, for the purpose of this CRADA, shall be regarded as beyond the control of the Party in question: Acts of God; acts or omissions of any government or agency thereof; compliance with requirements, rules, regulations, or orders of any governmental authority or any office, department, agency, or instrumentality thereof; fire; storm; flood; earthquake; accident; acts of the public enemy; war; rebellion; insurrection; riot; sabotage; invasion; quarantine; restriction; transportation embargoes; or failures or delays in transportation.

ARTICLE XXV: ADMINISTRATION OF CRADA

It is understood and agreed that this CRADA is entered into by the Contractor under the authority of its prime contract with DOE. The Contractor is authorized to and will administer this CRADA in all respects, unless otherwise specifically provided for herein. Administration of this CRADA may be transferred from the Contractor to DOE or its designee with notice of such transfer to the Participant, and the Contractor shall have no further responsibilities except for the confidentiality, use, and/or nondisclosure obligations of this CRADA.

ARTICLE XXVI: RECORDS AND ACCOUNTING FOR GOVERNMENT PROPERTY

The Participant shall maintain records of receipts, expenditures, and the disposition of all Government property in its custody related to the CRADA.

ARTICLE XXVII: NOTICES

A. Any communications required by this CRADA, if given by postage pre-paid, first class U.S. Mail addressed to the Party to receive the communication, shall be deemed made as of the day of receipt of such communication by the addressee, or on the date given if by verified fac-simile. Address changes shall be given in accordance with this Article and shall be effective thereafter. All such communications, to be considered effective, shall include the number of this CRADA.

B. The addresses, telephone numbers, and facsimile numbers for the Parties are as follows:

ARTICLE XXVIII: DISPUTES

The Parties shall attempt to jointly resolve all disputes arising from this CRADA. If the Parties are unable to jointly resolve a dispute within a reasonable period of time, they agree to [process to be negotiated by the Parties]. To the extent that there is no applicable U.S. federal law, this CRADA and performance thereunder shall be governed by the law of the State of _____.

ARTICLE XXIX: ENTIRE CRADA AND MODIFICATIONS

A. It is expressly understood and agreed that this CRADA with its Appendices contains the entire agreement between the Parties with respect to the subject matter hereof and that all prior representations or agreements relating hereto have been merged into this document and are thus superseded in totality by this CRADA. This CRADA shall not be effective until approved by DOE.

B. Any agreement to materially change any terms or conditions of this CRADA or the Appendices shall be valid only if the change is made in writing, executed by the Parties hereto, and approved by DOE.

ARTICLE XXX: TERMINATION

This CRADA may be terminated by either Party upon ____days written notice to the other Party. This CRADA may also be terminated by the Contractor in the event of failure by the Participant to provide the necessary advance funding, as agreed in Article III.

In the event of termination by either Party, each Party shall be responsible for its share of the costs incurred through the effective date of termination, as well as its share of the costs incurred after the effective date of termination, and that are related to the termination. The confidentiality, use, and/or nondisclosure obligations of this CRADA shall survive any termination of this CRADA.

FOR CONTRACTOR:

BY_____

TITLE_____

DATE_____

FOR PARTICIPANT:

BY_____

TITLE_____

DATE_____

Source: Jacob N. Erlich and Michael Musick. Cooperative Research and Development Agreement Handbook. Federal Laboratory Consortium Handbook Series No. 5. Washington, D.C.: Federal Laboratory Consortium for Technology Transfer, 1994.

REFERENCES

American Association for the Advancement of Science (AAAS). March 2001. *U.S. R&D Funding by Performer.* Available at http://www.aaas.org/spp/dspp/rd/trendusp.pdf.

———. March 2001. *U.S. R&D Funding by Source.* Available at http://www.aaas.org/spp/dspp/rd/trendusr.pdf.

———. July 2001. *Trends in Federal R&D.* Available at http://www.aaas.org/spp/dspp/rd/trendtot.pdf.

Association of University Technology Managers Licensing Survey: FY2001 Survey Summary. 2001. Northbrook, IL: AUTM, Inc.

Brody, R. 1996. *Effective Partnering: A Report to Congress on Federal Technology Partnerships.* Washington, DC: Office of Technology Policy.

Chapman, R., and G. Lundquist. 1997. *Managing the Successful Transfer of Technology from Federal Facilities: A Survey of Selected Laboratories and Facilities in the Mid-Continent Region of the Federal Laboratory Consortium.* Littleton, Colo.: Chapman Research Group, Inc.

Crandall, B. C., ed. 1996. *Nanotechnology: Molecular Speculations on Global Abundance.* Cambridge, Mass.: MIT Press.

Darling, David. 1995. *Micromachines and Nanotechnology: The Amazing New World of the Ultrasmall.* Silver Burdett Press.

Davis, Julie L. and Suzanne S. Harrison. 2001. *Edison in the Boardroom (How Leading Companies Realize Value from Their Intellectual Assets).* New York: John Bailey & Sons.

Drexler, Eric. 1987. *Engines of Creation.* Anchor Books/Doubleday.

———. 1992. *Nanosystems: Molecular Machinery, Manufacturing and Computation.* John Wiley & Sons.

Edvinsson, L. M. Malone. 1997. *Intellectual Capital.* New York: Harper Business.

Endo, M., S. Dresselhaus, and S. Iijima, eds. 1996. *Carbon Nanotubes.* Elsevier Science.

Erlich, Jacob N., and Michael Musick. 1994. *Cooperative Research and Development Agreement Handbook.* Federal Laboratory Consortium Handbook Series No. 5. Washington, D.C.: Federal Laboratory Consortium for Technology Transfer.

Freitas, Robert A., Jr. 1999. *Nanomedicine.* Vol. 1, *Basic Capabilities.* Landes Bioscience.

Fujimasa, Iwao. 1995. *Micromachines: A New Era in Mechanical Engineering.* Oxford University Press.

Geisler, Eliezer. 2000. *The Metrics of Science and Technology.* Westport, CT: Quorum Books.

General Accounting Office (GAO). 1996. *Federal R&D Laboratories.* GAO/RCED/NSIAD-96-78R. Washington, D.C.: General Accounting Office.

————. 2001. *Technology Transfer: DOE Has Fewer Partnerships, and They Rely More on Private Funding.* Report to chairmen, Committee on Armed Services, House of Representatives and Senate. GAO-01-568. Washington, D.C.: General Accounting Office.

Gross, Clifford. 2002. *Nature Biotechnology,* Vol. 21.

Gross, C., U. Reischl, and P. Abercrombie. 2000. *The New Idea Factory.* Columbus, OH: Battelle Press.

Hoch, H., H. Craighead, and L. Jelinski. 1996. *Nanofabrication and Biosystems: Integrating Materials Science, Engineering, and Biology.* Cambridge University Press.

Mobley, J. 1999. "Licensing Is Key to Success at U.S. Federal Labs." *Les Nouvelles* 34 (1) (March): 30–34.

Muir, Albert E. 1997. *The Technology Transfer System.* Latham, N.Y.: Latham Book Publishing.

National Science Board. 2000. *Science and Engineering Indicators—2000.* NSB-00-1. Arlington, Va.: National Science Board.

Office of Scientific Research and Development. 1945. *Science, the Endless Frontier.* A report to the president by Vannevar Bush, director of the Office of Scientific Research and Development. Washington, D.C.: U.S. Government Printing Office.

Personal Communication with C. Gross. 2001. Mogee Research and Analysis Associates, Inc.

Regis, Ed. 1996. *Nano: The Emerging Science of Nanotechnology.* Vol. 1. Little, Brown & Company.

Ross, Philip E. 2001. *The Road to Lilliput.* San Francisco: Red Herring.

Soni, Som R. 1995. *Techtransfer and CRADA with Federal Laboratories.* Beavercreek, OH: Ad Tech.

Stewart, T. 1999. *Intellectual Capital, the New Wealth of Organizations.* New York: Doubleday.

Technology Innovation. 1994. Chapter 63 United States Code Annotated; Title 15, Commerce and Trade, sections 3701–3715. Prepared for the Federal Laboratory Consortium for Technology Transfer. St. Paul, Minn.: West Publishing.

U.S. Department of Commerce. 2000. *Tech transfer 2000: Making Partnerships Work.* Washington, D.C.: Office of Technology Policy.

U.S. Patent and Trademark Office. Internet site: http://www.uspto.gov/.

U.S. Senate. 1979. *University and Small Business Patent Procedures Act: Report of the Committee on the Judiciary.* Report No. 96–480. Washington, D.C.: U.S. Government Printing Office.

———. 1986. *Federal Technology Transfer Act of 1986: Report from the Committee on Commerce, Science, and Transportation.* Report No. 99–283. Washington, D.C.: U.S. Government Printing Office.

Weber, Steven J., Christopher J. Brasco, and Jack E. Kerrigan. 1999. Technology Transfer Revolution: Legislative History and Future Proposals. Presented at the Technology Transfer Conference, April 26, at the Ritz Carlton, Tysons Corner, Virginia.

INDEX

About the Authors

CLIFFORD M. GROSS is the founder and CEO of UTEK Corporation. The holder of eighteen patents and author of two previous books and numerous articles and papers, Gross has previously served as Research Professor and Director at the Center for Product Ergonomics, University of South Florida.

JOSEPH P. ALLEN is President of the Robert C. Byrd National Technology Transfer Center at Wheeling Jesuit University in West Virginia. Allen has also served as the Director of the Office of Technology Commercialization at the U.S. Department of Commerce.